D1249930

THE

LIFE AND WRITINGS

OF

MAJOR JACK DOWNING

AMS PRESS
NEW YORK

MAJOR JACK DOWNING,

OF DOWNINGVILLE.

THE

LIFE AND WRITINGS

OF

MAJOR JACK DOWNING,

Of Downingville,

AWAY DOWN EAST IN THE STATE OF MAINE.

WRITTEN BY HIMSELF.

[SEBA SMITH]

' What makes all doctrines plain and clear ?
About two hundred pounds a year.
And that which was proved true before,
Prove false again ? Two hundred more.'
                                        HUDIBRAS.

BOSTON:

LILLY, WAIT, COLMAN, & HOLDEN.

1833.

Library of Congress Cataloging in Publication Data

[Smith, Seba] 1792–1868.
    The life and writings of Major Jack Downing, of
Downingville.

    I. Title.
PS2876.L68 1973   818'.3'07   71-164785
ISBN 0-404-02168-9

Reprinted from the edition of 1833, Boston
First AMS edition published, 1973
Manufactured in the United States of America

AMS PRESS, INC.
New York, N.Y.   10003

TO

GINERAL ANDREW JACKSON,

PRESIDENT OF THE UNITED STATES,

This Book

IS RESPECTFULLY INSCRIBED,

BY HIS FAITHFUL FRIEND AND HUMBLE SERVANT,

MAJOR JACK DOWNING.

PREFACE.

Arter I got my book all done, and had looked it over every day as the printer went along with it, till I got clear to the last page, so as to see it was done right, the printer comes to me, and says he, we want a Preface now. A preface! says I, what in nater is that? Why, says he, it is something to fill up the two first pages with. But, says I, aint the two first pages filled up yet? I thought we had jest got through the last page; I hope our cake aint all turning to dough again. O, it's all right, says he, we always print the first pages last; all we want now is the preface, to fill up them are two first pages. Well, says I, but this is a pretty curious piece of business, this duin work backwards. I've hearn tell that Freemasons when they build their chimneys, begin at the top and work down, and that's what's got the Anti Masons so mad about it, that they are going to tear 'em all up, root and branch; but I never knew afore that folks printed the first end of a book last. But now, says I, Mr printer, if I've got to make this ere preface that you tell about, what must I put into it? O, says he, you must tell 'em something about the book; how you come to make it, and what's in it, and what it's good

1*

for, and the like of that. Well, says I, if that's all, I
guess I can work it out in short metre. In the first
place then, I made the book because I couldn't help it ;
if I hadn't made it, I dont believe but what I should
have split. And in the next place, I made it so as to
get my letters all together, out of the way of the rascally counterfeits, so that folks might know the good
eggs from the rotten ones. And about these counterfeits, I see the New York Daily Advertiser says they are
going to print a book of the counterfeit letters somewhere there or at Philadelphia. All I have to say about
it is, they are welcome to print as many letters as they
are a mind to, if they will only jest put their own names
to 'em. But he that will print his letters and put *my*
name to 'em, I think would steal a sheep.

And in the next place, as to what is in the book, I
guess folks will find that out fast enough, without my
telling them.

And in the last place, as to what it is good for, it will
tell folks more about politics, and how to get offices, than
ever they knew before in all their lives ; and what is the
best ont, it will be pretty likely to get me in to be
President.

MAJOR JACK DOWNING.

BOSTON, Nov. 14, 1833.

CONTENTS.

MY LIFE.

MY LETTERS.

APPENDIX.

View of Downingville, from Uncle Joshua's Barn-Yard.

MY LIFE.

*In which I tell considerable more about my Grandfather,
than I do about Myself.*

When we read about great men, we always want to
know something about the place where they live; therefore I shall begin my history with a short account of
Downingville, the place where I was born and brought
up.

Downingville is a snug, tidy sort of a village, situated
in a valley about two miles long, and a mile and a half
wide, scooped out between two large rugged hills that
lie to the east and west, having a thick forest of trees to
the north, and a clear pond of water, with a sandy
beach, to the south. It is about three miles from the
main road as you go back into the country, and is *jest
about in the middle of down east.* It contains by this time
a pretty considerable number of inhabitants, though my
grandfather Downing was the first person that settled
there, jest after he got back from sogering in the revolutionary war. It has a school-house, and a tavern,
and a minister, and a doctor, and a blacksmith, and a
shoe-maker, and folks that work at most all sorts of
trades. They have n't got any meetin house up yet, but
the school house is pretty large and does very well to
hold meetins in, and they have meetins very regular

2

every Sunday, the men filling up all the seats on one side of the school house and the women on the other.

They have n't got any lawyer in Downingville; there was one come once and sot out to settle there, and hired a room and put a sign up over the door with his name on it, and the word OFFICE in great large letters, so big you could read 'em clear across the road. A meeting of the inhabitants was called at the school house the next day, and after chawing the matter over awhile, it was unanimously agreed if the man wanted an office he should go somewhere else for it, for as for having an office-seeker in Downingville they never would. So they voted that he should leave the town in twenty-four hours, or they would take him down to the pond and duck him, and ride him out of town on a rail. A committee of twenty of the stoutest men in Downingville was appointed to carry the message to him, at which he prudently took the hint, and packed up and cleared out that afternoon. All the quarrels, and disputes and law-cases are always left out to uncle Joshua Downing, and he settles them all, by and large, at two shillings apiece, except where they have come to blows, and then he charges two and sixpence a piece.

The land in Downingville is most capital rich land, and bears excellent crops. I would n't pretend to say it 's equal to some land I've hearn tell of away off in Ohio, where the corn grows so tall they have to go up on a ladder to pick the ears off; and where a boy fell into the hole that his father had dug a beet out of, and they had to let down a bed-cord to draw him up again; and where pigs are so plenty that they run about the farms ready roasted, and some of 'em with knives and forks in their backs for any body who wants to eat. I would n't pretend that Downingville is any such sort of a place as that; but this I do say, he that is diligent and will plant his potatoes and corn early, and hoe them well, may always get a good crop, and live above board.

As I said afore, my grandfather, old Mr Zebedee Downing, was the first settler in Downingville. Bless his old heart, he's living yet, and although he is eighty-six years old, he attended a public caucus for the good of his country about two years ago, and made a speech, as you will find somewhere before you get through this book, where it tells about my being nominated for Governor of the State of Maine.

As it is the fashion, in writing the lives of great folks, to go back and tell something about their posterity, I spose I ought to give some account of my good old grandfather, for he was a true patriot, and as strong a republican as ever uncle Joshua was. He was born somewhere in the old bay State away back of Boston, and when the revolutionary war come on he went a sogering. Many and many a time, when I was a little boy, I've sot on the dye-pot in the corner till most midnight to hear him tell over his going through the *fatigue of Burgwine.* If one of the neighbors came in to chat awhile in an evening, my grandfather was always sure to go through with the fatigue of Burgwine ; and if a stranger was travelling through Downingville and stopt at my grandfather's in a warm afternoon to get a drink of water, it was ten chances to one if he could get away till my grandfather had been through the whole story of the fatigue of Burgwine. He used to tell it the best to old Mr Johnson, who used to come in regularly about once a week to spend an evening and drink a mug of my grandfather's cider. And he would set so patiently and hear my grandfather through from beginning to end, that I never could tell which took the most comfort, Mr Johnson in drinking the cider, or my grandfather in going through the fatigue of Burgwine. After Mr Johnson had taken about two or three drinks he would smack his lips, and says he, I guess, Mr Downing, you would have been glad to get such a mug of cider as this in the battle of Burgwine. Why yes, said my grandfather, or

when we was on the march from Cambridge to Peekskill either, or from Peekskill to Albany, or from Albany
to Saratogue, where we went through the fatigue of
Burgwine. Old Schyler was our gineral, said my grandfather, bracing himself back in his chair, and he turned
out to be a traitor, and was sent for, to go to Gineral
Washington to be court-martialed. Then gineral Gates
was sent to us to take the command, and he was a most
capital officer every inch of him. He had his cocked
hat on, and his regimentals, and his furbelows on his
shoulders, and he looked nobly, said my grandfather.
I can see him now as plain as if 'twas yesterday. He
wore a plaguy great stub cue, as big as my wrist, sticking out at the back of his neck as straight as a hand-
spike. Well, when Gates came we were all reviewed,
and every thing was put in complete order, and he led us
on, ye see, to take Burgwine. By daylight in the morning we were called out by the sound of the drum, and
drawn up in regiments, and the word was, ' on your
posts, march.' And there we stood marching on our
posts without moving forward an inch ; heads up, looking to the right ; we did n't dare to move an eye, nor
hardly to wink.

By and by along comes the old Gineral to inspect us,
riding along so stately, and that old stub cue sticking
out behind his head so straight, it seems as though I can
see him now right here before me. And then he addressed us, like a father talking to his children. Fellow soldiers, says he, this day we are going to try the
strength of Burgwine's forces ; now let every man keep
a stiff upper lip, go forward boldly and attack them
with courage, and you 've nothing to fear. O, he addressed us completely ; and then we marched off to
meet the inemy. By and by we begun to hear the balls
whizzing over our heads, and the inemy's guns begun
to roar like thunder. I felt terribly for a minute or two,
but we kept marching up, marching up, said my grand-

father, rising and marching across the floor, for we had
orders not to fire a gun till we got up so near we could
almost reach 'em with our bagonuts; and there was a
hundred drums all in a bunch rattling enough to craze
a nation, and the fifes and the bugles, continued my
grandfather, still marching across the floor, went tudle,
tudle, tudle, tudle — O, I can hear that very tune ringing in my ears now, as plain as if 'twas yesterday, and
I never shall forget it to my dying day. When we got
up so near the inemy that we could fairly see the white
of their eyes, the word was 'halt,' said my grandfather,
suddenly halting in the middle of the floor, and sticking
his head back as straight as a soldier — 'make ready;'
'twas did in a moment, continued my grandfather,
throwing his staff up against his shoulder, — 'take aim'
— 'twas did in a moment, fetching his staff down straight
before his eyes — 'fire' — then, O marcy, what a roar,
said my grandfather, striking his staff down on the
floor, and such a smother and smoke you could n't
hardly see your hand afore you. Well in an instant
the word was 'prime and load,' and as fast as we fired
we fell back in the rear to let others come up and take
their turn, so by the time we were loaded we were in
front and ready to fire again, for we kept marching all
the time, said my grandfather, beginning to march again
across the floor. But the inemy stood their ground and
kept pouring in upon us tremendously, and we kept
marching up and firing, marching up and firing, but
did n't gain forward an inch. I felt streaked enough,
for the balls were whistling over our heads, and sometimes a man would drop down on one side of me and
sometimes on t'other, but it would n't do for us to flinch
a hair; we must march up and fire and wheel to the
right and left, and keep it going. By and by the word
was, 'advance columns;' then, heavens and earth, how
light I felt, said my grandfather, quickening his march
across the floor. I knew in a moment the inemy was

2*

retreating, and it seemed to me I could have jumped over the moon. Well, we marched forward, but still kept firing, and presently we begun to come on to the inemy's ground; and then, O marcy, such a sight I never see before and never want to again: stepping over the dead bodies, and the poor wounded wretches wallowing in their blood, mangled all to pieces, and such screeches and groans, some crying out dont kill me, dont kill me, and others begging us to kill 'em to put 'em out of misery. O, it was enough to melt the very heart of a stone, said my grandfather, wiping the tears from his eyes.

But they need n't have been afraid of being hurt, for our Gineral was one of the best men that ever lived. He had the carts brought up immediately and all the poor wounded souls carried off as fast as possible where they could be taken good care of. He would n't let one of 'em be hurt any more than he would one of his own men. But it was a dreadful hot battle; we fit and skirmished all the afternoon and took a good many prisoners, and some cannon and ammunition. When it come night the inemy retreated to their fortifications, and we camped all night on the ground with our guns in our hands, ready at a moment's warning to pitch battle again. As soon as it was daylight we were all mustered and paraded again, and round come the old Gineral to see how we looked. He held his head up like a soldier, and the old stub cue stuck out as straight as ever. I can see it now as plain as I can see my staff, said my grandfather. And O, my stars, how he addressed us; it made our hearts jump to hear him. Fellow soldiers, says he, this day we shall make Burgwine tremble. If you are only as brave as you were yesterday we shall have him and all·his army before night. But Burgwine had slipped away in the night and got into a place stronger fortified. But he could n't get away; he was hemmed in all round; so we got him before it was over. We were five or six days skirmishing about it; but I cant tell you all, nor a quarter part ont.

But how was it you took Burgwine at last? said Mr Johnson, taking another drink of cider. O, he had to give up at last, said my grandfather. After we had skirmished a day or two longer, Gineral Gates sent word to Burgwine, that if he had a mind to march his army back into Canada, and leave every thing this side unmolested, he'd let him go peaceably. But Burgwine would n't accept it; he sent word back that 'he was going to winter with his troops in Boston.' Well, after we had skirmished round two or three days longer, and Burgwine got into such close quarters that he could n't get away any how, he sent word to Gineral Gates that he'd accept the offer and march back to Canada; but Gates sent word back to him again, 'You said you meant to winter in Boston, and I mean to make you as good as your word.' At last Burgwine see it was no use for him to hold out any longer, so he give all his men up prisoners of war. Then we were all paraded in lines a little ways apart to see them surrender. And they marched out and marched along towards us; and it was a most noble sight to see them all dressed out in their regimentals and their bagonuts glistening in the sun enough to dazzle any body's eyes. And they marched along and stacked their arms, and they all marched through between our lines looking homesick enough. I guess we felt as well as they did if our clothes want so good.

Well that was the end of the war in the northern states. There was a little skirmishing away off to the south afterwards, but nothing to be compared to that. The battle of Burgwine was what achieved our independence; it was the cap-stone of the war; there never was sich a gloris battle as that since the days of Cesar, nor Methuselah, no, nor clear back to Adam. I dont think

there ever was, said Mr Johnson, handing me the quart
mug and telling me to run and get another mug of cider ;
for before my grandfather could get through the fatigue
of Burgwine Mr Johnson would most always get to the
bottom of the mug.   When I brought in the second
mug, Mr Johnson took another sip and smacked his
lips, and says he, Mr Downing I should like to drink a
toast with you ; so here 's health and prosperity to the
apple-trees of Downingville.   Mr Downing, what will
you drink to us ? said he, handing the mug to my
grandfather.   Why, I dont keer about any cider, said
my grandfather [for he is a very temperate man, and
so are all the Downings remarkably temperate] but I
will jest drink a little to the memory of the greatest and
the bravest Gineral that this world ever see yet; so
here 's my respects to old Gineral Gates' stub cue.   By
this time my grandfather having poured out of him the
whole fatigue of Burgwine ; and Mr Johnson having
poured into him about three pints of cider, they would
both of them feel pretty considerably relieved, and Mr
Johnson would bid us good night and go home.

I take it that it was hearing these stories of my grandfather's bravery told over so often in my younger days,
that made me such a military character as to induce the
President to appoint me to the command at Madawaska,
and also to go to South Carolina to put down the Nullifiers.   But I 'm getting a little before my story, for I
have n't got through with my grandfather yet, and my
father comes before I do too.   As I said afore, my
grandfather was the first settler in Downingville.   When
he got through sogering in the revolutionary war, he
took a notion he 'd go and pick him out a good lot of
land away down east to settle on, where there was land
enough to be had jest for whistling for it, and where his
boys would have a chance to do something in the
world.   So he took grandmother and the two boys, for
father and Uncle Joshua were all the boys he had then,

and packed them into a horse waggon, and took an axe
and a hoe and a shovel, and some victuals, and a bed
tick to put some straw in, and a gun and some blankets
and one thing another, and started off down east. He
drove away into Maine till he got clear to the end of
the road, and then he picked his way along through the
woods and round the pond five miles further, till he got
to the very spot where Downingville now is, and there
he stopt and baited his horse, and while grandmother
and the boys sot down and took a bit of a luncheon,
grandfather went away up top of one of the hills to
take a view of the country. And when he come down
again, says he, I guess we may as well ontackle, for I
dont believe we shall find a better place if we travel all
summer. So he ontackled the old horse, and took the
waggon and turned it over against a great oak tree, and
put some bushes up round it and made a pretty comfortable sort of a house for 'em to sleep in a few nights,
and then he took his axe and slashed away amongst the
trees. But that old oak never was cut down; it 's the
very same one that stands out a little ways in front of
grandfather's house now. And poor old grandmother as
long as she lived, for she 's been dead about five years,
always made a practice once a year, when the day come
round that they first camped under the old oak, to have
the table carried out and set under the tree, and all
hands, children and grand-children, had to go and eat
supper there, and the good old lady always used to tell
over the whole story how she slept eight nights under
the waggon, and how they were the sweetest nights' rest
she ever had.

Well, grandfather he smashed away among the trees,
and he soon had a half a dozen acres of 'em sprawling,
and while they were drying in the sun he went to
work and built him a snug little log house, and made
two stools to set on, one for him and one for grandmother, and a couple of blocks for the boys. He made

a stone fireplace in one corner of the house, and left a hole in one corner of the roof for the smoke to go out, and he got it all fixed as nice as a new pin, and then they moved into it; and I've heard grandmother say more than a hundred times, that she raly believed she took more comfort in that log house, than ever a queen took in a palace.

When the leaves and the twigs of the trees that grandfather had cut down had got considerable dry in the sun, he went out one warm clear afternoon and sot fire to 'em. The wind was blowing a considerable of a breeze from the southward, and the fire spread almost as fast as a horse could run. Grandmother used to say it was the grandest sight she ever see, to see them are six acres of trees all in a light flame at once, and the fire streaming up as high as the tallest pines, sometimes in a broad red sheet, and sometimes in narrow strips that went up rolling and bending like ten thousand fiery dragon's tongues. After the fire had gone through it grandfather went to work to clear it up. He picked up the limbs and bits that were left and threw 'em in heaps and sot fire to 'em again, and he laid sticks across the large logs that were too heavy to move, and *niggered* them off with fire, and then roolled them up in piles and sot fire to 'em again and burnt 'em all up smack smooth. Then he went to work and planted the ground all over to corn, and potatoes, and punkins, and beans, and squashes, and round near the house he planted water-millions, and mush-millions, and cowcumbers, and beats and carrots and tarnips; and grandmother carried out a whole apron full of seeds of all kinds of arbs that ever grew in old Massachusetts, and sowed 'em all round, and they come up as thick as hops.

After this the family of old Mr Zebedee Downing always lived like heroes and never knew what it was to be in want. They had ten children, and a smart likely set of boys and gals they were too, and they all lived to grow up, and were all married and well to do in the world. Father, whose name was Solomon, was the oldest boy, and as they grew up, the hardest of the work naturally fell upon him, and as grandfather begun to get along considerable in years, father had to take the principal care of the farm. So that he was always called a hard-working boy and a hard-working man. He had a quiet peaceable disposition, and was never known to quarrel with any body, and scarcely ever to speak a hash word. He was always out as soon as it was light in the morning, and worked as long as he could see at night, and let the weather be what it would, cold or hot, rain or shine, his day's work was never left undone. But this hard work, and going out in the wet and cold so much, brought on the rumaties and made an old man of him before he was fifty. For ten years past he has n't been able to do hardly any thing, and he can't get about now half so smart as grandfather, although he is twenty-two years younger.

Uncle Joshua was the next oldest, and he was as different from father as a toad wants a tail. He was a clear shirk, and never would work if he could help it. But he was always good natured, and full of his pranks, and kept his clack agoing the whole day long; so that the boys used to like him, and whenever they wanted to have any frolic or fun they always used to go to him to take the lead. As he grew up he took to reading considerable, and after they begun to have newspapers at Downingville he was a master hand to read newspapers and talk politics, and by the time he was twenty-five years old he knew more about politics than any other man in Downingville. When he was thirty years old he was chosen Moderator of the town meeting, and has been chosen to that office every year since. He's been a squire a good many years, and has held most all the offices in town one after another, and is on the whole considered the foremost man in Downingville. He is now Post Master of the United States for Downingville, an office which I was the means of helping him to by my acquaintance with the President. Uncle Joshua has been a considerable of a trading sort of a character, and he 's got pretty well afore hand, so that he lives in a nice two story house, painted red, with a good orchard round it, and owns a good farm, and a saw-mill, besides considerable wild land.

I cant stop now to tell about the rest of my uncles and ants, for I've got so many letters to put into this book that if I stop to tell about one half of my relations there would n't be room enough for the letters ; and it would n't do to leave them out, for they contain all the history of my public life. So I may as well break right off from the rest of 'em, and begin to tell about myself.

I believe I was born somewhere about the year seventeen hundred and ninety-five, more or less, and mother says I was the smartest baby that she ever see. I dont speak of this by way of bragging, but as I am writing a history to go before the world, I'm bound to be impartial. She says before I was a week old I showed that I was real grit, and could kick and scream two hours upon the stretch, and not seem to be the least bit tired that ever was. But I dont remember any thing about this. The first I remember, I found myself one cold November day, when I was about five years old, bareheaded and barefoot, sliding on the ice. It had been a snapping cold night, and in the morning the pond was all froze over as smooth as glass, and hard enough to bear a horse. All the boys in the neighborhood, and most all the gals, turned out and had a fine frolic that day, sliding and running on the pond. Most of the larger boys had shoes, but we little fellers that want big enough to wear shoes had to tuff it out as well as we could. I carried a great pine chip in my hand, and when my feet got so cold I could n't stand it no longer, I'd put the chip down and stand on that a little while and warm 'em, and then at it to sliding again like a two year old.

When I got to be considerable of a boy I used to have to work with father on the farm. But it always seemed to go rather against my grain, and father used to say that I did n't love work a bit better than uncle Joshua did, without he'd give me my stent, and then he said I would spring to it and get it done by noon, and go off round the pond in the afternoon fishing or hunting musquash. I think I took the most comfort in catching musquash of any thing I used to do. There was a good deal of pleasure in catching pickerel; to take a long fishing pole and line, and go down to the pond in the morning, and stand on a log whose top limbs run away off into the water, and throw the hook off and bob it about on the top of the water, and see a great pickerel jump and catch it, and wait a minute or two for him to get it well into his mouth, and then pull him ashore, kicking and jumping and flouncing—this was most capital fun, but it want quite equal to musquashing. I had a little steel trap, and I used to go down at night to the bank of a brook that run into the pond, and set the trap on the bank just under water, and fasten it by a line to a stake or a tree, and put a bit of a parsnip on a stick and place it over the trap a little above the water, and then go home and sleep as well as I could for dreaming of musquashes, and as soon as it was cleverly light in the morning go down to the pond and creep along where the trap was sot, with my heart in my mouth, wondering if it was sprung or no, and come along to the stake and see no trap, but the line drawn straight out into the water, then take hold of the line and draw up the trap, and see it rising up through the water fast hold of a great plump musquash, as dead as a drownded rat and full of fur as a beaver, this was fun alive; it made me feel as nicely as though I was hauling up a bucket of dollars. The summer I was fourteen years old I catch-

3

ed enough to buy me a fur hat, and a pair of shoes, and a new jacket and trowses; and enough to buy me a pretty good new suit of clothes almost every summer after that till I was twenty. Howsomever I used to stick to the farm pretty well, and help father along all I could, for after I got old enough to think more about it, it used to hurt my feelings to see the old gentleman work so hard. And many a time when he has taken hold of a hard job to do, I have gone to him and took it out of his hands, and said, now father you go into the house and set down and rest you, and let me do this. And the old gentleman would turn round, but I could see the water come into his eyes, and he would say, 'Well Jack, you are a kind boy, let folks say what they will of you;' and then he would take his staff and walk away into the house.

We used to have a school in Downingville about three months in the winter season and two months in the summer, and I went to the winter school three winters, from the time I was twelve till I was fifteen. And I was called about the best scholar of my age that there was in school. But to be impartial, I must confess the praise did n't always all belong to me, for I used sometimes to work headwork a little in order to get the name of being a smart scholar. One instance of it was in reading. I got along in reading so well, that the master said I read better than some of the boys that were considerable older than I, and that had been to school a dozen winters. But the way I managed it was this. There was cousin Obediah was the best reader there was in school, and as clever a boy as one in a thousand, only his father had n't got no orchard. So I used to carry a great apple to school in my pocket every day and give to him to get him to set behind me when I was reading, where he could peak into my book, and when I come to a hard word, have him whisper it to me, and then I read it out loud. Well, one day I was reading along so, pretty glib, and at last I come to a pesky great long crooked word, that I could n't make head nor tail to it. So I waited for Obediah. But it proved to be a match for Obediah. He peaked, and squinted, and choked, and I was catching my breath and waiting for him to speak ; and at last he found he could do nothing with it, and says he, ' skip it.' The moment I heard the sound I bawled out, *skip it*. What's that ? said the master, looking at me as queer as though he had catched a weazel asleep. I stopt and looked at the word again, and poked my tongue out, and waited for Obediah. Well, Obediah give me a hunch, and whispered again, ' skip it.' Then I bawled out again, *skip it*. At that the master and about one half the scholars yaw-hawed right out. I could n't stand that ; and I dropt the book and streaked it out of school, and pulled foot for home as fast as I could go, and I never showed my head in school again from that day to this. But for all that, I made out to pick up a pretty good education. I got so I could read and spell like a fox, and could cypher as far as the rule of three. And when I got to be about twenty years old, I was strongly talked of one winter for schoolmaster. But as a good many of the same boys and gals would go to me, that were in the school when I read ' skip it,' I did n't dare to venture it for fear there would be a sort of a snickering among 'em whenever any of the scholars come to a hard word.

So I jogged along with father on the farm. But let me be doing what I would, whether it was hoeing pota-toes, or pitching hay, or making stone wall, or junking and piling logs, I never could feel exactly easy ; some-thing seemed to keep ringing in my ears all the time, and saying I was made to do something else in the world besides this. And an old woman that come along and told fortunes, when she come to tell mine, said that wherever I should go and whatever I should undertake to do, I should always get to the top of the ladder. I believe I have mentioned it somewhere in one of my letters. Well, this made me keep a thinking so much the harder, and wondering what I should be in the world, and although I used to stick to my work as steady as any of the boys, yet I used to feel as uneasy as a fish out of water. But what made me think most about it was father. He always used to stand to it I was smarter than common boys, and used to tell mother she might depend upon it, if I lived and nothing did n't happen to me, I should some day or other raise the name of the Downings higher than it ever had been yet.

At last father drempt a dream, that put the cap-stone upon the whole of it. He dreampt that I was out in the field hoeing potatoes, and he stood leaning over his staff, as he very often used to do, looking at me. By and by he said I stopt hoeing, and stood up and leaned my chin on my hoe handle, and seemed to look up towards the sky; and he said I looked as calm as the moon in a clear summer night. Presently my hat begun to rise up gradually, and dropt off on to the ground, but I stood still. Then he said the top of my head begun to open, and a curious green plant begun to sprout up out of it. And it grew up about two feet, and sent out ever so many young branches with broad green leaves, and then the little buds begun to open and roll out great clusters of the most beautiful bright flowers one above another that ever he see in all his life. He watched 'em till they all got blowed out into a great round bunch, as big as a bushel basket; and then he waked up, and he felt so he got right out of bed and walked the floor till morning. And when we all got up, he sot down and told the dream over to I and mother. Mother sot with her pocket handkerchief wiping the tears out of her eyes all the time he was telling of it; and I felt as though my blood was running cold all over me. But from that time I always felt sure the time would come when Downing-ville would n't be big enough to hold me, and that I should do something or other in the world that would be worth telling of; but what it would be I could n't think.

Well, I kept jogging along on the farm after the same old sort, year after year, so long, and there did n't nothing happen to me, that sometimes I almost begun to give it up, and think sure enough it was all nothing but a dream. Still I kept having spells that I felt terrible uneasy, and was tempted forty times to pack up and go and seek my fortune. I might tell a good deal more about my life, and my uncles and ants and cousins, and the rest of the neighbors: but I begin to feel a most tired of writing my life, and believe I shall have to serve it pretty much as I planted my watermillion seeds. And that was this. When I was about six or seven years old, our folks give me a pint of watermillion seeds and told me to go out into the field and plant 'em for myself, and I might have all I could raise. So off I goes tickled enough. And I went to work and punched little holes down in the ground and put in one seed to time along in a row, three or four inches apart, till I got about half the seeds planted. It was rather a warm afternoon and I begun to feel a little tired, so I took and dug a hole and poured the rest of the seeds all in together, and covered 'em up, and went into the house. Well, mother asked me if I 'd planted my seeds; yes mam, says I. What, all of 'em, says she? Yes mam, says I. But you 've been very spry, says she, how did you get them done so quick? O, says I, easy enough; I planted 'em in a *hill and a row*. And when they begun to come up they found em in a hill and a row sure enough. So I believe I shall have to pour the rest of my life into a hill, and let it go.

To come then right to the pint — I dont mean the pint of watermillion seeds, but the pint in my life which seemed to be the turning pint — In the fall of the year 1829 I took it into my head I 'd go to Portland. I had

3*

heard a good deal about Portland, what a fine place
it was, and how the folks got rich there proper fast;
and that fall there was a couple of new papers come
up to Downingville from there, called the Portland
Courier and Family Reader; and they told a good
many queer kind of things about Portland and one thing
another; and all at once it popped into my head, and I
up and told father, and says I, I 'm going to Portland
whether or no; and I 'll see what this world is made of
yet.   Father stared a little at first, and said he was
afraid I should get lost; but when he see I was bent
upon it, he give it up; and he stepped to his chist and
opened the till, and took out a dollar and give to me,
and says he, Jack, this is all I can do for you; but go,
and lead an honest life, and I believe I shall hear good
of you yet.   He turned and walked across the room,
but I could see the tears start into his eyes, and mother
sot down and had a hearty crying spell.   This made
me feel rather bad for a minute or two, and I almost
had a mind to give it up; and then again father's dream
came into my mind, and I mustered up courage, and
declared 1 'd go.   So I tackled up the old horse and
packed in a load of ax handles and a few notions, and
mother fried me some dough-nuts and put 'em into a box
along with some cheese and sassages, and ropped me up
another shirt, for I told her I did n't know how long I
should be gone; and after I got all rigged out, I went
round and bid all the neighbors good bye, and jumped in
and drove off for Portland.

Ant Sally had been married two or three years before
and moved to Portland, and I inquired round till I found
out where she lived, and went there and put the old
horse up and eat some supper and went to bed.   And the
next morning I got up and straightened right off to see
the Editor of the Portland Courier, for I knew by what
I had seen in his paper that he was jest the man to tell
me which way to steer.   And when I come to see him

I knew I was right; for soon as I told him my name and what I wanted, he took me by the hand as kind as if he had been a brother; and says he, Mr. Downing, I 'll do any thing I can to assist you. You have come to a good town ; Portland is a healthy thriving place, and any man with a proper degree of enterprise may do well here. But says he, Mr. Downing, and he looked mighty kind of knowing, says he, if you want to make out to your mind, you must do as the steamboats do. Well, says I, how do they do ? for I did n't know what a steam boat was, any more than the man in the moon. Why, says he, they *go ahead.* And you must drive about among the folks here jest as though you were at home on the farm among the cattle. Dont be afraid of any of 'em, but figure away, and I dare say you will get into good business in a very little while. But says he, there 's one thing you must be careful of, and that is not to get into the hands of them are folks that trades up round Huckler's Row ; for there 's some sharpers up there, if they get hold of you, would twist your eye teeth out in five minutes. Well after he had gin me all the good advice he could I went back to Ant Sally's again and got some breakfast, and then I walked all over the town to see what chance I could find to sell my ax handles and things, and to get into business.

After I had walked about three or four hours I come along towards the upper end of the town where I found there were stores and shops of all sorts and sizes. And I met a feller, and says I, what place is this ? Why this says he, is Huckler's Row. What, says I, are these the stores where the traders in Huckler's Row keep ? And says he, yes. Well then, thinks I to myself, I have a pesky good mind to go in and have a try with one of these chaps, and see if they can twist my eye teeth out. If they can get the best end of a bargain out of me, they can do what there aint a man in Downingville can do, and I should jest like to know what sort of stuff

these ere Portland chaps are made of. So in I goes
into the best looking store among 'em. And I see some
biscuit lying on the shelf, and says I, Mister, how much
do you ax apiece for them are biscuit ? A cent apiece,
says he. Well, says I, I shant give you that, but if you
've a mind to, I 'll give you two cents for three of 'em,
for I begin to feel a little as though I should like to take
a bite. Well, says he, I would n't sell 'em to any body
else so, but seeing it 's you I dont care if you take 'em.
I knew he lied, for he never see me before in his life.
Well he handed down the biscuits and I took 'em, and
walked round the store awhile to see what else he had
to sell. At last, says I, Mister, have you got any good
new cider ? Says he, yes, as good as ever you see.
Well, says I, what do you ax a glass for it ? Two cents,
says he. Well, says I, seems to me I feel more dry than
I do hungry now. Aint you a mind to take these ere
biscuit again and give me a glass of cider ? And says he
I dont care if I do ; so he took and laid 'em on the shelf
again, and poured out a glass of cider. I took the
cider and drinkt it down, and to tell the truth it was
capital good cider. Then, says I, I guess it 's time for
me to be a going, and I stept along towards the door.
But, says he, stop Mister. I believe you have n't paid
me for the cider. Not paid you for the cider, says I,
what do you mean by that ? Did n't the biscuit, that I
give you jest come to the cider ? Oh, ah, right, says
he. So I started to go again ; and says he, but stop,
Mister, you did n't pay me for the biscuit. What, says
I, do you mean to impose upon me ? do you think I am
going to pay you for the biscuit and let you keep 'em tu ?
Aint they there now on your shelf, what more do you
want ? I guess sir, you dont whittle me in that way.
So I turned about and marched off, and left the feller
staring and thinking and scratching his head, as though
he was struck with a dunderment. Howsomever, I did
n't want to cheat him, only jest to show 'em it want so

easy a matter to pull my eye teeth out, so I called in
next day and paid him his two cents. Well I staid at
Ant Sally's a week or two, and I went about town every
day to see what chance I could find to trade off my ax
handles, or hire out, or find some way or other to begin
to seek my fortune.

And I must confess the editor of the Courier was about
right in calling Portland a pretty good thriving sort of a
place; every body seemed to be as busy as so many bees;
and the masts of the vessels stuck up round the wharves
as thick as pine trees in uncle Joshua's pasture; and the
stores and the shops were so thick, it seemed as if there
was no end to 'em.   In short although I have been round
the world considerable, from that time to this, all the way
from Madawaska to Washington, I 've never seen any
place yet that I think has any business to grin at Portland.

At last I happened to blunder into the Legislater ; and
I believe that was the beginning of my good luck.   I see
such queer kinds of carrying on there, that I could n't
help setting down and writing to cousin Ephraim to tell
uncle Joshua about it; because he always wanted to know
every thing that's going on in politics. So I went to the
editor of the Portland Courier, for I had got out of money,
and asked him if he would be so good as to lend me
ninepence to pay the postage. And he said he would
with all his heart. But he could tell me a better way
than that ; if I had a mind to let him have the letter he
would send it up in the Courier and it would'nt cost any
postage at all. So I let him have it, and fact, he went
right to work and printed it in the Courier as large as
life. He said he would n't let any body see it but cousin
Ephraim ; but somehow or other it leaked out and was
all over the Legislater the next morning, and every body
was inquiring for Mr Downing. Well this kind of got
me right into public life at once ; and I 've been in public
life ever since, and have been writing letters and rising

up along gradually one step after another, till I 've got up along side of the President, and am talked of now pretty strong for President myself, and have been nominated in a good many of the first papers in the country.

All my public life pretty much may be found in my letters. And I shall put 'em into this book along one after another jest as they come, from the time I first sent that letter in the Portland Courier to cousin Ephraim till this time. I don't know but some of the politics in 'em will want a little explaining along by the way, so I have got my friend the editor of the Portland Courier, to put in some notes wherever he thinks they want 'em.

MY LETTERS.

Together with a few from Cousin Nabby, and Uncle Joshua, and Cousin Ephraim, and so on; containing a pretty considerable account of my public life from Jinuary 1830 to November 1833.

[*Note by the Editor.* The political struggle in the Legislature of Maine in the winter of 1830 will long be remembered. The preceding electioneering campaign had been carried on with a bitterness and personality unprecedented in the State, and so nearly were the parties divided, that before the meeting of the Legislature to count the votes for Governor both sides confidently claimed the victory. Hence the members came together with feelings highly excited, prepared to dispute every inch of ground, and ready to take fire at the first spark which collision might produce. A fierce war commenced at the first moment of the meeting, and continued for about six weeks without intermission, before they succeeded in organizing the government. It was during this state of things that Mr Downing fortunately happened to drop into the Legislature, when his prolific genius was at once fired to record the scenes that were passing before him, for the edification not only of the present generation but of remote posterity. In explanation of the first letter, it may be remarked, that as soon as the Representatives had assembled, Albert Smith, Esq. of Nobleborough, the present Marshal of Maine, called them to order, and nominated Mr White of Monmouth, Chairman, who was declared elected without ceremony, and took the chair. After he had occupied it two days Mr Goodenow was elected Speaker.]

LETTER I.

In which Mr Downing tells about choosing Speaker.

Portland, Monday, Jan. 18, 1830.
To Cousin Ephraim Downing up in Downingville.

DEAR COUSIN EPHRAIM. — I now take my pen in hand to let you know that I am well, hoping these few lines will find you enjoying the same blessing. When I come down to Portland I did n't think o' staying more than three or four days, if I could sell my load of ax handles, and mother's cheese, and cousin Nabby's bundle of footings; but when I got here I found uncle Nat was gone a freighting down to Quoddy, and ant Sally said as how I should n't stir a step home till he come back agin, which wont be this month. So here I am, loitering about this great town, as lazy as an ox. Ax handles dont fetch nothing, I could n't hardly give 'em away. Tell cousin Nabby I sold her footings for nine-pence a pair, and took it all in cotton cloth. Mother's cheese come to five-and-sixpence; I got her half a pound of shushon, and two ounces of snuff, and the rest in sugar. When uncle Nat comes home I shall put my ax handles aboard of him, and let him take 'em to Boston next time he goes; I saw a feller tother day, that told me they'd fetch a good price there. — I've been here now a whole fortnight, and if I could tell ye one half I've seen, I guess you'd stare worse than if you'd seen a catamount. I've been to meeting, and to the museum, and to both Legislaters, the one they call the House, and the one they call the Sinnet. I spose uncle Joshua is in a great hurry to hear something about these Legislaters; for you know he's always reading newspapers, and talking politics, when he can get any body to talk with him. I've seen him, when he had five tons of hay in the field well made, and a heavy shower coming up, stand two hours disputing with squire W. about Adams and Jackson, one calling Adams a tory and a fed, and the other saying Jackson was a murderer and a fool; so they kept it up, till the rain began to pour down, and about spoilt all his hay.

Uncle Joshua may set his heart at rest about the bushel of corn that he bet long with the post-master, that Mr Ruggles would be Speaker of that Legislater, they call the House; for he's lost it, slick as a whistle. As I

had n't much to do, I 've been there every day since
they 've been a setting. A Mr White of Monmouth was
the Speaker the two first days ; and I cant see why they
did n't keep him in all the time ; for he seemed to be a
very clever good-natured sort of man, and he had such a
smooth pleasant way with him, that I could n't help feeling sorry when they turned him out and put in another.
But some said he was n't put in hardly fair ; and I dont
know as he was, for the first day when they were all coming in and crowding round, there was a large fat man,
with a round, full, jolly sort of a face, I suppose he was
the captain, for he got up and commanded them to come
to order, and then he told this Mr White to whip into the
chair quicker than you could say Jack Robinson. Some
of 'em scolded about it, and I heard some, in a little
room they called the lobby, say 'twas a mean trick ; but
I could n't see why, for I thought Mr White made a capital Speaker, and when *our* company turns out you know
the captain always has a right to do as he 's a mind to.

They kept disputing most all the time the two first
days about a poor Mr Roberts from Waterborough.
Some said he should n't have a seat, because he adjourned
the town meeting, and was n't fairly elected. Others
said it was no such thing, and that he was elected as
fairly as any of 'em. — And Mr Roberts himself said he
was, and said he could bring men that would swear to it,
and good men too. But notwithstanding all this, when
they came to vote, they got three or four majority that
he should n't have a seat. And I thought it a needless
piece of cruelty, for they want crowded, and there was
a number of seats empty. But they would have it so,
and the poor man had to go and stand up in the lobby.

Then they disputed awhile about a Mr Fowler's having
a seat. Some said he should n't have a seat, because
when he was elected some of his votes were given for his
father. But they were more kind to him than they were
to Mr Roberts ; for they voted that he *should* have a seat ;

and I suppose it was because they thought he had a lawful right to inherit whatever was his father's. They all
declared there was no party politics about it, and I dont
think there was; for I noticed that all who voted that **Mr
Roberts** *should* have a seat, voted that **Mr Fowler** should
not; and all who voted that **Mr Roberts** should *not* have
a seat, voted that **Mr Fowler** *should.* So, as they all voted *both* ways, they must have acted as their consciences
told them, and I dont see how there could be any party
about it.

It's a pity they could n't be allowed to have two speak-
ers, for they seemed to be very anxious to choose **Mr
Ruggles** and **Mr Goodenow.** They two had every vote,
except one, and if they had had *that,* I believe they would
both have been chosen; as it was, however, they both came
within a humbird's eye of it. Whether it was **Mr Ruggles** that voted for **Mr Goodenow,** or **Mr Goodenow** for
Mr Ruggles, I can't exactly tell; but I rather guess it was
Mr Ruggles voted for **Mr Goodenow,** for he appeared to
be very glad that **Mr Goodenow** was elected, and went up
to him soon after **Mr Goodenow** took the chair, and shook
hands with him as good-natured as could be. I would
have given half my load of ax handles, if they could both
have been elected and set up there together, they would
have been so happy. But as they can't have but one
speaker at a time, and as **Mr Goodenow** appears to understand the business very well, it is not likely **Mr Ruggles** will be speaker any this winter. So uncle Joshua
will have to shell out his bushel of corn, and I hope it
will learn him better than to bet about politics again. If
he had not been a goose, he might have known he would
loose it, even if he had been ever so sure of getting it;
for in these politics there's never any telling which way
the cat will jump. You know, before the last September
election, some of the papers that came to our town had
found out that *Mr Hunton* would have five thousand
majority of the votes. And some of the other papers had

found out that *Mr Smith* would have five thousand majority.   But the cat jumped 'tother way to *both* of 'em ; for
I cant find yet as either of 'em has got *any* majority.
Some say Mr Hunton has got a *little* majority, but as far
from five thousand as I am from home.   And as for **Mr**
Smith, they dont think he has any majority at all.   You
remember, too, before I came from home, some of the
papers said how there was a majority of ten or fifteen
national republicans in the Legislater, and the other papers
said there was a pretty clever little majority of *democratic
republicans*.   Well, now every body says it has turned
out jest as that queer little paper, called the Daily Courier, said 't would.   That paper said it was such a close
rub, it could n't hardly tell which side would beat.   And it
's jest so, for they 've been here now most a fortnight acting
jest like two boys playin see-saw on a rail.   First one
goes up, then 'tother ; but I reckon one of the boys is
rather heaviest, for once in awhile he comes down chuck,
and throws the other up into the air as though he would
pitch him head over heels.

In that 'tother Legislater they call the Sinnet, there
has been some of the drollest carryins on that you ever
heard of.   If I can get time I 'll write you something
about it, pretty soon.   So I subscribe myself, in haste,
your loving cousin till death.

JACK DOWNING.

LETTER II.

*In which Mr Downing tells about poor Mr Roberts having
to stand up.*

[*Note by the Editor.* It was the rule at the meeting of the
Legislature to admit all to a seat who could produce a certificate of
their election, which certificate was considered *prima facia* evidence that they were duly returned as members. The Portland
Argus and Advertiser were the leading papers of the two parties ;
and as matters began to grow worse and worse in the Legislature,
the Argus constantly affirmed that the democratic republicans used
every endeavor in their power to organize the government and
proceed in the public business, but that the Huntonites would not
let them. And the Advertiser as constantly affirmed, that the national republicans used their utmost endeavors to proceed in the
public business, but the Jacksonites would not let them.]

Portland, Jan. 22, 1830.

To Uncle Joshua Downing up in Downingville.

DEAR UNCLE JOSHUA. — I spose you learnt by my letter t'other day to cousin Ephraim, that you had lost the
bushel of corn you bet about the Speaker in the Legislater ; I mean that Legislater they call the House ; for
Mr White got it first, and then Mr Goodenow got it, and
he's kept it ever since. And they say he'll be Speaker
all winter, although he don't *speak* near so much as
some the rest of 'em. There's lawyer Ruggles, of
Thomaston, that used to be Speaker, and folks say he
made a very smart one. And there's lawyer Boutelle,
of Waterville, who's got eyes sharp enough to look
through any body, and who makes 'em all as still as
mice when he speaks. And there's lawyer Smith of
Nobleborough ; he looks very much like a man I saw
in the museum, that they called Daniel Lambert, only
he is'nt quite so large ; but my patience, he's a real
peeler for speaking, and sometimes he pours out his
voice so as to make me jump right up on my feet. If

I was going to bet who would be Speaker next year, I should bet upon him before any body else. And there's lawyer Bourne, of Kennebunk, and lawyer Kent, of Bangor, and lawyer Norton, of Milburn, and doctor Burnham, of Orland, and doctor Shaw of Wiscasset, and doctor Wells, of Freeport, and parson Knowlton, of Montville, and parson Swett, of Prospect, and some others, if I could only think of 'em. Now, most any of these speak more than Mr Goodenow does; and still Mr Goodenow is called the Speaker, because they voted that he should be. They've disputed two days more about that poor Mr Roberts having a seat. I can't see why they need to make such a fuss about it. As they've got seats enough, why don't they let him have one, and not keep him standing up for three weeks in the lobby and round the fire; its a plaguy sight worse than being on a standing committee, for they say the standing committees have a chance to set most every day. But in the dispute about Mr Roberts last Wednesday and Thursday, the difficulty seemed to be something or other about a *primy facy* case. I don't know what sort of a case 'twas, but that's what they called it. Some said he hadn't got any *primy facy* case, and he mus'nt have a seat till he had one. The others stood to it that he *had* got one, and a very good one; Mr Ruggles said it was full as good a one as the gentlemen from Portland had. And they read above twenty papers that they called depositions, about the town meeting at Waterborough; but they didn't seem to say any thing about the *primy facy* case. About one half of 'em said the town meeting was adjourned, and t'other half said .twas'nt. And one of the depositions said there was some of 'em at the meeting agreed that Mr Roberts should n't be elected at any rate; and if they could n't prevent it any other way, they agreed to keep up a row till midnight. And when they brought in candles in the evening, they knocked 'em all over, and put 'em out. So they all

4*

had to clear out; and some said there was a vote to adjourn the meeting, and some said Mr Roberts adjourned it alone, and some said 'twasn't adjourned at all. And one of the depositioners said Mr Roberts offered to give him as much rum as he would drink, if he would only say the meeting was fairly adjourned. But all the depositions didn't convince but sixty-nine members of the House that Mr Roberts had a *primy facy* case; and there were seventy-five convinced t'other way. So, after they had disputed two days, they voted again that Mr Roberts shouldn't have a seat yet.

O dear, uncle Joshua, these Legislaters have got the State into a dreadful pickle. I've been reading the Portland Argus and the Portland Advertiser, and it's enough to scare a Bunker Hill sojer out of his seven senses, to see what we are all coming to. According to these papers, there are two very clever parties in the State, that are trying with all their might to save us from ruin. They are called *democratic republikins*, and *national republikins;* and you'd be pefectly astonished to see how hard they've worked, as these papers say, in both Legislaters, to set things right, and get business a going on well, so that we can have a governor, and live in peace and harmony, and not break out into a civil war, and all be ruined in a bunch. But it's doubtful if they'll make out to save us after all; for there is such a set of Jacksonites and Huntonites, that are all the time a plotting to bring us to destruction, that I tell ye what 'tis, if something isn't done pretty soon, it'll be gone goose with us.

These Jacksonites and Huntonites seem to have a majority in the Legislaters; and they've been making a proper bother for a most three weeks, so that the democratic republikins and the national republikins could n't do nothing at all. And sometimes I'm really afraid they'll have to break up and go home without doing any thing; and if they do, they say we shall all be afloat, and there's no knowing where we shall land. The republikins appointed a committee to count the votes for governor, and the committee told 'em t'other day, there was 39 majority for Mr Hunton, and he was elected. But then these Jacksonites and Huntonites went to disputing about the matter; and some say they will dispute it this fortnight yet. What a blessing it would be if the Legislaters were all democratic and national republikins. The people are growing pretty mad at all this botheration, and I can't tell what'll be the end on't. But I shall write again to you or cousin Ephraim pretty soon. So I remain your loving neefu till death.

JACK DOWNING.

P. S. I concluded to send my letters in the Daily Courier to save postage — the printer said he would n't show them to any body.

———

LETTER III.

In which Cousin Nabby advises Mr Downing to come home.

Downingville, Jan. 30, 1830.

DEAR COUSIN JACK. — If you were only here, I would break the handle of our old birch broom over your back for serving me such a caper. Here I have been waiting three weeks for that cotton cloth you got for the footings; and you know the meeting-house windows were to have been broke a fortnight ago, if I had got it. And then I had to tell Sam, I was waiting for some cotton cloth. He tried to keep in with all his might, but he burst out a laughing so, I'm a good mind to turn him off. But if I do, *you and he will be both in the same pickle.* You had better let them *legislaters* alone; and if you can't sell your ax handles, take 'em and come home and mind your business. There is Jemima Parsons romping about with the school-master, fair weather and foul. Last Wednesday she went a sleigh-riding with him, and to-night she's going to the singing-school, and he is going to carry her. Last night she came over to our house, and wanted me to go to uncle Zeke's to borry their swifts, she said, when she knew we had some, and had borried them a dozen times. I said nothing, but went with her. When we got there, who should we find but the school-master. — I know Jemime knew it, and went there purpose to have him go home with her. She never askt for the swifts. Coming home, the master askt her if she had seen your last letter. She said yes, and began to laugh and talk about you, just as tho' I was no relation. She said she guessed them legislaters would try to make a governor out of *you* next, if you staid there much longer. One of them steers you sold to Jacob Small that week you went to Portland, died t'other day; and he says if we have no governor this year, he wont pay you a cent for 'em. So you have lost your steers and Jemima Parsons, jest by your dallying about there among them legislaters. I say you had better come home, and see to your own business. I spose father and brother Eph. would like to have you stay there all winter and tell 'em about the governors and legislaters, but ant wants her tea, and I want my cotton cloth, so I wish you'd make haste home and bring 'em.   Your loving Cousin,

                                        NABBY.

To Mr Jack Downing.

LETTER IV.

In which Uncle Joshua tells how he went to Boston, and took dinner with the Gineral Court.

[*Note by the Editor.* This letter came through the Boston Daily Advertiser, and there has always been some doubt whether it was really written by that respectable and stanch patriot, Joshua Downing, Esq. The Major says he has often asked him the question, at which his uncle Joshua would always shake his head and laugh, but give no answer. It is written, however, in the pure style of the Downing family, which is the strongest evidence we can have that the letter is genuine.]

Letter from Joshua Downing, in Boston, to his nephew, Jack Downing, in Portland.

DEAR NEPHEW,—I left home just after your letter to your cousin Ephraim got there, and I didn't get a sight of your letter to me that you put into the Courier at Portland, until I saw it in the Daily Advertiser in Boston, and I guess Mr Hale is the only person in Boston who takes that are little Courier, so you was pretty safe about the letter not being seen, as the printer promised you. — How I happened to see it here, you will find out before I have got through with this letter. I guess you wont be a little struck up when you find out that I'm in Boston — but I had best begin at the beginning and then I shall get thro' quicker.

After seeing your letter to Ephraim as I said before, I concluded it wouldn't be a bad scheme to tackle up and take a load of turkies, some apple-sauce, and other notions that the neighbors wanted to get to market, and as your uncle Nat would be in Boston with the ax handles, we all thought best to try our luck there. Nothing happened worth mentioning on the road, nor till next morning after I got here and put up in Elm street. I then got off my watch pretty curiously, as you shall be informed. I was down in the bar room, and tho't it well enough to look pretty considerable smart, and now and then compared my watch with the clock in the bar, and found it as near right as ever it was — when a feller stept up to me and ask'd how I'd trade? and says I, for what? and says he, for your watch — and says I, any way that will be a fair shake — upon that says he, I'll give you *my* watch and five dollars. — Says I, its done! He gave me the five dollars, and I gave him my watch. Now, says I, give me *your* watch — and, says he, with a loud laugh, I han't got none — and that kind a turn'd the laugh on me. Thinks I, let them laugh that lose. Soon as the laugh was well over, the feller thought he'd try the watch to his ear — why, says he, it dont go — no, says I, not without its carried — then I began to laugh — he tried to open it and couldn't start it a hair, and broke his thumb nail into the bargain. Won't she open, says he? Not's I know on, says I — and then the laugh seemed to take another turn.

Don't you think I got off the old Brittania pretty well, considrin? And then I thought I'd go and see about my load of turkies and other notions. I expected to have gone all over town to sell my load, but Mr Doolittle told me if I'd go down to the new market, I should find folks enough to buy all I had at once. So down I goes, and a likely kind of a feller, with an eye like a hawk and quick as a steeltrap for a trade, (they called him a 4th staller,) came up to the wagon, and before you could say Jack Robinson, we struck a bargain for the whole cargo — and come to weigh and reckon up, I found I should get as much as 10s6d more than any of us calculated before I left home, and had the applesauce left besides. So I thought I'd jist see how this 4th staller worked his card to be able to give us so good a price for the turkies, and I went inside the market-house, and a grander sight I never expect to see! But it was the 3d staller, instead of the 4th, had my turkies

all sorted and hung up, and looking so much better that
I hardly should known 'em. Pretty soon, a gentleman
asked the 3d staller what he asked for turkies? Why,
says he, if you want something better than you ever saw
before, there's some 'twas killed last night purpose for
you. You may take 'em at 9d, being it's you. I'll give
you 12 cents, said the gentleman, as I've got some of
the General Court to dine with me, and must treat well.
I shant stand for half a cent with an old customer, says
he. And so they traded; and in about the space of half
an hour or more, all my turkies went into baskets at that
rate. The 4th staller gave me 6d a pound, and I began
to think I'd been a little too much in a hurry for trade —
but's no use to cry for spilt milk. Then I went up to the
State House to see what was going on there; but I
thought I'd get off my apple-sauce on my way — and
seeing a sign of old clothes bartered, I stepped in and
made a trade, and got a whole suit of superfine black
broadcloth from from top to toe, for a firkin of apple-
sauce, (which didn't cost much I guess, at home.)

Accordingly I rigged myself up in the new suit, and
you'd hardly known me. I did n't like the set of the
shoulders, they were so dreadful puckery; but the man
said that was all right. I guess he 'll find the apple
sauce full as puckery when he gets down into it — but
that 's between ourselves. Well, when I got up to the
State House I found them at work on the rail road —
busy enough I can tell you — they got a part of it made
already. I found most all the folks kept their hats on
except the man who was talking out loud and the man
he was talking to — all the rest seemed to be busy about
their own consarns. As I did n't see any body to talk to
I kept my hat on and took a seat, and look'd round to
see what was going on. I had n't been setting long
before I saw a slick-headed, sharp-eyed little man,
who seemed to have the principal management of the
folks, looking at me pretty sharp, as much as to say who

are you ? but I said nothing and looked tother way — at last he touched me on the shoulder — I thought he was feeling of the puckers. Are you a member ? says he— sartin says I — how long have you taken your seat ? says he. About ten minutes, says I. Are you qualified ? says he. I guess not, says I. And then he left me. I did n't know exactly what this old gentleman was after — but soon he returned and said it was proper for me to be qualified before I took a seat, and I must go before the governor! By Jing ! I never felt so before in all my born days. As good luck would have it, he was beckoned to come to a man at the desk, and as soon as his back was turned I give him the slip. Jest as I was going off, the gentleman who bought my turkies of the 4th staller took hold of my arm, and I was afraid at first that he was going to carry me to the Governor — but he began to talk as sociable as if we had been old acquaintances. How long have you been in the house, Mr Smith, says he. My name is Downing, said I. I beg your pardon, says he — I mean Downing. It 's no offence, says I. I hav'nt been here long. Then says he in a very pleasan way, a few of your brother members are to take pot-luck with me to day, and I should be happy to have you join them. What 's pot-luck said I. O, a family dinner, says he — no ceremony. I thought by this time I was well qualified for that without going to the Governor. So says I, yes, and thank ye too. How long before you 'll want me, says I. At 3 o'clock, says he, and gave me a piece of paste board with his name on it — and the name of the street, and the number of his house, and said that would show me the way. Well, says I, I dont know of nothing that will keep me away. And then we parted. I took considerable liking to him.

After strolling round and seeing a great many things about the State House and the marble immage of Gin. Washington, standing on a stump in the Porch, I went out into the street they call Bacon street, and my stars!

what swarms of women folks I saw all drest up as if they were going to meeting. You can tell cousin Polly Sandburn, who you know is no slimster, that she need n't take on so about being genteel in her shapes — for the genteelest ladies here beat her as to size all hollow. I dont believe one of 'em could get into our fore dore — and as for their arms — I should n't want better measure for a bushel of meal than one of their sleeves could hold. I shant shell out the bushel of corn you say I 've lost on Speaker Ruggles at that rate. But this puts me in mind of the dinner which Mr. ———— wants I should help the Gineral Court eat. So I took out the piece of paste board, and began to inquire my way and got along completely, and found the number the first time — but the door was locked, and there was no knocker, and I thumpt with my whip handle, but nobody come. And says I to a man going by, dont nobody live here ? and says he yes. Well, how do you get in ? Why, says he, ring; and says I, ring what ? And says he, the bell. And says I where 's the rope ? And says he, pull that little brass nub ; and so I gave it a twitch, and I 'm sure a bell did ring; and who do you think opened the door with a white apron afore him ? You could n't guess for a week a Sundays — so I 'll tell you. It was Stephen Furlong, who kept our district school last winter, for 5 dollars a month, and kept bachelor's hall, and helped tend for Gineral Coombs a training days, and make out muster rolls. We was considerably struck up at first, both of us ; and when he found I was going to eat dinner with Mr. ———— and Gineral Court, he thought it queer kind of doings — but says he, I guess it will be as well for both of us not to know each other a bit more than we can help. And says I, with a wink, you 're half right, and in I went. There was nobody in the room but Mr. ———— and his wife, and not a sign of any dinner to be seen any where — though I thought

5

now and then when a side door opened, I could smell
cupboard, as they say.

I thought I should be puzzled enough to know what
to say, but I had 'nt my thoughts long to myself. Mr
——— has about as nimble a tongue as you ever heard,
and could say ten words to my one, and I had nothing
to do in the way of making talk. Just then I heard a
ringing, and Stephen was busy opening the door and
letting in the Gineral Court, who all had their hats off,
and looking pretty scrumptious, you may depend. I
did 'nt see but I could stand along side of 'em without
disparagement, except to my boots, which had just got
a lick of beeswax and tallow — not a mite of dinner yet,
and I began to feel as if 'twas nearer supper-time than
dinner-time — when all at once two doors flew away
from each other right into the wall, and what did I see
but one of the grandest thanksgiving dinners you ever
laid your eyes on — and lights on the table, and silver
candlesticks and gold lamps over head — the window
shutters closed — I guess more than one of us stared at
first, but we soon found the way to our mouths — I made
Stephen tend out for me pretty sharp, and he got my
plate filled three or four times with soup, which beat all
I ever tasted. I shan't go through the whole dinner
again to you — but I am mistaken if it cost me much
for victuals this week, if I pay by the meal at Mr Doolittle's, who comes pretty near up to a thanksgiving
every day. There was considerable talk about stock
and manufactories, and lier bilities, and rimidies, and a
great loss on stock. I thought this a good chance for
me to put in a word — for I calculated I knew as much
about raising stock and keeping over as any of 'em.
Says I to Mr ———, there's one thing I've always ob-
served in my experience in stock — just as sure as you
try to keep over more stock than you have fodder to
carry them well into April, one half will die on your
hands, to a sartinty — and there's no remedy for it —

I've tried it out and out, and there's no law that can make a ton of hay keep over ten cows, unless you have more carrots and potatoes than you can throw a stick at. This made some of the folks stare who did 'nt know much about stock — and Steve give me a jog, as much as to say, keep quiet. He thought I was getting into a quog-mire, and soon after, giving me a wink, opened the door and got me out of the room into the entry.

After we had got out of hearing, says I to Steve, how are you getting on in the world — should you like to come back to keep our school if I could get a vote for you ? — not by two chalks says Steve — I know which side my bread is buttered better than all that — I get 12 dollars a month and found, and now and then some old clothes, which is better than keeping school at 5 dollars and find myself and work out my highway tax besides — then turning up the cape of my *new coat*, says he, I guess I've dusted that before now — most likely, says I, but not in our district school. And this brings to mind to tell you how I got a sight of your letter. They tell me here that every body reads the Boston Daily Advertiser, because there is no knowing but what they may find out something to their advantage, so I thought I would be as wise as the rest of them, and before I got half through with it, what should I find mixed up among the news but your letter that you put into that little paper down in Portland, and I knew it was your writing before I had read ten lines of it.

I hope I've answered it to your satisfaction.

Your respectful uncle,   JOSHUA DOWNING.

P. S.   Mr Topliff says your uncle Nat is telegraphed, but I'm afraid the ax handles wont come to much — I find the Boston folks make a handle of most any thing they can lay hold of, and just as like as not they'll make a handle of our private letters if they should see them.

N. B.   You spell dreadful bad, according to my notion

— and this proves what I always said, that our district has been going down hill ever since Stephen Furlong left it.

[*Note by the Editor.* In order that the reader may understand the progress of the war in the Legislature, it should be remarked that the parties in the Senate were equally divided. There were eight Huntonites, or national republicans, and eight Smithites, or democratic republicans, and four vacancies. The battles therefore in the Senate were more serious, obstinate, and protracted, than they were in the House. They balloted regularly for President every day for about a fortnight. To illustrate the state of affairs at that time, a couple of extracts from the Portland Courier in relation to the balloting in the Senate are subjoined.]

From the *Portland Courier, Jan.* 1830.

Saturday forenoon the House having adjourned at an early hour, we repaired to the Senate Chamber with the view of standing watch awhile. We arrived just in the height of a spirited skirmish, or what might almost be called a battle ; but the room was crowded, and the doorway so impenetrably thronged, that we could gain no entrance. There was scarcely room for a man to wedge his nose in, unless it were a remarkably thin and sharp one. From the subdued and regular hum within, there was evidently a debate going on, but we being somewhat low in stature, and a solid phalanx of six-footers standing before us, we were left in the unpleasant predicament of stretching up on tiptoe without catching a single glimpse of the scene, and holding our hands behind our ears without distinguishing a syllable that was uttered.

The debate however soon subsided. We learnt afterwards from inquiry, that it related to the subject of forming a convention with the House for the purpose of filling vacancies, before the Senate was organized ; the 8 Huntonites voting in favor of the proposition, and the 8 Smithites against it. A vote was then passed to proceed to ballot for President again ; and luckily for

us, the ballot boxes were out in the lobby, and out came
the messenger, cutting his way like a hero, (we like to
have said, hero of New Orleans, but happened to think
some would say we were taking *sides*,) we simply say
then, he cut his way through the dense ranks of specta-
tors, like a hero, and we crept in through the breach
he had made. The committee collected the votes for
President, and retired. In about ten minutes they returned, and declared the result; 7 for Mr Dunlap, 7
for Mr Kingsbury, and 2 scattering.

They collected the votes again, and retired as before,
and returned as before, and declared the same result.
Again they proceeded in the same round, and came in
the third time, and stood ready to declare. The spec-
tators had become so accustomed to the report, that they
were whispering it off in advance of the Committee,
like a mischievous and sinful boy running ahead of some
good old country Deacon, who always uses the same
words in prayer. — Judge then, ye readers of the Courier, what unspeakable astonishment prevailed, when
from the lips of the Chairman fell the startling words,
8 for Sanford Kingsbury, 6 for Robert P. Dunlap, and
2 scattering.

The effect was like that of a clap of thunder in the
dead of winter : some faces grew longer, and some
grew shorter ; in some eyes there was a look of wild
ness ; in others a leering complacency, that seemed to
say, ' your're dish'd at last; while some confounded
knowing glances from other quarters visibly replied,
' not as you know on.' And to be sure these last were
in the right ; for round they went the fourth time, collected the ballots, counted them, and came in again —
expectation was on tiptoe, and speculation was very
busy. Some thought this ballot would settle the question, but others doubted. The Committee declared, and
the same old tune greeted the ears of the audience

— 7 for Mr Dunlap, 7 for Mr Kingsbury, and 2 scattering.

Another extract from the same.

A new Tune. — We have to pitch our pipe to a new tune this morning. The second great battle of the session was fought, or rather terminated yesterday afternoon. After a regular engagement for eight days in succession, during which time the regular armies of Huntonites and Smithites in the Senate were drawn up face to face, forenoon and afternoon, exchanging some half a dozen shots every day, and then retiring by mutual consent, and sleeping upon their arms, the conflict was ended yesterday afternoon by a *ruse de guerre* on the part of the Huntonites, which led them to victory without bloodshed. The Senate met in the afternoon at three o'clock, and proceeded to their usual round of duties. The committee received the votes for President, and retired, and came in again, and declared in the strains of the old tune, 7 for Mr Dunlap, 7 for Mr Kingsbury, and 2 scattering. They proceeded again, and came in as before. It was the *fiftieth* ballot since the commencement of the session; and had a *fifty pounder* been unexpectedly discharged in the room, it would hardly have produced a stronger sensation, than the declaration of the Committee, when they piped away in the following new tune : whole number of votes 15. Necessary to a choice 8 : JOSHUA HALL has 8, ROBERT P. DUNLAP 6, JAMES STEELE 1, Blank 1. We shall not attempt to describe the coloring of faces, the wildness of eyes, or the biting of lips that ensued ; for, not arriving in season we did not see them. But we have no doubt from the remarks of those who were present, that the occasion would have furnished a scene for painting, full equal, if not surpassing, that in the House on the choice of Speaker. After the first consternation had subsided,

Mr Hall was declared duly elected President of the Senate. Whereupon he rose in his place, and thanked the gentlemen of the Board for the confidence they had placed in him. He doubted his abilities to discharge properly the duties assigned him ; but under present circumstances he would accept the trust. He accordingly took the Chair.

[*Note by the Editor.* Mr Hall, or Elder Hall, as he was usually called, was a democratic republican, but was chosen President exclusively by the national republican votes, he throwing a blank vote himself. He was a short, fleshy, good hearted old gentleman, a minister of the Methodist denomination, and knew much more about preaching than he did about politics. The democratic republicans after their first consternation at his election had subsided, fearing that he had actually gone over to the enemy, took measures to have a private consultation with him immediately after adjournment. This interview resulted in nailing the old gentleman to his former political faith, and he stuck to the party like wax during the remainder of the session. So the Senate was still divided, eight to eight, except when the four new Senators elected by the national republicans to fill the vacancies, attempted to act.]

LETTER V.

In which Mr Downing tells what a hobble the Legislature got into, in trying to make so many Governors.

Portland, Feb. 1, 1830.

To Cousin Ephraim Downing up in Downingville.

DEAR COUSIN EPHRAIM. — I spose you expected me to write to you agin long afore now and tell you something more about these legislaters, and I meant to, but I could n't very well; for I'll tell you jest how twas. — Some days, when the legislater would get into a plaguy hobble, I would think to myself, well, soon as they get out of this snarl, I'll write to cousin Ephraim and tell him all about it ; but before they got fairly out of that, they'd be right into another ; and if I waited till next

day to see how that ended, my keesers! before night
they'd all be higgledy piggle in a worse hobble than
they'd ever been in afore. So if I wait to tell you how
it comes out, I believe I shall have to wait till haying
time. Another thing I've been waiting for, was to tell
you who was Governor. — But, O dear, I cant find out
half so much about it now, here in this great city of
Portland, where all the Governors live, as I could six
months ago among the bear traps and log houses in our
town, way back in the woods. Last August, you know,
according to the papers we were going to have two
Governors right off, sure as rates; Mr Hunton and Mr
Smith. Well now its got to be the first of February,
and we haven't got *one* yet. And although the governor-
makers have had four or five under way for a month
past, some think it very doubtful whether they will get
one done so as to be fit to use this year. There's Mr
Hunton, and Mr Smith, and Mr Cutler, and Mr Goodenow, and Mr Hall, have all been *partly* made into Governors; but when in all creation any of 'em will be *finished,* I guess it would puzzle a Philadelphy lawyer to
tell. I stated in my letter to uncle Joshua, that there
were two very clever parties in the legislater, the democratic republikans and the national republikans; and
they are so, and very industrious, and try to make things
go on right; and I really believe, if the confounded
Jacksonites and Huntonites didn't bother 'em so, they'd
make us a Governor, as quick as I could make an ax
handle. It is enough to do any body's heart good to see
how kind and obliging these democratic republikans and
national republikans are to each other, and how each
party tries to help the other along; and its enough to
make any body's blood boil to see the Jacksonites and
Huntonites, jest like the dog in the manger, because they
cant eat the hay themselves, snap at these two clever
parties the moment either of 'em sets out to take a
mouthful. I'll jest give you an instance of the kindness

that these two clever parties show to each other. — You
know the constitution says when we haven 't any Governor the President of the Sinnet must be Governor,
and when we have 'nt any President of the Sinnet, the
Speaker of the House must be Governor. So when
Governor Lincoln died Mr Cutler was Governor for
awhile, because he was last year President of the Sinnet. Mr Goodenow is a national republikan, and when
he was elected Speaker of the House, the democratic republikans told him as there was no President of the
Sinnet elected yet, it belonged to him to be Governor,
and tried as hard as though he had belonged to their
own party, to encourage him to go right into the council chamber and do the governor's business. But the
national republikans didn't dare to let him go, for he
was elected by only one majority, and they said if he
should leave the chair, it wouldn't be five minutes before
a Jacksonite would be whisked into it, and then the two
clever parties would all be up a tree. Well, jest so twas
in the Sinnet after Elder Hall was elected President,
only the bread was buttered on tother side. Elder Hall is
a democratic republikan, and there was a great deal tougher scrabble to elect him, than there was to choose the
Speaker of the House. But as soon as he was elected,
the national republikans went to him very kindly, and
said, ' Elder Hall, by the provisions of the constitution
you are now fairly Governor of the State till another
governor is qualified. Dont be bashful about it, but
please to walk right into the Council chamber, and do
the governor's business.' But the democratic republikans said, that would never do, for if he should, the Sinnet Board would be capsized in an instant and the Huntonites would rule the roast. — So there was a pair of
Governors spoilt when they were more than half made,
jest by the mischief of the Jacksonites and Huntonites.
And the consequence is, that Mr Cutler has to keep doing the Governor's business yet, whether he wants to or

not, and whether it is right for him to, or not. They
say the poor man is a good deal distressed about it, and
has sent to the great Judges of the Supreme Court to
know whether it's right for him to be Governor any
longer or not. If the Judges should say he mus'nt be
Governor any longer, we shall be in a dreadful pickle.
Only think, no Governor, and no laws, but every body
do jest as they're a mind to. Well, if that should be
the case, I know one thing, that is, Bill Johnson will get
one good flogging for calling me a mean puppy and a
coward last summer; I've longed to give it to him ever
since; and if the Legislater don't make a governor this
winter, I shall come right home, and Bill must look out.
What a pity 'tis they should waste so much time trying
to make so many governors; for, if they should make
a dozen, we shouldn't want to use but one this year;
and it is thought if they had all clapt to and worked
upon one instead of working upon so many, they might
have had him done more than three weeks ago.

Your lovin cuzen til death,
JACK DOWNING.

LETTER VI.

*In which Mr Downing describes a sad mishap that befel
the House of Representatives.*

[*Note by the Editor.* After a stormy debate in the House in relation to forming a Convention of the two branches to fill the vacancies in the Senate, the national republicans finally carried the day;
whereupon the democratic republicans, having remonstrated to the
last, took their hats and marched out of the House in a body, about
sixty in number, headed by Mr Smith of Nobleborough. The
national republicans of the two branches, however, held the Convention, and filled the vacancies in the Senate, and the next day
the democratic republicans returned to their seats.]

Portland, Tuesday, Feb. 2, 1830.

DEAR COUSIN EPHRAIM,—I have jest time to write you a short *postscript* to a letter that I shall send you in a day or two. We have had a dreadful time here to-day. You know the wheels of government have been stopt here for three or four weeks, and they all clapt their shoulders under to-day, and give 'em a lift; and they started so hard, that as true as you're alive, *they split both Legislaters right in tu.* Some say they are split so bad, they can't mend 'em again, but I hope they can though; I shall tell you all about how 'twas done, in a day or two. I've been expecting a letter from you, or some of the folks, sometime. As I've got pretty short of money, I wish you would send 'em in the *Daily Courier*, so I shant have to pay the postage.

Your hearty cousin,

JACK DOWNING.

———

LETTER VII.

In which affairs take a more favourable turn.

Portland, Feb. 3, 1830.

COUSIN EPHRAIM,—I thought I would jest write you another little *postscript* to my letter that I was going to send you in a day or tu, and let you know that the legislaters want split so bad as some folks tho't for. They've got 'em both mended agin, so that they set 'em agoing to day afore noon. But in the arternoon, that legislater they call the Sinnet, got stuck, and in trying to make it go, it rather seemed to crack a little; so they stopt short till to-morrow. Its been jostled about so, and got so weak an' rickety, some are afraid it will give out yet, or *split in tu agin.*

JACK DOWNING.

LETTER VIII.

In which Mrs Downing urges her son to come home.

Downingville, Feb. 6, 1830.

MY DEAR SON, — Its a good while since I writ a letter, and I almost forget how; but you stay down there to Portland so long, I kind of want to say something to you. I have been churning this morning, and my hand shakes so I cant hardly hold my pen still. And then I am afraid the news I've got to tell, will be such a blow to you, it makes me feel sort of narvous. Last Sunday the schoolmaster and Jemima Parsons had their names stuck up together in the meeting-house porch. — Now I hope you wont take on, my dear Jack; for if I was you, I should be glad to get rid of her so. I guess she's rather *slack*, if the truth was known : for I went in there one day, and she'd jest done washing the floor; and I declare, it looked as grey as if she'd got the water out of a mud puddle. And then she went to making pies without washing her hands, or shifting her apron. They made me stop to supper, but I never touched Jemime's pies. There's Dolly Spaulding, I'm sure she's likelier looking than Jemime Parsons, if 'twant for that habit she's got of looking two ways at once. If she's making a soup, one eye is *always* in the pot, if t'other *does* look up chimney. She's as good a cook as ever was born, and neat as wax-work. Sally Kean was to our house spinning linen t'other day, because I burnt my hand so bad trying out lard I couldn't hold the thread, and she said Dolly had more sheets and pillow-cases than you could count for one while, and she is always making blankets and coverlids. She has sold footings enough to buy her half a dozen silver spoons and a case of knives. When I was young, such a gal would had a husband long ago. The men didn't use to ask if a gal looked one way, or two ways with her eyes, but whether she was neat and smart; only if she had thin lips and peaked nose, they were sometimes a little shy of her.

O Jack, I'm afraid these legislaters will be the ruination of you! 'Twill make you jest like your uncle Joshua. You know he had rather stand and dispute about politiks any time, than work on his farm, and talking will never build a stone wall or pay our taxes.

I dont care so much about the shushon as your poor cousin Nabby does about the cotton cloth. But your father has got the rumatise dreadfully this winter; and its rather hard for him to have to cut all the wood and make the fires this cold winter. I cant see what good twil do for you to stay in Portland any longer, and I think you had better come home and see a little to the work on the farm.

Your loving mother,
MARY DOWNING.

LETTER IX.

In which Mr Downing tells about trigging the wheels of government.

Portland, Thursday, Feb. 11, 1830.

DEAR COUSIN EPHRAIM. — I 've wrote you three *post-scripts* since I wrote you a letter, and the reason is, these

6

Legislaters have been carryin on so like all possest, and
I 've been in looking at 'em so much, I could n't get time
to write more than three lines at once, for fear I should be
out of the way, and should miss seeing some of the fun.
But thinkin you 'd be tired of waiting, I tried to get the
printer to send my letter yesterday ; but he told me right
up and down he could n't. I told him he must, for I
ought to sent before now. But he said he could n't, and
would n't, and that was the upshot of the matter, for the
paper was chock full, and more tu, of the Governor's
message. Bless my stars, says I, and have we got a
Governor done enough so he can speak a message?
Yes, indeed we have, says he, *thanks be to the two great
republikin parties*, who have saved the State from the
anarkee of the Jacksonites and Huntonites ; the Governor
is done, and is jest a going into the Legislater, and if
you 'll go right up there, you can see him. So I pushed
in among the crowd, and I got a pretty good squeezin
tu ; but I got a good place, for I could elbow it as well
as any on 'em. And I had n't been there five minutes,
seemingly, before we had a Governor sure enough ; and
a good stout, genteel looking sort of a man he was tu, as
you would see in a whole regiment, taking in captains
and all. Nobody disputed that he was finished pretty
workmanlike ; and he ought to be, for they 'd been long
enough about it. So they concluded to swear him in, as
they call it, and he took a great oath to behave like a
Governor a whole year. Some say the wheels of government will go along smooth and easy now, as a wheel-
barrow across a brick yard ; but some shake their heads,
and say the wheels will be jolting over rocks and stumps
all winter yet ; and I dont know but they will, for the
Governor had n't hardly turned his back upon 'em and
gone out, before they went right to disputing agin as
hard as ever. I was a good mind to run out and call the
Governor back to still 'em. But I could n't tell where
to look for him, so they got clear of a drubbing that time.

I know he 'd a gin it to 'em if he 'd been there ; for what
do you think was the first thing they went to disputing
about ? It was how many Governor's speeches they
should print this winter ; jest as if the Governor could n't
tell that himself. Some wanted three hundred, and some
five hundred, and some seven or eight hundred. Finally
they concluded to print five hundred ; and I should think
that was enough in all conscience, if they are all going
to be as long as that one they printed in the Courier
yesterday. In the next place, they took up that everlasting dispute about Mr Roberts' having a seat ; for if
you 'll believe me, they 've kept that poor man standing
there till this time.

I'll tell you how tis, Cousin Ephraim, we must con-
trive some way or other to keep these Jacksonits and
Huntonites out of the Legislater another year, or we
shall be ruin'd ; for they make pesky bad work, triging
the wheels of government. They've triged 'em so much
that they say it has cost the State about *fifteen thousand
dollars* a'ready, more than 'twould, if they had gone
along straight without stopping. So you may tell uncle
Joshua that besides that bushel of corn he lost in betting
about the Speaker, he'll have to shell out as much as *two
bushels more* to pay the cost of triging the wheels. Jin-
goe ! sometimes when I've seen the wheels chocked with
a little trig not bigger than a cat's head, and the whole
legislater trying with all their might two or three days,
and couldn't start it a hair, how I've longed to hitch on
my little speckled four-year-olds, and give 'em a pull ;
if they wouldn't make the wheels fly over the trigs in a
jiffy, I wont guess agin. 'Tother day in the great convention, when both Legislaters met together to chuse
some Counsellors, Mr Boutelle and Mr Smith of Nobleborough tried to explain how 'twas the wheels of government were trig'd so much. Mr Boutelle, as I have
told you a-fore, is a national republican, and Mr Smith
is a democratic republican. They differed a little in

their opinion. Mr Boutelle seemed to think the trigs
were all put under by *one class of politicians*, and from
what he said, I took it he meant the Jacksonites. He
said ever since the Legislater began, the moment they
started the wheels, that class of politicians would throw
under a chock and stop 'em; and which ever way they
turned, that class of politicians would meet 'em at every
corner and bring 'em up all standin. Mr Smith seemed
to think *another* class of politicians had the greatest hand
in it, and it was pretty clear that he meant the Huntonites.
He said when they first got here, that class of politicians
sot the wheels of government rolling the *wrong way;*
they put the big wheels forward, and the Legislater had
been going backwards ever since, jest like a lobster.
And the Huntonites not only trig'd the wheels, whenever
they begun to roll the right way; but as soon as the
'blessed Governor' was done they trig'd him tu; and
though he had been done four days, they wouldn't let
him come into the Legislater so that their eyes could be
blest with the sight of him. So from what I can find
out, the Jacksonites and Huntonites both, are a trouble-
some contrary set, and there must be some way con-
trived to keep 'em out of the Legislater in future.

It seems soon after you got my first letter, uncle
Joshua tackled up, and started off to Boston with a
load of turkeys and apple-sauce. I had a letter from
him t'other day, as long as all out doors, in the Boston
Advertiser. He says he got more for the turkeys than
he expected tu; but I think it's a plaguy pity he did'nt
bring 'em to Portland. I know he'd got more than he
could in Boston. Provision kind is getting up here
wonderfully, on account of these Legislaters being likely to stay here all winter; and some think they'll be
here half the summer tu. And then there's sich a cloud
of what they call lobby members and office hunters, that
the butchers have got frightened, and gone to buying up
all the beef and pork they can get hold on far and near,

for they are afraid a famine will be upon us next. Howsomever, uncle Joshua did well to carry his ' puckery apple-sauce' to Boston. He could 'nt get a cent for't here ; for every body's puckery and sour enough here now.

Give my love to father and mother and cousin Nabby. I shall answer their letters as soon as I can.

Your lovin Cousin.

JACK DOWNING.

———

LETTER X.

In which Mr Downing advises his uncle Joshua to hold on to his bushel of corn, because the Legislature had begun to 'rip up their duins.'

Portland, Friday, Feb. 12, 1830.

Postcript to uncle Joshua.

☞ THIS WITH CARE AND SPEED.

DEAR UNCLE, — If you have'nt paid over that are bushel of corn yet, that you lost when you bet Mr Ruggles would be Speaker, hold on to it for your life, till you hear from me agin, for I aint so clear but you may save it yet. They've gone to rippin up their duins here, and there's no knowing but they may go clear back to the beginning and have another tug about Speaker. At any rate, if your bushel of corn is'nt gone out of your crib yet, I advise you by all means to keep it there.

Tell 'squire N. the question is'nt settled yet ; and you wont shell out a single kernel till it is fairly nailed and clinched, so it can't be ript up agin. I'll tell you what tis, uncle Josh, the Supreme Court beats the Jacksonites and Huntonites all hollow for trigging the wheels. You know after they had such a tussle for about a week

6*

to chose Elder Hall President of the Sinnet, and after he come in at last all hollow, for they said he had a majority of eight out of sixteen, they went on then two or three weeks nicely, duin business *tie and tie*, hard as they could. Then up steps the Judges of the Supreme Court and tells Mr Hall he was governor, and ought to go into the Council Chamber. They seemed to be a little bit thunder struck at first. But they soon come to agin, and Elder Hall got out of the chair and Mr Kingsbury got into it, and they jogged along another week, duin business as hard as ever. They said all the chairs round the table ought to be filled, so they changed works with the House and made four more Sinneters. So having four good fresh hands come in, they took hold in good earnest and turned off more business in two days, than they had done in a month before.

Then up steps the Supreme Court agin and tells 'em their cake is all dough; for they hadn't been duin constitutional. This was yesterday; and it made a dreadful touse. They went right to work rippin up and tarrin away what they'd been duin; and before nine o'clock in the evening they turned out the four new Sinneters, out of their chairs and appointed a committee to begin to make four more. They took hold so hash about it, I spose some the rest of the Sinneters begun to be afraid they should be ript up tu; so they clear'd out, I guess near about half on 'em, and have n't been seen nor heard of to day. Some of 'em that had more courage went in and tried to du business; but there wasn't enough of 'em to start an inch. They sent a man all round town in the forenoon and afternoon to tell 'em to come in and go to work, but he could n't find hide nor hair of one of 'em. Elder Hall said *he guessed they must be somewhere in a convention.*

Some say they'll rip up the new Councillors next, and then the Governor, cause the new Sinneters helpt make 'em all. But there's one comfort left for us, let the cat jump which way 'twill; if Mr Hunton is'nt a constitutional Governor, Elder Hall is; the Judges have nailed that fast. So I think Bill Johnson will get off with a whole skin, for I shant dare to flog him this year. If they go clear back to the Speaker, and decide it in favor of your bushel of corn, I shall let you know as soon as possible.

Your lovin neffu,

JACK DOWNING.

LETTER XI.

In which Mr Downing describes some queer duins in the Senate.

[*Note by the Editor.* The democratic republicans insisted that the Convention which filled the vacancies in the Senate was not constitutional, and refused to recognize the new members at the Board, and the President refused to count their votes. After considerable turmoil the four new Senators withdrew; in consequence of which several others of the same party withdrew also, so that there was not a quorum left to do business. After two or three days, however, they returned, and the new senators re-asserted their claims to a seat. Great confusion ensued; the President refused to count their votes; and taking the votes of the other members, he declared the Senate adjourned. The national republicans refused to consider it an adjournment, kept their seats, and began to talk of re-organizing the Senate by choosing a new President. Elder Hall, therefore, fearing the chair would be immediately filled again if he left it, kept his seat, but still repeatedly declared the Senate adjourned. The particulars of the scene are more minutely described in the following letter.]

To Cousin Ephraim Downing up in Downingville.

Portland, Wednesday, Feb. 17, 1830.

DEAR COUSIN EPHRAIM, — Here I am yet, and have n't much else to du, so I might as well keep writin to you; for I spose uncle Joshua 's in a peck of trouble

about his bushel of corn. I'm pesky fraid he'll lose it
yet; for they dont seem to rip up worth a cent since the
first night they begun. The truth was they took hold
rather tu hash that night; and rippin up them are four
new Sinneters so quick, they scart away four or five more
old ones, so they did n't dare to come in again for tu days.
And that threw 'em all into the suds, head and ears. It
was worse than trigging the wheels, for it broke the Sinnet wheel right in tu, and left it so flat, that all Job's
oxen never could start it, if they hadn't got it mended
again. They tried, and tried, to keep duin something,
but they couldn't du the leastest thing. One time they
tried to du something with a little bit of a message that
was sent to 'em on a piece of paper from the House.
The President took it in his hand, and held it up, and
asked 'em what was best to du with it. Some of 'em
motioned that they'd lay it on the table; but come to
consider on it, they found they couldn't according to
the constitution, without there was more of 'em to help.
They said they couldn't lay it on the table, nor du nothin
at all with it. I was afraid the poor old gentleman
would have to stand there and hold it till they got the
wheel mended agin. But I believe he finally *let it drop*
on the table; and I spose there was nothin in the constitution against that.

They got the wheel mended Monday about eleven er
clock, so they could start along a little. But them are
four new Sinneters that they ript up Thursday night,
come right back agin Monday, and sot down to the
great round table; and stood tu it through thick and
thin, that they want ript up, and no sich thing. — Well,
this kicked up a kind of a bobbery among 'em, so they
thought they'd try to journ. The President counted
'em, and said they were journed and might go out. One
of the new Sinneters said the President didn't count
right, and they want journed a bit; and they must set
still and have an overhauling about it.

So they set down agin, all but four or five that put on their hats and great coats and stood backside of the room. The room was chock full of folks looking on, and the President told 'em the Sinnet was journed and they might as well go out, but they did seem to keer tu, and they put their hats on and began to laugh like fun. The President sot still in his cheer, for I spose he thought if he left it, some of them are roguish fellers would be gettin into it. The man that keeps order, told the folks they must take their hats off when they were in the Sinnet; but they said they wouldn't, cause the Sinnet was ajourned. Then the man went and asked the President if the Sinnet was all ajourned, and the President said 'twas, and there was no doubt about it. And the folks felt so tickled to think they could wear their hats when the Sinneters were setting round the great table, that they kind of whistled a little bit all over the room.

Finally, after settin about half an hour, another man got up and motioned to ajourn, and the President got up and put it to vote agin. He told 'em if they wanted to ajourn, they must say ah, and they all said ah this time, and cleared out in five minutes.

But about this rippin up business; instead of rippin up the councillors, as some thought they would, both legislaters met together to-day, and called in four of the councillors, and nailed 'em down harder with an oath.

They've sot the committees to work like fun now, and its thought they'll turn off business hand over hand; for you know its almost March, and then the great Supreme Court meets here. And they say they have a grand jury that picks up all disorderly and mischievous folks, and carries 'em in to court, and the court puts 'em in jail. These legislaters have been cuttin up such rigs here all winter, that they begin to look pretty shy when any thing is said about the first of March, and I

dont believe the grand jury 'll be able to find a single
mother's son of 'em when the court gets here.

From your cousin,
JACK DOWNING.

————

LETTER XII.

*In which Mr Downing hits upon a new idea for making
money out of the office-seekers that were swarming round
the new Governor.*

Postscript to Ephraim.

Portland, Feb. 23, 1830.

Dear Cousin. — As soon as you get this, I want you
to load up the old lumber-box with them are long slick
bean-poles, that I got out last summer. I guess I shant
make much by my ax handles, for I can't sell 'em yet ;
I han't sold but tu since I've been here ; and the sea's
been froze over so that uncle Ned hant got in from
Quoddy yet, and I hant had any chance to send my ax
handles to Boston. But if I loose on the ax handles, I
shall make it up on the bean poles if you only get 'em
here in season. Do make haste as fast as you can, and
you shall share half the profits.

It ant to stick beans with nuther ; and I guess you'll
kind o' laff, when I tell you what tis for. You know when
we went to the court there was a man sot up in a box,
that they called a Sheriff, and held a long white pole in
his hand. Well I heard somebody say tother day that
there was more than a hundred folks here that wanted
to get a Sheriff's pole ; and I happened to think that
them are bean poles would make cute ones. But you
must get 'em here afore the Governor makes his appint-

ments, or it 'll be gone goose with us, about it, for we couldn't sell more than half a dozen arter that.

From your Cousin,
JACK DOWNING.

————

LETTER XIII.

Cousin Ephraim in trouble.

———————— Feb. 25, 1830.

DEAR JACK. — Here I am, about half way to Portland, with one shu of the old lumber box broke down, and tother one putty rickety. Its about half the way bare ground, and the old hoss begins to be ruther wheezy. But you know I don't give up for trifles, when there's a chance to make a spec. Soon as I got your letter bout the bean poles, I made business fly. Mother put me up a box of beef and dough-nuts, and I fed old grey, and tackled up, and all loaded and ready to start in tu hours; and if I live I shall get the bean poles there at some rate or other fore long; but I'm fraid I may be late. If you know the Governor, I wish you'd just ask him to keep his appointments back a little while; he shant loose nothin by it, if the poles sell well. I shall have to go the rest of the way on wheels, and I want you to see if you cant hire one of the government wheels and come and meet me, for the plagy fellers here wont trust me with their wheels till I get back. Besides if I could get one of the wheels of government, I'm thinking I could get along a good deal faster; for I met a man jest now from Portland that said they've got them are wheels going now like a buz. He said there was no wheels in the country that could go half so fast; and he thinks they work a good deal better for being split up and mended so much.

Grandfather said they would want as many cockades as Sheriff polls; and so he put in his old continental one, that he had in the revolution.

P. S.   I hope you'll get the government wheels to come arter the poles, for I want some that are putty easy *trig'd*, cause the hills are ruther slippery.

Your Cusin,

EPHRAIM DOWNING.

———

LETTER XIV.

In which Mr Downing describes a severe tug at the wheels of government.

[*Note by the Editor*.   The opinion of the Judges of the Supreme Court having been asked, they decided that the vacancies in the Senate were not constitutionally filled, and that the subsequent doings of the Legislature were consequently void.]

Portland, March 3, 1830.

To Cousin Ephraim Downing, stuck by the way.

You sent word to me in your letter t'other day, that you had got to bare ground, and broke down one shu of the lumber box, and wanted me to get the wheels of Government and come up after the poles.   I tried to get 'em, but they would 'nt let 'em go; and they said 'twould 'nt be any use if I did; for I could 'nt get more than ten rods before the wheels would be trig'd.   They were expecting of 'em to be trig'd every day, they said; for the Judges had sent a monstrous great trig to the Governor, and told him if they went to start the wheels forward any, he must clap it under; for they must 'nt go forward a bit more, and must roll the wheels back a good ways, till they found the right road.   Well, sure enough, Tuesday, when they was goin along a little easy, some on 'em threw the trig right under, and it brought 'em up with a dreadful jolt.

And then, my stars, if the Sinneters didn't go at it tie and tie, like smoke. The national republicans pulled one way, and the democratic republicans 'tother, with all their might, jest as you and I used to set down and brace our feet against each other, and take hold of a stick to see which could pull tother up. They pulled and grinned all day, but nary side couldn't pull up toth- er. The national republicans said they wouldn't stop for that little trig, nor no notion of it; and they pulled the wheels forward as hard as they could. The demo- cratic republicans braced their feet tother way, and said the wheels shouldn't move another inch forward; they had got on to a wrong road, and the Judges had put that trig there to keep 'em all from goin to destruction; and they tried all day as hard as they could to roll the wheels back to find the right road. They pulled like my little tu year olds all day, but I couldn't see as they started the wheels backwards or forwards a single hair. This morning they hitched on and took another jest sich a pull. The national republicans said they knew the road as well as the Judges did, and they were goin right and wouldn't touch to go back; the road was a good plain smooth road, and there wasn't a mite of danger in goin on. The democratic republicans said they could hear some pretty heavy thundering along that road, and they'd not go another step that way; but they stood tu it they want afraid of the thunder. The national republicans said they'd heard thunder before now, and seen dread- ful black clouds all over the sky, and they'd seen a fair afternoon and a bright rainbow after all that. So they pulled and disputed, and disputed and pulled, till most noon, and then they concluded to stop and breath upon it till to-morrow, when I spose they will spit on their hands to make 'em stick and begin as hard as ever.

I hope you'll make haste and get the poles along; if

7

you cant get any wheels up there, you better tie up a
couple of bundles of 'em and swing 'em acrost the old
horse, saddle-bags fashion.   You'll get well paid for it,
if you get 'em here in season.   Your cousin,

                                    JACK DOWNING.

———

LETTER XV.

*In which Mr Downing tells what it means to set up a
candidate for office.*

                          Portland, Tuesday, March 16, 1830.
To Uncle Joshua Downing up in Downingville.

DEAR UNCLE JOSHUA — I guess by this time, its so
long since I writ home, you almost begin to think Jack
is sick or dead, or gone down to Quoddy long with uncle
Nat, or somewhere else.   But you needn't think any
sich thing, for here I am sticking to Portland like wax,
and I guess I shant pull up stakes agin this one while.
The more I stay to Portland the better I like it.   Its a
nation fine place ; there's things enough here for any
body to see all their life time.   I guess I shall tell you
something about 'em before summer's out.   These Legislaters haven't done nothin scarcely worth telling about
this most a fortnight.   I've been in most every day jest
to take a squint at 'em.   There was n't hardly a bit of
a quarrel to be heard of from one day's end to another.   They were all as good natured and loving as a
family of brothers, that had been living out all summer,
and had jest got home together at thanksgiving time.
They kept to work as busy as bees upon pieces of paper
that they called Bills.   Sometimes they voted to read
'em once, sometimes twice, and sometimes three times.
At last the sun begun to shine so warm, that it made 'em

think of planting time, and at it they went, passing Bills *by the gross*, [probably a mistake for *to be engrossed*, — editor,] till they settled 'em away like a heap of corn at a husking, before a barnful of boys and gals. And they've got so near the bottom of the heap, they say they shall brush out the floors in a day or two more, and start off home. I spose they wont mind it much if they do brush out some of the ears without husking ; they've had their frolic and their husking supper, and I guess that's the most they come for. It seems to me, uncle Joshua, it costs our farmers a great deal more to husk out their law-corn every winter than it need tu. They let tu many noisy talking fellers come to the husking. I've always minded, when I went to a husking, that these noisy kind of chaps seem to care a good deal more about what they can get to eat and drink, than they du about the corn ; and them are that don't make much fuss, are apt to husk the most and make the cleanest work.

O dear, uncle, there's a hot time ahead. I almost dread to think of it. I'm afraid there is going to be a worse scrabble next summer to see who shall go to the great State husking than there was last. The Hunton-ites and Smithites are determined to have each of 'em a governor agin next year. They've sot up their candi-dates on both sides ; and who in all the world should you guess they are ? The Huntonites have sot up Mr Hunton, and the Smithites have sot up Mr Smith. You understand what it means, I spose, to set up a candi-date. It means the same that it does at a shooting match to set up a goose or a turkey to be fired at. The rule of the game is that the Smithites are to fire at Mr Hunton, and the Huntonites are to fire at Mr Smith. They think it will take a pretty hard battle to get them both in. But both parties say they've got the constitu-tion on their side, so I think likely they'll both beat.

They've been piling up a monstrous heap of ammunition this winter, enough to keep 'em firing all summer; and I guess it wont be long before you'll see the smoke rising all over the State, wherever there's a newspaper. I think these newspapers are dreadful smoky things; they are enough to blind any body's eyes any time. I mean all except the *Daily Courier* and *Family Reader*, that I send my letters in; I never see much smoke in them. But take the rest of the papers, that talk about politics, and patriotism, and republicanism, and federalism, and Jacksonism, and Hartford Conventionism, and let any body read in one of 'em half an hour, and his eyes will be so full of smoke he can't see better than an owl in the sunshine; he would n't be able to tell the difference between a corn-stalk and the biggest oak tree in our pasture.

You know, uncle, these Legislaters have had some dreadful quarrels this winter about a book they call the constitution: and had to get the Judges of the great Court to read it to 'em. They made such a fuss about it I thought it must be a mighty great book, as big agin as grandfather's great bible. But one day I see one of the Sinneters have one, and my stars, it was n't so big as my old spelling book. Thinks I to myself, if ax handles will by one, I'll have one and see if I cant read it myself. So I went into a store where they had a nation sight of books, and asked 'em for a constitution. They showed me some nice little ones, that they asked a quarter of a dollar apiece for. I was out of money, so I told the man I'd give him four good white oak ax handles, well finished, for one: and he said, being 'twas me, I might have it. So now I've got a constitution of my own, and if I find I can read it, I shall let you know something about what's in it before a great while.

Your neffu,

JACK DOWNING.

LETTER XVI.

*In which Mr Downing tells how the Legislature cleared
out, and how Elder Hall went home.*

To Cousin Ephraim Downing up in Downingville.

Portland, Monday, March 22, 1830.

Cousin Ephraim, — I kind of want to say a few more
words to you about the Legislaters. You know they
came together here in the first of the winter in a kind of
a stew, and they had storms and tempests among 'em all
the time they staid here, and finally they went off Friday in a sort of whirlwind or hurricane, I dont know
which. Some folks say they hope it will blow 'em so
far they wont get back again. — But I guess there aint
much danger of that ; for you know squire Nokes always used to say the bad penny will return. They were
dreadful kind of snappish the last day they were here ;
they couldn't hardly touch a single thing without quarrelling about it. — They quarrelled about paying some
of the folks they hired to work for 'em ; and they quarrelled ever so long about paying them are four Sinneters
that were chosen in the convention ; and at last they got
to quarrelling like cats and dogs to see if they should
thank the President and Speaker for all the work they've
done this winter. But they had to thank 'em at last.
And then Mr Goodnow, the Speaker in that Legislater
they call the House, got up and talked to 'em so pleasant,
and kind, and scripture-like, it made 'em feel a little
bad ; some of 'em couldn't hardly help shedding tears.
I tho't them are, that had been quarrelling so, must feel
a little sheepish.

That are Elder Hall, that was President of the Sinnet, seemed to be the most poplar man in the whole
bunch of both Legislaters. There wasn't one of the rest
7*

of 'em that could work it so as to make both parties like 'em. But some how or other, he did. The national republicans liked him so well, that they all voted for him for President; and the democratic republicans liked him so well, that they all voted to thank him when they went away. And I dont so much wonder at it, for he seemed to me to be about the cleverest, good natured old gentleman that ever I see.

Its true the old gentleman had rather hard work to keep the wheels of government going in the Sinnet this winter; and they would get trig'd every little while in spite of all he could do. I spose this made him rather shy of all kinds of wheels; for he wouldn't go home in a stage, nor a waggon, nor a shay. These kind of carts all have wheels, and I spose he thought they might get trig'd and he wouldn't hardly get home all summer. So he concluded to go by water; and he went aboard a vessel Saturday night, and sailed for down east; and as true as you are alive, before the next day noon the wheels of the vessel got trig'd; tho' they said the vessel didn't go on wheels, but some how or other it got trig'd, and back they came next day into Portland again, and there they had to stay till Monday, because the wind didn't blow according to the constitution. But President Hall you know isn't the man to leave his post in time of difficulty; so he never adjourned, nor came ashore, but stuck to the rack till Monday, when a good constitutional breeze sprung up, and they sot sail again. And I wish him a pleasant passage home, and peace and happiness after he gets there; for as I said afore, I dont think there's a cleverer man any where down east.

I was going to tell you something about a town meeting that I've been tu to day; but as uncle Joshua is sleckman and survayor I spose he would like to hear about it more than you, so I guess I shall write to him.

From your cousin,
JACK DOWNING.

LETTER XVII.

In which Mr Downing hints to Uncle Joshua that he has a prospect of being nominated for Governor.

To Uncle Joshua Downing up in Downingville.

Portland, April 14, 1830.

UNCLE JOSHUA, — I spose you remember that are story about the two dogs, that uncle Joe Downing used to tell; how they got to fighting, and snapped and bit, *till they eat each other up, all but jest the tip ends of their tails.* Now I never could exactly see through that story, enough to know how it was done, till lately. I almost thought it was was a kind of tough yarn, that had been stretched a good deal. But fact, uncle, I begin to think it 's true, every word on't; for there 's something going on here as much like it as two peas in a pod. The Portland Argus and the Portland Advertiser, have fell afowl of each other and gone to biting one another's noses off. And if they keep on as they 've began, I guess before summer is out they 'll not only eat each other all up, tails and all, but I believe they are going to devour them are tu outrageous wicked parties, that plagued the legislature so all winter; I mean the Jacksonites and the Huntonites. They 've only been at it a week or two, and they 've made quite a hole into 'em aready. The Advertiser eats the Jacksonites, and the Argus eats the Huntonites, and they are thinning of 'em off pretty fast. This will be a great comfort to the State, as it will give the two republican parties a chance to do something another winter. The Advertiser has eat up the Jacksonites in some places away down east, such as Eastport and so on, and away up tother way in Limerick, and Waterborough, and Fryeburg.

And the Argus has eaten up the Huntonites in Newfield, and Sanford, and Berwick, and Vinalhaven, and so on. All these towns on both sides now have good fair *republican majorities*. I spose about by the middle of next August they 'll get 'em all killed off so there wont be the skin of a Jacksonite or Huntonite left to be sent to the next legislature.

I hope, uncle Joshua, you will be more careful about meddling with politics; for so sure as you get hitched on to the Jackson party or the Hunton party, these barking, deep mouthed creatures will fix their teeth upon you, and you 'll be munched down before you know it.

There 's one thing, uncle, that seems to wear pretty hard upon my mind, and plagues me a good deal; I have n't slept but little this tu three nights about it. I wish you would n't say any thing about it up there amongst our folks, for if it should all prove a fudge, they 'd be laughing at me. But I tell it to you, because I want your advice, as you 've always read the papers, and know considerable about political matters; tho' to be honest I dont spose any one knows much more about politics by reading the papers, after all.

But what I was going to tell you, is — now, uncle, dont twist your tobacco chaw over to tother corner of your mouth and leer over your spectacles, and say Jack 's a fool — what I was going to tell you, is this: I see by a paper printed down to Brunswick, that they talk of *nominating me for Governor* to run down Smith and Hunton. Think of that, uncle; your poor neefu Jack, that last summer was hoeing about among the potatoes, and chopping wood, and making stone walls, like enough before another summer comes about, will be Governor of the State. I shall have a better chance to flog Bill Johnson then, than I should last winter, if we had n't had no Governor nor no laws; for I spose a Governor has a right to flog any body he 's a mind to.

But that 's nither here nor there, uncle; I want your serious advice. *If they nominate me, had I better accept?* Sometimes I 'm half afraid I should n't understand

very well how to du the business; for I never had a
chance to see any governor business done, only what I
see Elder Hall du in the Sinnet chamber last winter.
Poor man, that makes me think what a time he had
going home. I wrote to you before that he went by water,
and that the vessel got trig'd by an unconstitutional
wind the first day and had to come back again. And he
must have found a good many hard trigs after that, for
he did n't get home til 2d day of April.

Where he was, in that dreadful storm the 26th of
March I have n't heard. But I should think after standing the racket he did last winter in the legislater, and
then this ere storm at sea, he never need to fear any
thing on land or water again in this world.

I wish you 'd write me what you think about my being
a candidate for Governor, and whether you think I
could get along with the business. Considerable part of
the business I should n't be a mite afraid but what I
could du; that is, *the turning out and putting in.* I
know every crook and turn of that business; for I
dont believe there 's a boy in our county, though I say it
myself, *that 's turned out and tied up more cattle than I
have.* And they say a Governor has a good deal of this
sort of work to du.

No more at present from your loving neefu,
JACK DOWNING.

LETTER XVIII.

*In which Uncle Joshua discovers remarkable skill in the
science of politics, and advises Mr Downing by all means
to stand as a candidate for governor.*

Downingville, April 18, 1830.

To my neffu, Jack Downing, at Portland.

DEAR JACK — I never felt nicer in my life than I did
when I got your last letter. I did think it was a kind of
foolish notion in you to stay down there to Portland all
winter, and then hire out there this summer. I thought
you better be at home to work on the farm ; for your
father, poor old gentleman, is hauled up with the ruma-
tize so, he wont be able to du hardly a week's work this
summer. But I begin to believe Jack knows which side
his bread is buttered yet. For if you can only run
pretty well as a candidate for Governor, even if you
shouldn't be elected, it will be worth more to you than
the best farm in this County. It will be the means of
getting you into some good office before long, and then
you can step up, ye see, from one office to another till
you get to be Governor. But if the thing is managed
right, I am in hopes you'll get in this time, and the
Downings will begin to look up, and be somebody. Its
a very good start, your being nominated in that are paper down to Brunswick. But there's a good deal to be
done yet, to carry it. I'm older than you are, and have
seen more of this kind of business done than you, and of
course ought to know more about it. Besides, you know
I've always been reading the papers. Well, in the first
place, you must fix upon the name of your party ; I'm
thinking you better call it *the democratic national republican party*, and then, ye see, you'll haul in some from
both of the two clever parties in the State. As for the
Jacksonites and Huntonites, I wouldn't try to get any

support from them; for after such rigs as they cut up in
the Legislater last winter, the people back here in the
country dont like 'em very well. I think it would hurt
you to have any thing to do with 'em. Then you must
get a few of your friends together in Portland, no matter
if there aint no more than half a dozen, and pass some
patriotic resolutions, and then publish the duins of the
meeting in the paper, headed THE VOICE OF THE PEOPLE:
and then go on to say, at a numerous and respectable
meeting of democratic national republicans held in Portland at such a time, &c.

Resolved unanimously, that we have perfect confidence
in the exalted talents, the unspotted integrity, and well
known patriotism of *Mr Jack Downing*, [or perhaps it
should be the Hon. Jaçk Downing] and that we cheer-
fully recommend him to the people of this State as a
candidate for the office of Governor.

Resolved, that his well known attachment to the interests, the principles, and usages of the democratic national republican party, eminently entitles him to their
confidence and support.

Resolved, as the sense of this meeting, that nothing
short of the election of that firm patriot, the Hon. Jack
Downing, can preserve the State from total, absolute,
and irretrievable destruction.

Resolved, that a County Convention be called to ratify
the doings of this meeting, and that the democratic national republicans in other counties be requested to call
conventions for the same purpose.

Resolved, that the proceedings of this meeting be published in all the democratic national republican newspapers in the State.

We will then get up such a meeting in this town, and
pass some more highly patriotic resolutions and send
'em down, and you must have 'em put into the paper
headed A VOICE FROM THE COUNTRY. And then we must
get a few together somewhere, and call it a *county con-*

vention, and keep rolling the snow ball over, till we wind up the whole State in it. Then, ye see, about the first of August we must begin to pin it down pretty snug in the papers. Kind of touch it up some how like this: extract of a letter from a gentleman of the first respectability in York County to the central committee in Portland. 'The democratic national republicans here are wide awake ; York County is going for Mr Downing, all hollow : we shall give him in this county at least a thousand majority over both Smith and Hunton.' Another from Penobscot : 'three quarters of the votes in this county will be given to Mr Downing : the friends of Smith and Hunton have given up the question, so satisfied are they that there is no chance for them.'

Another from Kennebec : 'from information received from all parts of the State, upon which perfect reliance may be placed, we are enabled to state for the information of our democratic national republican friends, that there is not the least shadow of doubt of the election of Mr Downing. It is now rendered certain beyond the possibility of mistake, *that he will receive from five to ten thousand majority over both the other candidates.*'

If this don't carry it, you'll have to hang up your fiddle till another year. And after the election is over, if you shouldn't happen to get hardly any votes at all, you must turn about with perfect indifference, and say the democratic national republicans *didn't try* — made no effort at all — but will undoubtedly carry the election next year all hollow.

P. S. If you get in, I shall expect my son Ephraim to have the office of Sheriff in this County, for he's got some of the bean poles left yet, that he sot out to carry to market last winter. The other offices we'll distribute at our leisure.

Your affectionate old uncle,
JOSHUA DOWNING.

LETTER XIX.

In which Mr Downing gives his opinion about newspapers.

Portland, March 30, 1830.

DEAR UNCLE JOSHUA — In my last letter to Ephraim, I said I should write to you pretty soon something about the Portland Town Meeting. As you've been sleckman and survare a good many years, I spose you'd like to hear about sich kind of things. And I spose I might tell you about a good many other things tu, that you don't have much chance to know about away up there; and aunt Sally says I ought tu; for she says I have a great many advantages living here in Portland, that folks can't have up in the country, and if I should write to some of you once or twice a week, she thinks it would be time well spent. So I shall spend part of my evenings, after I get my day's work done, in writing letters. I don't know but I forgot to tell you that I had hired out here this summer. I get eight dollars a month and board, and have the evenings to myself. I go to school three evenings in a week, and aunt Sally says she can begin to see that I spell better already. The printer of the Courier and the Family Reader, that sends my letters for me, is very kind; he does'nt ask any thing for sending my letters, and he gives me as many newspapers as I can get time to read. So I spend one evening in a week reading newspapers, and set up pretty late that evening tu. And besides I get a chance to read awhile most every morning before the rest of the folks are up; for these Portland folks are none of your starters in the morning. I've known my father many a time, before the rhumatiz took the poor old gentleman, to mow down an acre of stout grass in the morning, and get done by that time one half the Portland folks leave off snoring. Sometimes I think I better be up in the country tu, mowing

8

or hoeing potatoes, or something else, instead of reading newspapers. Its true they are bewitching kind of things, and I like well enough to read 'em, but jest between you and me, they are the worst things to bother a feller's head about, that you ever see. In one of my letters, you know, I said newspapers were dreadful *smoky* things, and any body couldn't read in 'em half an hour without having their eyes so full of smoke they couldn't tell a pig-sty from a meeting house.

But I'm thinking after all they are more like *rum* than smoke. You know rum will sometimes set quite peaceable folks together by the ears, and make them *quarrel* like mad dogs — so do the newspapers. Rum makes folks act very *silly* — so do the newspapers. Rum makes folks *see double* — so do the newspapers. Sometimes rum gets folks so they can't see at all — so do the newspapers. Rum, if they take tu much of it, makes folks *sick to the stomach* — so do the newspapers. Rum makes folks go rather *crooked*, reeling from one side of the road to t'other — and the newspapers make one half the politicians *cross their path* as often as any drunkard you ever see. It was the newspapers, uncle Joshua, that made you *bet* about the Speaker last summer, and lose your bushel of corn. Remember that, uncle, and dont believe any thing you see in the papers this summer, unless you see it in the Daily Courier or Family Reader; and dont you believe them neither if ever you see them smoke like the rest of the papers.

As I was a saying about my evenings, I spend one evening a week reading that little book called the constitution, that kept our legislaters quarrelling all winter. You know I bought one for four ax-handles; I find I can read it considerable easy, most all of it without spelling, and when I get through I shall tell you something about it.

A queer thought, uncle, has just popt into my head: I guess I should make a capital member of Congress —

for this letter is just like one of the Congress speeches.
It begun about the town meeting, but not a bit of a word
is there in it from beginning to end about the town meeting, after you get over the text.   But I find by reading
the papers that when a Congress man speaks all day
without touching his subject, he makes a motion to adjourn, and goes at it again the next day.   So I believe I
must say good night to you now, and try it again the
next leisure evening.

Your loving neffu,

JACK DOWNING.

LETTER XX.

*In which Mr Downing tells how to distinguish one republi-
can party from another.*

Portland, June 9, 1830.

UNCLE JOSHUA, — Did you ever see tu dogs get to
quarrelling about one bone ?   How they will snap and
snarl about it, especially if they are hungry.   Sometimes one will get it into his mouth and hook it away
like smoke, and t'other arter him full chisel.   And when
he overtakes him they'll have another scratch, and drop
the bone, and then t'other one'll get it, and off he goes
like a shot.   And sometimes they both get hold together,
one at one end and one at t'other, and then sich a tug-
ging and growlin you never see.   Well now, when they
act so, they act jest like the Portland Argus and Portland Advertiser ; two great big growlers, they are all the
time quarrelling about their *Republikin*, to see which
shall have it.   If the Advertiser says any thing about his
republikin, the Argus snaps at it, and says 'tisn't your

republikin, its mine. You no business to be a republikin, you are a Federalist.

And when the Argus says any thing about his republikin, the Advertiser flies up, and says, you no business to be a republikin, you're a Jacksonite. And so they have it up hill and down, bark, bark, and tug, tug, and which 'll get the republikin at last I cant tell. Sometimes they get so mad, seems as though they'll tear each other all to pieces, and there's forty thousand folks setting of 'em on and hollering stooboy. Now there wasn't any need of all this quarrel, for each of 'em had a republikin last winter ; the Argus had a democratic one, and the Advertiser had a national one, and they got 'em mixed by leaving off the *chrissen names*. And I guess it would puzzle a Philadelphy lawyer to tell 'em apart without their names, for their republikins are as much alike as tu peas in a pod.

The Advertiser never should say *republikin* alone, but *national* republikin, and the Argus never should say republikin alone, but *democratic* republican. And then it seems as though each one might know his own bone, and knaw it without quarrelling.

I thought, uncle, I'd jest tell you a little about this ere business, because I know you always want to find out all the kinks about politiks.

Your neffu,
JACK DOWNING.

P. S. I dont hear any thing yet about the convention up there that you promised to make to nominate me for Governor. I think its time it was out ; for I am afraid Mr Hunton and Mr Smith will get the start of me, if I aint under way soon. J. D.

Grand Caucus at Downingville.

From the Portland Courier of July 21, 1830.

☞ THE LONG AGONY OVER, ✍

And the Nomination out.

We delay this paper something beyond the usual hour of publication in order to lay before our readers the important intelligence received yesterday from Downingville. — This we have been able to accomplish, tho' not without extraordinary exertions and extra help. But the crisis is important, we had almost said appalling, and demands of every patriotic citizen of Maine the highest sacrifices in his power to make. The important proceedings of the grand convention at Downingville reached here, by express, yesterday about a quarter before 3 o'clock **P. M.** having travelled the whole distance, notwithstanding the extreme high temperature of the weather, at the rate of thirteen and a half miles an hour. And but for an unfortunate occurrence, it would undoubtedly have reached here at least three hours earlier. *Capt. Jehu Downing*, who with his characteristic magnanimity and patriotism volunteered to bring the express the whole way, having taken a very high spirited steed for the first ten miles, was unfortunately thrown to the ground in attempting to leap a barrier which lay across the road. Two of his ribs were broken by the fall, and his right arm so badly fractured that it is feared amputation must be resorted to, besides several other severe contusions on various parts of the body. We are happy to hear however that Doctor Zachariah Downing, who on hearing the melancholy intelligence very promptly repaired to the spot to offer his professional services, pronounces the Captain out of danger, and also that the Captain bears his misfortune with his accustomed fortitude, expressly

8*

declaring that the only regret he feels on the occasion is the delay of the express. Here is patriotism, a devotedness to the welfare of the country, and to genuine democratic national republican principles, worthy of the days of the revolution.

Lieut. Timothy Downing forwarded the express the remainder of the way with the utmost despatch, having run down three horses, one of which died on the road. — But we keep our readers too long from the gratifying intelligence received.

Grand Democratic National Republican Convention.

Downingville, Monday, July 19, 1830.

At a large and respectable meeting of the democratic national republicans of Downingville and the neighboring parts of the state, convened this day at the centre school house, the meeting was called to order by the venerable and silver-haired patriarch, old *Mr Zebedee Downing*, who had not been out to a political meeting before for the last twenty-five years. The venerable old gentleman stated in a few feeling remarks the object of the meeting; that he had not meddled with politics since the days of Jefferson; but that now in view of the awful calamities which threatened to involve our country in total ruin, he felt it his duty the little remaining time he might be spared from the grave, to lift up his voice and his example before his children, grand children, and great grand children whom he saw gathered around him, and encourage them to save the country for which he had fought and bled in his younger years. After the enthusiastic applause elicited by these remarks, the old gentleman called for the nomination of a chairman, and JOSHUA DOWNING, ESQUIRE was unanimously called to the chair, and *Mr Ephraim Downing* appointed Secretary.

On motion of Mr Jacob Downing, voted, that a committee of five be appointed to draft resolutions to lay before this meeting. Whereupon Jotham Downing, Ichabod Downing, Zenas Downing, Levi Downing, and Isaiah Downing, were appointed said committee, and after retiring about five minutes, they returned and reported the following preamble and resolutions.

Whereas an awful crisis has arrived in the political affairs of our country, our public men all having turned traitors, and resolved to ruin the country, and make us and our children all slaves forever; and whereas our ship of state and our ship of the United States, are both driven with tremendous violence before the fury of the political tempest, and are just upon the point of being dashed upon the breakers of political destruction ; and whereas, nothing short of the most prompt and vigorous exertions of the patriotic democratic national republicans of this state and of the United States can avert the impending danger,

And whereas, the Jacksonites, and Adamsites, and Huntonites, and Smithites, have so multiplied in the land, and brought things to such a pass, that our liberties are unquestionably about to receive their doom forever :

Therefore Resolved, that it is the highest and most sacred duty of every patriotic Democratic National Republican in the State, to arouse himself and buckle on his political armour, and make one last, one mighty effort, to save the state and the country, and place the constitution once more upon a safe and firm foundation.

Resolved, that the awful crisis of affairs in this State requires a firm devoted patriot, a high-minded and gifted statesman, and a uniform unwavering Democratic National Republican, for chief magistrate.

Resolved, that in this awful crisis, we believe the eyes of all true patriots are turned upon

THE HON. JACK DOWNING,

late of Downingville, but since last winter a resident in
Portland, the capital of the State.

Resolved, that we have the fullest confidence in the
talents, integrity, moral worth, tried patriotism, and unwavering and unchangeable sterling Democratic National
Republicanism of the *Hon. Jack Downing*, and that his
election to the office of Governor in September next,
and nothing else, can save the State from total, unutterable, and irretrievable ruin.

Resolved therefore, That we recommend him to the
electors of this State as a candidate for said office, and
that we will use all fair and honourable means, and, if
necessary, will not stick at some a little *dis*-honourable,
to secure his election.

Resolved, That we disapprove of personal crimination
and re-crimination in political contests, and therefore
will only say of our opponents, that we think them no
better than they should be, and that they unquestionably mean to destroy the land we live in.

Resolved, That it be recommended to all the patriotic
democratic national republicans throughout the State, to
be up and doing; to call county meetings, town meetings, school district meetings, and village and bar-room
meetings, and proceed to organize the party as fast as
possible, by appointing standing committees, and central
committees, and corresponding committees, and bearers
and distributers of handbills; and in short by doing every thing that the good of the cause and the salvation of
the country requires.

Resolved, conditionally, That in case General Jackson should be likely to be re-elected, we highly and cor-
dially approve of his administration, and believe him to
be second to none but Washington; but in case he should
stand no chance of re-election, we resolve him to be the
ignorant tool of a corrupt faction, plotting to destroy the
liberties of the country.

Resolved, That the thanks of this convention be presented to Miss Abigail Downing, for the use of her school room this afternoon, she having with a generous patriotism dismissed her school for that purpose.

Resolved, That the proceedings of this convention, signed by the Chairman and Secretary, be published in the *Portland Daily Courier*, and the *Family Reader*, the official organs of the Hon. JACK DOWNING's correspondence, and any other genuine Democratic National Republican papers in the State.

JOSHUA DOWNING, *Chairman.*
Attest : EPHRAIM DOWNING, *Secretary.*

We are assured by Lieutenant Timothy Downing, with whom we had a short interview, that the best spirit prevailed in the convention ; not a dissenting voice was heard, and all the resolutions passed unanimously. We add an extract or two from private letters.

From Ephraim Downing, to the Hon. Jack Downing.

" Well Jack, if you don't acknowledge we've done the thing up in style, you're no gentleman and not fit for Governor. I wish you to be very particular to keep the Sheriff's office for me.—Father says cousin Jeremiah has thrown out some hints that he shall have the Sheriff's office. But butter my ristbands, if you do give it to him you'll go out of office again next year, that's positive. Jere's a clear factionist, you may rely upon that. No, no, stick to·your old friends, and they'll stick to you. I'm going to start to-morrow morning on an electioneering cruise. I shall drum 'em up about right. You only keep a stiff upper lip, and you'll come in all hollow."

From Joshua Downing, Esq. to the Hon. Jack Downing.

" Dear Jack, things look well here ; with proper exertions I think you may rely upon success. I am in great haste, and write this jest to tell you to be sure and not promise a single office to any mortal living, till I see you.

These things must be managed very prudently, and you will stand in need of the counsel of your old uncle. I think I could do as much good to the State by being appointed Land Agent, as any way ; but I'll determine upon that when I see you.

N. B. Make no promises. Your affectionate uncle,
JOSHUA.

LETTER XXI.

In which Mr Downing tells about the Portland town-meeting.

Portland, September 15, 1830.

DEAR UNCLE JOSHUA. — The great battle, that 's been coming on all summer, is over, and the smoke jest begins to blow away a little, so that we can look round and see who 's killed, and who 's wounded so bad they cant get over it, and who 's driven off the field, and who stands their ground and cries victory. I 've been looking out for you here ever since yesterday noon, for I thought if it looked up there, as though I stood any chance to be elected governor, you would be right down here as quick as possible, driving night and day, to see about them are *offices.* For you know you promised to help me fix 'em, and told me I must not give away one of 'em till you come. And you may depend on it I should a held on to 'em to the bat's end, till you did come, let who would come arter 'em. But as you have n't got here yet, I 'm afraid I did n't run very well up there, so I thought I would write to you and see what 's the matter. If I did n't run any better up there than I did down here to Portland, I would n't give a cent to be a candidate any

longer this year; for I might run till I was gray, and not
be elected. However, worst come to worst, I know what
I can do. If Judge Smith's got in, and they say about
here he 's gone all hollow, I 'll see if I cant work it so
as to get an office under him. — You see I kept pretty
still along for sometime before election, and I guess I can
manage it so as to make him think I lectioneered for
him, and then I 'll follow him up, tooth and nail, till he
gives me an office. I 'll try for sheriff first, and if I cant
get that, I 'll try for Clark of the Courts, for they say
that 's a pretty good office. And if he says he has given
them all away, I 'll try for Land Agent, for you know
I 've been about the woods a good deal; and if he says
that belongs to Dr Rose, I 'll try to be a Post Master
somewhere, or a door keeper to the Legislater, or some
sich like. And if he says these are all gone tu, I 'll tell
him if he 'll give me a fair price, I 'll water his horse and
brush his boots. And if he wont let me do that, I say
burn his boots, I 'll run against him again next year.

I spose you would like to know something about how
the election turned out down here. Soon as the bell
rung, I sot out to go to the town hall, but before I got
half way there, I met chaises, and waggons, and another
kind of chaises, that went on four wheels and was shut
up close as a hen-coop, all driving *'tother way*, jehu like.
What is the matter? says I; who 's beat? But along
they went snapping their whips without answering me a
word, and by their being in sich a terrible hurry I thought
sure enough they had got beat, and the enemy was arter
'em. So I steered round into another street to get out
of the way for fear they should get a brush at me; but
there was as many more of 'em driving like split down
that street tu. Where upon arth are they all going, says
I, to a feller that overtook me upon the full run. Going?
says he; why to bring 'em to the polls, you goose head:
and away he went by me in a whisk. When he said
poles, I thought that cousin Ephraim must have come in

with a load, as they 'd be likely to fetch a good price
about this time, and I concluded all that running and
driving was to see who should have the first grab at 'em.
I called to him to tell me where Ephraim was, but he
was out of hearing.

So I marched along till I got to the town hall, and
they were flocking in thick as hops.   When I got within two or three rods of the house a man come along
and handed me a vote for Mr Smith; I stept on the side
walk and another man handed me a vote for Mr Hunton; and I went along towards the door and another
man handed me a vote for Mr Smith, and then another
handed me one for Mr Hunton.   And then I went to go
up stairs into the hall, and there was a row of about
twenty men, and all of 'em gave me a vote, about one
half for Smith and one half for Hunton.   And before I
got through the hall to the place where they were firing
off their votes, they gave me about twenty more ; so if
I had been a mind to vote for Smith or Hunton I could
have gin 'em a noble lift ; but that wasn't what I was
arter.   I was looking out for the interests of my constituents at Downingville.   And when I come to see
among so many votes, not one of 'em had my name on
it, I began to feel a little kind of streaked.

I went out again, and I see the chaises and waggons
kept coming and going, and I found out that bringing of
'em to the polls meant bringing of 'em to vote.   And I
asked a feller that stood there, who them are men, that
they kept bringing, voted for.   Why, says he, they vote
for whichever goes arter 'em, you goose-head you.   Ah,
says I, is that the way they work it ?   And where do
they bring 'em from ?   O, says he, down round the
wharves, and the outskirts of the town and any where
that they can catch 'em.   Well, well, thinks I to myself, I've got a new rinkle, I see how this business is
done now.   So off I steered and hired a horse and waggon, and went to hunting up folks to carry to town meet-

ing. And I guess before night I carried nearly fifty there, of one sort and another; and I was sure to whisper to every one of 'em jest as they got out of the waggon, and tell 'em my name was Jack Downing. They all looked very good natured when I told 'em my name, and I thought to be sure they would all vote for me. But how was I thunderstruck when the vote was declared, and there was 1008 for Mr Smith, 909 for Mr Hunton, 4 for Mr Ladd, and one or two for somebody else, and not *one* for me. Now was 'nt that too bad, uncle? Them are faithless politicians that I carried up to the town-meeting! if I only knew who they were, they should pay for the horse and waggon, or we'd have a breeze about it.

Write soon, for I am anxious to know how they turned out in Downingville.

Your loving neffu,
JACK DOWNING.

LETTER XXII.

Return of votes from Downingville.

To the Hon. Jack Downing, Portland.

Downingville, Monday Eve, September 13, 1830.

DEAR JACK,—I have just returned, puffing and blowing, from town-meeting, and have only time to tell you that we gave you a confounded good run here. If your friends in the rest of the State have done their duty, you are elected by an overwhelming majority. The vote in this town for governor stood as follows:—

Hon. JACK DOWNING,	87
Hon. Samuel E. Smith,	00
Hon. Jonathan G. Hunton,	00

9

Capt. Jehu Downing is elected representative ; it was thought to be due to him by the party for his magnanimous exertions in carrying the express to Portland at the time you were nominated by our grand convention.

In great haste, your uncle,
JOSHUA DOWNING.

LETTER XXIII.

In which Mr Downing hits on a new plan to get an office.

Portland, Dec. 13, 1830.

DEAR UNCLE JOSHUA : — I am tired of hard work, and I mean to have an office some how or other yet. Its true I and all our family got rather dished in the governor business ; if I'd only got in, they should every soul of 'em had an office, down to the forty-ninth cousin. But its no use to cry for spilt milk. I've got another plan in my head ; I find the United States offices are the things to make money in, and if I can get hold of a good fat one, you may appoint a day of thanksgiving up there in Downingville, and throw by your work every one of you as long as you live.

I want you to set me up for member of Congress up there, and get me elected as soon as you can, for if I can get on to Washington I believe I can work it so as to get an office some how or other. — I want you to be particular to put me up as a Tariff man. I was agoing to take sides against the tariff so as to please Gineral Jackson and all his party, for they deal out the offices now a days, and you know they've been mad enough with the tariff to eat it up. But the Portland Advertiser has been blowin away lately and praising up the tariff and telling what a fine thing tis, and fact, *it has brought the old gineral round.* His great long message to Congress has just got along here, and the old gentleman says the tariff wants a little mending, but on the whole it's a cute good thing, and we must n't give it up.

Your lovin neffu,

JACK DOWNING.

LETTER XXIV.

In which Cousin Sarah compares the society of Portland with that of Downingville.

[*Note by the Editor.* This is not aunt Sally who was married and living in Portland; but a niece who had been there a short time at school.]

Portland, Dec. 22, 1830.

To Cousin Nabby Downing.

Now I do beg of you, my dear Nabby, never to joke me, as you did in your last letter, about the Portland beaux. Why, if I thought any thing about sich matters, I would a great deal sooner marry Sam Josslyn. He is educated enough to know the age of his cows and oxen, to know how to cultivate a field of corn, or a patch of potatoes ; can read his bible, and say the ten commandments, and what is better, Sam can *keep* them all. Besides these accomplishments, you know Sam has a snug little farm of his own, free from mortgages or any other embarrassments, is sober, active, and industrious, and I doubt not, has cast many a sheep's eye at my good cousin Nabby. These are good substantial prospects, which it is hardly worth while to overlook, and which it would be rather difficult to find among the Portland beaux. I have often heard uncle Joshua, who is now the most wealthy man in Downingville, tell how he com-

menced business with a capital of only *one dollar*, and
how some young wags of the village came in and made
a good deal of sport by purchasing up all his stock.
But he didn't care for their jokes, he added the profits
of his sale to his capital, and commenced business
again ; and by good management, economy in his dress
and frugality in his living, he soon put himself beyond
the reach of want or waggery. I have always admired
the perseverance and economy of my good uncle, and
have contrasted it with the management of our Portland
merchants. They often commence business with even
less capital than uncle Joshua ; but then their stock is
worth perhaps five or six thousand dollars. They cut a
great dash for a few months, and then, if they are un-
married, begin to ogle the girls in order to choose a
wife. And what do you think are the requisites for a
wife here, Cousin Nabby ? You say she must be capa-
ble, neat, industrious and amiable. No indeed, my dear,
such things are scarcely ever thought of here. She
must have a smattering of French, must be able to drum
the music out of a piano, to sing and dance, or all in
one word, she must be *genteel.* Well, such girls are
plenty enough down here, and a wife is soon obtained.
They hire a large house, furnish it elegantly, obtain
servants, go to parties, balls and the theatre, make jams,
and morning calls, and then *fail.* The wife goes home
again to her mother's, with the addition of an innocent
babe, and the young broken merchant is off to the south
to look after business again. Now do you not think this
a refined and intellectual state of society ? You will
not wonder that I am attached to the unsophisticated
manners and simple habits of our own village. Do not
think from what I have said, there are no people of in-
tellect here, for I assure you there is a choice brother-
hood whom we sometimes meet at social parties and
lectures, but they are so accustomed to the weak and
frivolous of our sex, that their conversation is almost

wholly confined to each other. Have you made any additions to our little library since I left home? If you are not too bashful, tell Sam to *read* these long winter evenings, instead of spending his time in making axe handles and goad sticks. Cousin Jack has got his head so full of politics, that I doubt whether he sells one for him, this winter. Tell Uncle Joshua if he has any more apple sauce to sell this winter, to send it down in the old lumber box by Ned, and if he must needs send his letters to Jack through the Courier, be sure and not to say one word about the apple sauce, for you dont know how queer it looks to see governors and goad-sticks, politics and pan-dowdy, ballot-boxes and bean-poles, all jumbled up together.

Your loving Cousin,
SARAH DOWNING.

LETTER XXV.

In which Mr Downing tells how Cousin Jehu went to the Legislature, and had to go back after his primy facy case.

Portland, Tuesday Jan. 11, 1831.

DEAR UNCLE JOSHUA,—Cousin Jehu and I got down here the Monday before the Legislater met, and sich a dragging time of it, as we had through the mud, I guess you never see. More than three quarters of the way, it was as bad as ploughing mash-meadow in April. The waggon wheels sometimes went in almost up to the hub, and we had to get out and lift and pry as hard as the Legislater used to, last winter, to get the wheels of government agoing. Your poor old hoss is nearly done tu. But we shall doctor him up as well as we can, so as to get him home again. Next day we went round to see how the market was. Your apple-sass fetched a good

price. We sold it to a Jacksonite tavern-keeper. He
said he wanted a little something to sour his dinners a
little mite ; for his boarders were all Jacksonites, and
they'd got the upperhand so now days, that they complained their victuals was all too sweet. Your boiled
cider went off at a real round price tu. Why, how
much did you boil that cider down ? It was so strong,
that a gill of it would knock a man down any time. We
sold it to a Huntonite tavern-keeper. He said his boarders were all Huntonites, and he didn't know what the matter was, but they seemed to be rather down in the mouth
lately, and he wanted a little something to start their
ideas and keep their sperits up. So he gin us jest what
we asked. Ax handles dont fetch nothing hardly. The
bean poles turned middling well, though they dont go off
so glib as they did last year. I find folks are a little
more shy about buying of 'em for sheriff poles than
they used to be, for they say when a man gets one,
there's no knowing as it will be any use to him more
than one year. Howsomever, we sold a few of 'em
right out, and made a pretty good spec in 'em. And we
bargained away a number more *upon condition that they
should want 'em.* Cousin Nabby's footings fetched the
same they did last year, that is ninepence a pair, and
we got her a nice piece of cotton cloth for 'em. Tell
aunt Keziah we got for her bundle of urbs a pound of
good shushon and a quarter of snuff. We shall send
'em all up in the waggon by Jim.

But Jim will have to wait here till cousin Jehu gets
back again, for he took the other hoss Wednesday and
started off like a stream of lightning for Downingville.
Now I spose you will be a little struck up at that, till I
tell you the reason of it, but the fact was he came away
from home and forgot to bring his *primy facy* case.
And we met one of the members Tuesday night and
got to speaking about it, and he said it would be
of no use to think of getting a seat in the House with-

out one, for they were going to be very particular, and nobody would be allowed to take a seat in the House unless he could show a good fair *primy facy* case. Well then, said cousin Jehu, the jig is up with me, for as true as eggs is bacon I left mine at home. But, finally, after considerin upon it, we concluded 'twas best for him, as he was a pretty smart rider, to start off and get it, and come back again as quick as possible. But he might have been saved all that trouble, if he had only known how it would turn out. For when the members got together Wednesday morning, they appointed a committee to go round among 'em and take the *primy facy* cases and count 'em, and see if there was enough to make a corum. I dont know as I can tell exactly what sort of a thing a corum is, but they said the constitution wouldn't let 'em do any thing till they had a corum, and it took a hundred and thirty *primy facy* cases to make one.

One of the Huntonites made a motion that the committee should examine the primy facy cases, and not count any but what was good.—But the Jacksonites said no, they should count 'em all first, and they'd take their seats and go to work, and have another committee afterwards to examine 'em. They disputed about it a little while pretty sharp; but at last the republicans begun to get a notion that it was only jest meant to trig the wheels of government, and it stuck in their crops so they couldn't bear it any longer, and they up foot and gave the trig such a kick, I guess the Huntonites nor Jacksonites neither wont find it again this winter.

So they let them all take their seats with such kind of primy facy things as they had got, and went to choosing officers.

There aint but a few Huntonites and Jacksonites in the Legislater this year, and its lucky there isn't, for there is no telling how much mischief they did last winter. There is so few of them are two rascally parties here now, that are trying to ruin the country, that 'tis thought the republicans will be able to keep the wheels agoing and get along without much trouble.

I have a good deal more to write to you, but haven't time in this letter. Elder Hall is here, but he is not President this year. He thinks rotation in office is all the beauty of republicanism, so he gave up the chair this year to Mr Dunlap.

Cousin Sally has got most through her second quarter's schooling here, and when she gets through, I dont know but I should advise you to take her home, for she grows so vain and accomplished, as they call it, that I dont think it 'll do her much good. Jest look at her last letter that she sent up in the Courier, and see how lady-like she talks. And then in order to be mighty nice, she must needs sign it Sarah ; as if the good old name of Sally, that her mother gave her, wasn't good enough for her.

Tell cousin Jehu to make haste back again, for the Legislater's rattling along so with their business that he'll hardly get a finger in the pie if he isn't here soon. They've made a Governor, and some Councillors, and a Secretary of State, and a Treasurer, and a State Printer, besides doing a good many other things, and it hasn't took half so long as it did last winter to say poor Mr Roberts shouldn't have a seat. This in haste.

Your lovin neffu,
JACK DOWNING.

LETTER XXVI.

In which Nabby describes the temperance of Downingville.

Downingville, Jinerwary 20, 1831.

To Cousin Sarah Downing, at School down to Portland.

I should like to know, cousin Sarah, if you have heard down there to Portland any thing about a *temperance society*. If you have just write and tell me what it means.

You know father wants to know the meaning of every
thing, and so I walked tu miles over to the school-master's
to borry Mr Walker's dictionary to see what it meant;
and after all I want no wiser than I was afore, for there
was n't one word in it about temperance societies. Tother
day father sot in the shop door, wondering if Jack would
go to the Congress or not, when a proper great fat red-
faced man came in, and opened a long paper with more
names on it than I could read in a week, — and says he,
Mr Downing, I want you to sine your name to this paper.
Father took hold of the paper with one hand, and run
tother up under his hat, jest as he always does when he
tries to think ; and, my friend, says he, I dont know as I
quite understand what this ere means. Why, says he,
by putting your name down, you promise not to drink
any rum yourself, nor to let any of your family. My conscience, father understood it then, I can tell you, he
hopped rite out of his chair, and I guess the temperance
man was gone in no time. Well, after father had time
to consider a little he began to feel afraid he had n't
used the man exactly right ; for, said he, may be all
places aint like Downingville. I remember reading in
the newspaper of some places where they drink rum as
we do water, and get so drunk that they tumble about on
the ground. And may be the man did n't know but
what we drank it here. And if he was trying to do good
he was n't so much to blame after all. Indeed, Sam,
said he, for Mr Josslyn came in while he was talking,
I 've been told there are shop keepers who retale rum by
the half jill, to men who drink it at their counters, and
some can actually bare that enormous quantity two and
three times in a day. I never see Sam's eyes so
big, Sarah ; he look'd as if he wanted to say, that 's a
whacker, Mr Downing ; and so thinks I, I will write to
Sarah, and she 'll tell me all about it.

Your loving cousin,   NABBY.

P. S. I tried to tell what father said in his own words,

cause you always like to hear him talk. Sam says
Sarah dont understand such things ; the libry is only fit
for folks like her and the schoolmaster. A farmer ort
to stick to his ox bows and goard sticks. And I believe
he 's half rite, Sarah, for I dont believe you are so happy for trying to no so much ; ever since you took to
study, I see you dont laugh half so hearty as you used
to, and you look sober three times as often. I 'm afraid
you will be a spoilt girl for the country, Sarah ; you 'd
better leave your hard words and come up here and sing
at your wheel all day, churn butter and milk the cows,
go to slay rides and quiltings, and be as good and happy
as you used to be. I love you, Sarah, and always shall,
and I believe Sam would like you as well as he duz me, if
twant for your learnin. There, I wont say another
word, for I 'm half cryin now.   N.

LETTER XXVII.

In which Mr Downing gives a description of the Ladies'
Fair.

Portland, Friday, Jan. 28, 1831.

My Dear Cousin Nabby, — It's a great while since
I writ to you, for you know when I write politics I always have to send it to uncle Joshua, cause he loves
dearly to dig into sich things, and when I write about
bringing bean poles and apple-sass to market, I have to
send to cousin Ephraim, cause he's the boy to do that
are ; but when I write about the ladies and sich like I
send it right to you ; and I've got a master mess to tell
you this time, as ever you heard in all your life. I dont
know where bouts to begin, and when I get begun I'm
afraid I never shall know where to leave off ; for if I

should try to tell you all about it, I dont know but you
would get to be as old as aunt Keziah before I should
get through. Howsomever, I'll try to give you a little
smattering of it, and I might as well begin before I go
any further, for I spose by this time you're all of a didder to know what I mean. Well then, to let you into
the mistery, we've had the *ladies fair* here, and of all
the scrapes that ever I see this beats the cap-shief; In-
dependant was nothing tu it hardly. I'll tell you how
they come to have it. There's a woman here that takes
care of a whole flock of little gals, what hant got nobody else to take care of 'em ; they call her the Orphan
Asylum. And they said she hadn't got money enough
to buy bread and milk for 'em all, and clothes to wear
in this cold weather. And so the ladies, for you know
Nabby, they are always kind hearted sort of creatures,
thought they'd put their heads together and see if they
couldn't get some money for her. So they agreed to
have what they call a fair — that means a place where
every sort of nicknack that was ever made or thought
of, and some that never was thought of before, are brought
together to sell. Well, you know the women can do
most any thing if they set out. So, as soon as they set
this afloat, it went through the town like a buzz. All
the ladies and gals went to work like smoke, making
up things for the fair.

And they were in sich a taking about it, they couldn't
do any thing else for two months. — When the men
went home to their dinners they'd fret and scold 'cause
'twant ready. Now dont scold, the woman would say,
for the gals have been so busy making them are little
frocks and pin-cushions and needle-books for the fair,
that they never thought of its being one o'clock so soon.
And when the old bachelors went up to bed, down they'd
come again sputtering along, and want to know what's
the reason their bed want made. Then the chamber
gal would jump as if she'd gone out of her skin ; well

there now, says she, as true as I'm alive, I've been so busy to day making that are dicky for the fair, that I never thought a word about the beds. Well, last Tuesday they got 'em all ready, and carried 'em into the great town hall, that's as big agin as uncle Joshua's forty foot barn, and paraded 'em out to sell. And they put it into the papers that they should be ready by six o'clock in the evening for customers. But the funniest of it all was, they charged every body ninepence a piece jest for coming in to buy their things whether they bought any thing or not. And if they went out a minute or two and come in again, they had to pay ninepence more. That's a plaguy good way to keep shop, they make money so fast by it. — Some of the young fellers kept going out and coming in again every few minutes, I spose jest to show the gals that come with 'em that they'd a good pocket full of ninepences and want stingy of 'em.

But I'm getting before my story. All day Tuesday the chaps were flying round getting their 5 dollar bills changed to go to the fair. As for me, I hadn't only a one dollar bill, and I did n't dare to show that to nobody for fear of the debety sheriffs, for they begin to look out pretty sharp after we disappointed office seekers now-a-days, and if they catch us with a dollar they nab it quick enough I tell ye. Howsomever, I borried a ninepence of a feller that used to work long with me last summer, and I told him I didn't doubt but what I could pay him next day, for most all the lobby members of the Legislater would be to the fair, and bein the sheriffs aint appointed yet, I should stand a good chance to bargain away a few of cousin Ephraim's bean poles; and I'm to have half for selling. So as soon as the clock struck six, I took my ninepence, and up I trudged and went right into the fair, jest like any body else; and my stars! sich another sight I dont think there ever was afore. I thought I'd seen most all the world since I left Downingville, but bless me, come to look around

here I found I hadn't hardly begun to see it yet. I never
see any thing that lookt so bright before, unless it was
when uncle Zekiel's barn burnt down. There was a
master sight of candles and lamps stuck up round the
windows and all over the great hall, and along in the
middle of it there hung down two great bunches of green
spruce tops as big as a hogset, and they were stuck full
of lamps all over 'em. I believe they called 'em *tallow
chandlers*, or some sich name. The folks kept coming
and pouring in as thick as bees, and at last the hall got
chock brim full, and then if there wasn't a crowdin and
squeezin time I'll never guess agin. They had to look
out for toes, I can tell 'em ; I was glad I left my corns
to home, for if I hadn't I should had 'em smashed all to
pieces forty times.

You might as well try to crawl through a woodpile as
to think of getting round any where in the hall, only jest
where the crowd happened to carry you. A chap that
stood pretty near me said to an old white headed gentleman, have you been over there to the old witch tother side of the hall to have your fortune told ; O no, says
he, *I have n't been jam'd that way yet*. As I was tussling
along to try to get a peep at some of the tables, I got
stuck fast between three stout women, and to move
another inch I couldn't if I was to be whipped. And
some how or other my head got jam'd under one of
their bonnets, but 'twas none of my duins though, and
says she, sir, I'll thank you to take your head out of
my face. Yes mam, says I, I will as soon as that lady's
head behind mine gets a little loose, so I can pull mine
back. But I had tough work to breath before I could
get command of my own head agin, I tell ye. Well,
at last I tussled along or was jam'd along some how or
other pretty near some of the tables, so that I could kind
o' peep over on to 'em sometimes. And sich a mess of
pretty things and queer things as they had there to sell
I never set eyes on before. And then, O sich a pretty

row of gals along behind the tables for shop-keepers, all dressed up so fine, and laughing out of both of their eyes so like little witches, and holding up their pretty things in their little white hands, and asking every body to buy 'em. O Nabby, I never felt the want of money so much before in all my life. Soon as I looked at 'em I wished I had a thousand dollars to spend. And *if I'd only been elected Governor*, as I ought to have been, and should have been if our party had only been a little better organized, I'd a made the money fly well, you may depend upon't ; for I think governors at sich times ought to be generous and set good examples. Now I think on't tell uncle Joshua I've seen the *real genuine republican party*. It was at the fair; there was old folks and young folks, and men and women, and boys and gals, and all sorts and sizes of folks mixed up together higgledy piggledy, and every one said and did jest what they'd a mind to. If this wasn't the republican party I dont know what is.

It looked funny to see every body buying every thing that was offered to 'em, and paying jest what they asked for it. And the queerest of it was, if you bought a thing that came to a ninepence, and handed 'em a quarter of a dollar to pay for it, they would chuck the quarter into the money draw, and you might whistle for your change ; they would n't give you back a cent. Only think ; if the stupid shop-keepers would only learn that are fashion, and charge all the gals that come arter patterns ninepence every time they come into their stores, and when any body buys any thing of 'em never give any change back, how fast they might get rich. There was young fellers buying pin-balls, and old bachelors buying doll-babies, and some of 'em *nigger babies* tu, and every body buying what they did n't want, more than a toad wants two tails.

At one end of the hall there was a great table covered all over with cakes and candy and apples and plums, and all kinds of luscious things, all brought in to help along the Orphan Asylum. A man would send in some apples that he sold in his store at two for a cent, and then go and get his children and post off to the hall, and pay ninepence apiece to go in, and then buy the apples and give two cents apiece for 'em.

One gal come along nibbling off a piece of cake about as big as two fingers, and another one says to her, what did you give for that? A shilling, says she; I thought I would do something to help along the Asylum. By and by she come along again cramming down a handful of plums and a great apple. Says 'tother one, says she, what did you give for them? Ninepence, says she; I should n't think of buying any thing at all, if it want for helping along the Asylum. By and by I saw her crounching a stick of candy, such as commonly sells for a cent. What did you give for that, says t'other one. Three cents, says she. Dear soul, thinks I, how very kind you are to help along the Asylum.

By and by I got joggled along up towards another table, and who should I see there, but a *witch!* Some called her the witch of Endor, that we read about in the Bible, and some said it was one of the Salem witches. She looked bad enough to be any one of 'em. She was a little peaked nosed dried up thing; about two feet high, and she stood there upon the table to tell folks their fortunes. She had a little staff in her hand that pointed down on to a little wheel that had every body's fortune written down on it. They 'd give the wheel a whirl and when it stopped, the fortune they wanted to tell any body would be right where the staff pointed. The old witch could n't, or else would n't read herself, so she had a pretty little roguish looking miss stand beside her to tell it off. They called her the priestess, but my stars, she did n't look no more like a minister's wife than you do, Nabby. They asked fourpence happeny apiece for telling fortunes. — Up stepped a smart looking little miss and gave the wheel a whirl and asked what her fortune was. Why, said the little witchee with a rogueish look ' at the annual return of this fair you will be introduced by your husband.' La me, said the miss, blushing, I 'm sure you cant make nothing by telling fortunes at fourpence apiece ; so she threw down half a dollar, and off she went. Then there came up a sober, thin, clever looking sort of a man, and gave a whirl, and the little priestess look'd him up in the face with a curl of the lip, and says she, ' a wolf in sheep's clothing — that suits your case exactly, sir.' And he turned away muttering, ' how upon earth come that little witch of a creature to know me ?'

Then up stepped another man, that they said was one of the Legislaters, and says he, how much do you ask for telling fortunes ? Only fourpence happeny says she. Well, says he, I believe I 'll have mine told, so he give a whirl, and after he heard his fortune, he handed a dollar to take out the fourpence happeny, and the rogueish priestess slipped it into the draw and turned right about, and went to waiting upon somebody else. And the poor man waited and waited for his change till he got tired — and then he drawed back out of sight.

But there, Nabby, I must stop before I tell you half ont, or I shall get my letter so long the printer wont send it ; for he threatens to charge me postage if I send sich long ones. But they had jest sich a scrape all the next day and next evening ; and the next evening after that, they sold all the trinkets they had left at vandue. I dont know how much money they got in the whole, but you may depend upon it 't was a real swad ; and I guess the Orphan Asylum woman might give the little gals gingerbread to eat this two years if she 's a mind to, and let 'em have new warm gowns and good shoes and stockings into the bargain. So here I must stop, and when I go to another fair you shall hear from me again.

Your loving cousin,

JACK DOWNING.

LETTER XXVIII.

In which Mr Downing tells how the Jacksonites in the Legislature had a dreadful tussle to pour a "healing act" down the throats of the Huntonites.

[*Note by the Editor.* The bitterness of feeling occasioned by the struggle for the ascendency between the two parties in 1830, still rankled in the breasts of the members of the Legislature in 1831. The Huntonites had acquired the ascendency the preceding session, but now the Jacksonites were in power, and they contended that the acts of the Huntonites in 1830 were unconstitutional and void. They therefore set about preparing a "healing act" to declare all the doings of the preceding Legislature *valid* in the lump. When this Bill was brought forward, it produced a storm in the Legislature, almost unparalleled. The Huntonites considered it altogether a useless provoking piece of political trickery. They contended that if the acts of the former Legislature were in fact unconstitutional, no law passed by this Legislature could make them constitutional; and considering it a wanton attempt to heap insult and odium upon them, they fought against it almost while life and breath remained. A fierce debate on the passage of this Bill was carried on for several days. But the Jacksonites had the power in their own hands, and the Bill was finally passed. The scene is somewhat minutely described in the two following letters.]

Portland, Feb. 4, 1831.

DEAR UNCLE JOSHUA. — If you got my postcript to this letter that I sent you yesterday, I spose you wont sleep nor eat much till you hear something more about it. So I thought I'd try to send you a little bit of a letter to-day. O dear, uncle, there's terrible times here again, and I'm half afraid it's agoing to be worse than it was last winter. The Legislater's been all in the wind this two or three days, pulling and hauling and fighting like smoke. The wheels of government are all stopt; I cant say as they are *trigged*, as they used to be last winter, but they are fairly stopped, because nobody dont pull 'em along; for when the members are all pulling each other's caps, how can they pull the wheels of government? They seemed to get along very well ever since they've been here till now, and I thought they most

10*

all belonged to them are two clever parties that tried so
hard to save the State last winter; I mean the democratic republicans and the national republicans. But
some how or other this week a quarrelsome gang of
Jacksonites and Huntonites has got into the Legislater
and kicked up such a bobbery, it seems as though they 'd
tare the State all to pieces. My heart 's been up in my
mouth a dozen times for fear the State would go to ruin
before I could get out of it; and I 've scratched round
and picked up what few bean-poles and ax-handles I
had left, and got all ready to set sail to Boston, for I'me
determined to be off before the State goes to rack. And
I advise you and all our friends at Downingville to pack
up as soon as you get this letter, and be all ready as
soon as you hear a cracking down this way to fly for
your lives away back into New-Hampshire or Vermont.
The trouble as near as I could understand it begun in
this way. The Jacksonites said the Huntonites worked
so hard last winter in trying to trig the wheels of government, and tare the constitution to pieces, that they made
themselves all sick, dreadful sick, and had n't got well
yet; and it was time to do something to try to cure 'em;
for their sickness was so catching that all the State
would be taken down with it in a little while, if they want
cured.

But the Huntonites said they want sick a bit; they
never was better in their lives; and moreover, it was
false that they had tried to trig the wheels of government last winter, or tear a single leaf out of the constitution; if any thing of that kind was done, they said
the Jacksonites did it, and as for taking doctor's stuff
they'd no notion of it. But the Jacksonites said 'twas
no use, the Huntonites were all sick, and they must take
some doctor stuff, and if they wouldn't take it willingly
they must be *made* to take it. So they went to work and
fixed a dose that they called a *healing act*, that they said
would cure all the Huntonites and any body else that had

catched the sickness of 'em. The Huntonites declared 'twas no use for 'em to fix it, for they never would take it as long as they lived, that's what they wouldn't; they were as well as any body, and they'd fight it out till next June before they'd take it. Howsomever, the Jackson-ites got their dose ready, and yesterday they carried it into the House of Representatives and told the Hunton-ites they must take it, and 'twould do 'em good. As soon as the Huntonites smelt of it, they turned up their noses, and said no, before they'd take that are plaguy dirty stuff they'd fight 'em all over the State, inch by inch. But the Jacksonites said 'twas no use, they might sniff as much as they pleased, it was the only thing that would cure 'em, and they must take it, and more than all that, they was the strongest and they *should* take it.

Some of the Huntonites looked pale as tho' they were a little grain frightened, and some of them looked red as though they were mad as a March hair. And some of 'em begun to talk to the Jacksonites and tell 'em how unreasonable it was to make 'em take doctor stuff when they want sick. They were well now, and like as not if they should take it; t'would make 'em all sick.

One of 'em, that talked like a very clever man got up and coaxed 'em to ask the Judges of the great Court if they thought there was any *need* of their taking sich a dose, or if it would do 'em any good if they did take it. But the Jacksonites said no, they shouldn't ask no sich questions. They understood the business well enough, they knew the Huntonites were sick, and they knew this would cure 'em, and swallow it they should. Well, the Huntonites see how 'twas gone goose with 'em, and they thought the only chance left was to put their hands over their mouths and fight and kick and scrabble with all their might and keep it out of their throats as long as they could. Still they tried to talk and reason with the Jacksonites about it. They asked 'em to let them have time to examine the medicine carefully and see what it was made of, or that they would tell 'em what it was made of, or why they thought it would do any good to take it. But the Jacksonites said they shouldn't tell 'em any thing about it, it would be 'casting pearls before swine,' and the good book said they mustn't do so.

The men who had fixed the dose knew what they were about, they had fixed it right, and the Huntonites must open their mouths and take it, and not parley any more about it. And now the real tusslé and the hard fight begun. The House seemed to be so full of Jacksonites and Huntonites that I guess there was n't but a few republicans left. And I could n't help minding that the Jacksonites took the seats of the democratic republicans, and the Huntonites took the seats of the national republicans. Well, the Jacksonites took the dose in one hand, and grab'd the Huntonites with the other, and tipped their heads back, and were jest agoing to pour it down their throats, when the Huntonites fetched a spring and kicked it away to the fourth day of April. But the Jacksonites run after it and got it back again in about half an hour, and clinched 'em again, and got all ready to pour it down; but jest as they got it almost to their lips, the Huntonites fetched another spring and kicked it away to the fourth of March. Away went the Jacksonites after it again, and brought it back, and clinched the Huntonites in the same manner as before, and they kicked it away again, but they did n't kick this time quite to the end of February.

So they kept it agoing all the forenoon, but every time the Huntonites kick'd the bitter dose away, it didn't go so far as it did the last time before. I spose they begun to grow tired and could n't kick so hard. Well, then they tried to adjourn so as to get some dinner, but the Jacksonites would n't let 'em. And they kept 'em there till four o'clock in the afternoon without any dinner, and I dont know but they thought the Huntonites would get so hungry after a while that they would swallow it down without much fuss. But it all would n't do, the nearer it come to 'em, the tighter the Huntonites gritted their teeth together, and I guess they'd a starved before they would take it. Well after the Jacksonites had tried nearly twenty times to pour down the bitter dose, and the Huntonites had kicked it away as many times, both parties seemed to be nearly tired out, and so they finally agreed to adjourn till nine o'clock this morning. I thought the Huntonites, if they once got out, would cut and run home and get clear of the plaguy stuff. But instead of that they all come in again this morning, and they've been at it again all day, hammer and tongs, the Jacksonites trying to pour it down, and the Huntonites fighting against it, tooth and nail.

How it 'll come out I cant tell. Whether the State will be ruined if they dont take it, I cant tell ; or whether it will cure them if they do take it, I can't tell. But I can assure you, dear uncle, there's a greater fuss here, than there was when the little boy said he run and jumped over a fence and tore his trowses as if the heavens and earth were coming to pieces. If we live through it, I shall let you know something more about it.

Your loving neffu,

JACK DOWNING.

LETTER XXIX.

In which Mr Downing tells how the Jacksonites at last got the 'healing act' down the throats of the Huntonites.

Portland, Saturday, March 5, 1831.

DEAR UNCLE JOSHUA. — I aint dead, but I spose you begin to feel kind of uneasy about me, bein I have n't writ home so long. Well, I'll tell you how 'twas ; I've had *this ere cold* and one thing another, so bad, I did n't feel hardly smart enough to write. And besides I got so skeer'd that night the Jacksonites poured their doctor

stuff, what they call the healing plaster, down the
throates of the Huntonites, that I did n't dare to go
nigh 'em agin for a good while for fear they'd pour some
of their pesky stuff down my throat. But I'm sorry I
did n't write afore, for I've let it alone so long now, that
my work has got desputly behindhand. When I writ to
you before, the Jacksonites were holding the Huntonites
by the hair of the head with one hand and trying to
cram the healing plaster down their throats with 'tother,
and the Huntonites were kicking and scrabbling, and
gritting their teeth together with all their might, and
doubling up their fists and stamping, and declaring up
hill and down, that they would never take it.   And they
were so upstropulous about it for a while, I did n't know
as they ever would swallow it. But the Jacksonites
were the stoutest, and held on to 'em like a dog to a
root, and kept 'em there all day and all the evening till
about midnight, and then the poor Huntonites seemed
to be a most dragged out. I fairly pitied 'em. Along
in the first of it they threatened pretty stoutly, and declared by every thing that's black and blue, if they had
to take this dirty dose and should happen to be strongest
next year, they'd make the Jacksonites take a dose
worth two of this. But all the threatening did n't do
any good ; and then they fell to begging and coaxing,
and that did n't do any good nother. The Jacksonites
said they should not only take it, but they should take it
that night before they slept. At last they got their
hands and feet tied, and kept bringing it up a little
nearer and little nearer to their mouths, and the Huntonites got so they could n't do nothing but *spit*. But
the Jacksonites did n't mind the spitting, for you know
it is n't for the doctor to stand about being spit upon a
little, when he's giving medicine. Just before the last
ont, the poor Huntonites rolled their eyes dreadfully,
and I believe some on 'em lost their senses a little ; one
of 'em took a notion that they were agoing to make him

swallow a whole live goose, feathers and all; and he
begged of 'em, if they would n't take out the gizzard
and 'tother inside things, that they'd jest pull out the pin
feathers, so that it would n't scratch his throat going
down. But they did n't pay no attention to him, and
just before the clock struck twelve they grabbed 'em by
the throat, and pried their mouths open, and poured it
in. The Huntonites guggled a little, but they had to
swallow it. A day or two arterwards they made some
of the Sinneters take it in the same way. They had
a considerable tussle for it, but not quite so bad as they
had in the House.

Some thought this healing dose would make the Huntonites worse, and some thought it would make 'em better. I've watched 'em ever since they took it whenever
I dared to go near the Legislater, and I cant see much
alteration in 'em. But that or something else has kicked
up a monstrous dust amongst other folks all over the
world amost. I've been looking over the newspapers a
little, and I never see the world in such a terrible hubbub before in all my life. Every body seems to be running mad, and jest ready to eat each other up. There's
Russia snapping her teeth like a great bear, and is just
agoing to eat up the Poles, I dont mean Ephraim's bean
poles, but all the folks that live in Poland; not that
are Poland up there where Mr Dunn lives, but that
great Poland over along side of Russia. And there's
the Dutch trying to eat up Holland, and the Belgians
are trying to eat up the Dutch, and there's 'five great
powers' trying to pour a healing dose down the throat
of the king of the Netherlands, and there's Mr O'Con-
nell trying to make the king of England and Parliament
take a healing dose, and there's Ireland jest ready to
eat up Mr O'Connel, and all the kings of Europe are
trying to eat up the people, and the people are all trying
to eat up the kings.

And our great folks in this country too, away off

there to Washington, have got into such a snarl, I guess
it would puzzle a Philadelphy lawyer to get 'em out of
it. There's the President and Mr Calhoun and Mr
Van Buren and the two great republican papers, and
half a dozen more of 'em, all together by the ears ; but
which of 'em will eat up the rest I don't know. I've
heard a good many guess that Mr Van Buren would eat
up the whole toat of 'em ; for they say although he's a
small man, there isn't another man in the country, that
can eat his way through a political pudding so slick as
he can. These are dreadful times, uncle ; I don't know
what 'll become of the world, if I dont get an office
pretty soon.

It seems to me there must be something out of the
way to make so much confusion in the world ; and I
hope the Legislater before they adjourn will pass a general healing act to cure all these difficulties. They 've
been talking about passing a healing act to cure our
state house up to Augusta, for they say its too small,
and they intend to bring it down here to Portland to
cure it. But I guess it 'll give 'em a pull, for they say
the Kennebeckers are master fellers to hold on.

They had a kind of a flusteration here to-day in the
Legislater. The Speaker 's cleared out, and left 'em,
because the Governor said he'd taken his turn sitting in
the *Chair* long enough, and he must go and sit on the
Bench awhile now. And then they went to work and
chose that good natured man from Monmouth for Speaker. I meant to a told you about them are two great
meetings they 've had here to make Governors and
Presidents and one thing another : but I hav'nt time to-
day.

One of 'em made Mr Smith Governor for next year
and Gineral Jackson President ; and 'tother made Mr
Sprague governor, and kind of put Mr Clay a brewing
for President.

If you think its best for me to run again for governor
another year I wish you'd call our friends together up
there and have me nominated, for there's nothing like
starting in season in these matters.

Your loving neffu,

JACK DOWNING.

LETTER XXX.

In which Mr. Downing dreams some poetry.

From the Portland Courier, April, 1831.

[*Legislative proceedings extra.* — On the evening before the adjournment of the Legislature, while the members of the House
were waiting for some bill to be engrossed, Mr. Shapleigh of Berwick presented an order, that a Committee be appointed to consider
the expediency of assessing an annual tax upon a certain class of
gentlemen commonly called Old Bachelors, to be appropriated for
the use and support of a certain class of ladies usually known by
the name of Old Maids, with leave to report by Bill or otherwise.
Mr McCrate of Nobleborough hoped the mover would offer his *rea-
sons* for the passage of the order. Mr. Delesdernier said he understood the order reflected upon his friend from Nobleborough ; he
therefore moved it be laid on the table, which motion was decided
in the negative.

Mr Baxter then remarked that he hoped gentlemen would reflect
before they went too far, and not commit an impropriety by way of
amusement. He moved that the order be indefinitely postponed,
which motion prevailed. While we were puzzling ourselves to
know what report we should make of these Legislative proceedings
our friend Jack Downing very opportunely, as he often does, came
in to our aid as follows.]

Portland, Saturday, April 2, 1831.

DEAR COUSIN NABBY,—I dont hardly know whether to
send this letter to you, or uncle Joshua. You know I
always send all the politics and Legislaters to uncle ;
but this ere one 's most all poetry, and they say that stuff
belongs to the ladies. So I believe on the whole I shall
send it to you. Dont you be skeer'd now because I 've

11

made some poetry, for I dont think it 'll hurt me ; I dont
feel crazy nor nothing.   But I 'll jest tell you how it
happened.   Last night I was in the Legislater and they
sot out to make a law to tax old bacheldors.   They tried
pretty hard to make it, and I thought one spell they 'd
get it.   I felt kind of bad about it because I knew it
would bear so hard upon cousin Obediah.   Well, I went
home and went to bed, and I dont know what the matter
was, but I had a kind of a queer night of it ; and when
I got up in the morning there was a soft sort of sickish
stuff kept running off of my tongue, jest like a stream
of chalk.   Pray tell me what you think of it ; here it is.

I dreamed a dream in the midst of my slumbers,
And, as fast as I dream'd, it was coined into numbers,
My thoughts ran along in such beautiful metre,
I 'm sure I ne'er saw any poetry sweeter.
It seem'd that a law had been recently made,
That a tax on old bachelors' pates should be laid.
And in order to make them all willing to marry,
The tax was as large as a man could well carry.
The Bachelors grumbled, and said 't were no use,
'T was cruel injustice and horrid abuse,
And declar'd that to save their own heart's blood from spilling,
Of such a vile tax they would ne'er pay a shilling.
But the Rulers determined their scheme to pursue,
So they set all the bachelors up at vendue.
A crier was sent thro' the town to and fro,
To rattle his bell, and his trumpet to blow,
And to bawl out at all he might meet in the way,
" Ho ! forty old bachelors sold here to day,"
And presently all the old maids in the town,
Each one in her very best bonnet and gown,
From thirty to sixty, fair, plain, red and pale,
Of every description, all flocked to the sale.
The auctioneer then in his labors began,
And called out aloud, as he held up a man,
" How much for a bachelor ? who wants to buy ? "
In a twink every maiden responded — " I — I."
In short, at a hugely extravagant price,
The bachelors all were sold off in a trice ;
And forty old maidens, some younger, some older,
Each lugged an old bachelor home on her shoulder.
                                                    JACK DOWNING.

LETTER XXXI.

In which Mr Downing tells how he got a new kink into his head, in consequence of the blow-up of President Jackson's first Cabinet.

Portland, April 26, 1831.

DEAR UNCLE JOSHUA, — I'm in considerable of a kind of a flusteration to-day, because I've got a new scheme in my head. New ideas, you know, are always apt to give me the agitations a little; so you mustn't wonder if my letter this time does have some rather odd things in it. I don't know when I've had such a great scheme in my head afore. But you know I was always determined to make something in the world, and if my friends 'll only jest stick by me, I shall make common folks stare yet. Some thought it was a pretty bold push my trying to get in to be governor last year; and some have laughed at me, and said I come out at the little end of the hòrn about it, and that I'd better staid up to Downingville and hoed potatoes, than to be fishing about for an office and not get any more votes than I did. But they can't see through a millstone so fur as I can. Altho' I didn't get in to be governor, its made me known in the world, and made considerable of a great man of me, so that I shall stand a much better chance to get an office if I try again. But I must make haste and tell you what I am at, for I am in a great hurry. I guess you'll stare when I tell you the next letter you'll get from me will be dated at Washington, or else somewhere on the road between here and there.

O, uncle, we have had some great news here from Washington; every body's up in arms about it, and can't hardly tell what to think of it. They say the President's four great Secretaries have all resigned;

only think of that, uncle. And they say their salaries were *six thousand dollars a-year* ; only jest think of that, uncle. Six thousand dollars a year. Why, a governor's salary is a fool to it. On the whole, I'm glad I didn't get the governor's office. I shall start for Washington to-morrow morning ; or I don't know but I shall start to night, if I can get ready, and travel all night. Its best to be in season in such things, and I shall have to go rather slow, for I've got pretty considerable short of money, and expect I shall have to foot it part way. I shall get there in about a fortnight, and I'm in hopes to be in season to get one of them are offices. I think it's the duty of all true republicans that have the good of the country at heart, to take hold and help the President along in these trying difficulties. For my part, I am perfectly willing to take one of the offices, and I hope some other good men will come right forward and take the others. What a shame 'twas that them are Secretaries should all clear out, and leave the poor old General to do all the work alone. Why, uncle, they'd no more patriotism than your old hoss.

But I must n't stop to parley about it now ; what I want to say is, I wish you to write a recommendation to the President for me to have one of his offices, and go round as quick as you can and get all our friends at Downingville to sign it, and send it on to Washington as fast as possible ; for it would be no more than right that I should show the President some kind of recommendation before he gives me the office. I want you to tell the President that I've always been one of his strongest friends ; and you know I always have spoke well of him, and *in fact he is the best President we ever had.* It might be well for you to quote this last sentence as an ' extract from a letter of the Hon. Jack Downing.' It would give the President some confidence in my friendship, and the ' Hon.' would convince him that I am a man of some standing in this State.

Now you keep up a good heart, uncle; you have always had to delve hard all your days up there on the old farm, and you've done considerable to boost me up into an office, and if I get hold of these six thousand dollars a year, you shall have a slice out of it that will make your old heels feel light again. I haven't named it to a single soul here except cousin Sally, and I want it to be kept a profound secret till I get the office, so as to make them are chaps that have been a sneering at me here, stare like an owl in a thunder shower. And, besides, if it should leak out that I was going, I'm afraid somebody else might get the start of me, for there are always enough that have their mouths open when it rains such rich porridge. But its like as not, the newspapers 'll blab it out before I get half way there. And you needn't think strange, if you see some of the Boston or New York papers in a few days saying, ' The Hon. Jack Downing passed through this city yesterday, on his way to Washington. It is rumored, that he is to be called upon to fill one of the vacant offices.' But I must stop, for it is time I was picking up my duds for a start. Sally has been darning my stockings all the morning. Love to Aunt and Cousin Nabby, and all of 'em. Good by. Your loving nephew,

JACK DOWNING.

LETTER XXXII.

In which cousin Sarah tells about cousin Jack's toes and elbows.

Portland, April 29, 1831.

DEAR NABBY. — One would suppose from Jack's letter to Uncle, that I was doing all in my power to assist him

11*

in prosecuting his ridiculous plans. But the truth is, Penelope's trials with her impatient lovers were nothing compared to mine with Jack. When the news came of the resignation of the members of the Cabinet at Washington, I had not seen him for some weeks; I sat by the window sewing, when in came Jack, and O Nabby, I shall despair of giving you a description. His toes and elbows, you know, were always lovers of freedom, and there they were peeping from their prison houses, so demure and so wo-begone, it almost made my heart ache. — Jack tried at first to make me swear secrecy; but I refused, and told him if he could not rely upon my discretion he better not say any thing. He seemed in high spirits, called me a dear cousin, and then revealed all his plans. I told him never to fear that I should divulge such ridiculous schemes; so preposterous, I wondered how they ever entered into the head of a Downing. I exhausted all my powers of persuasion and argument, to prevail upon him to let politics alone, and go back to Downingville, and take care of his farm and his poor infirm father and mother. He called me a little foolish school girl, that did n't know which side my bread was buttered; said I had better stick to my books and such kind of things, and let the business of the men alone; what did I know about politics! I must mind my work like a good gall, and when he was Secretary of State, he'd give me as fine a *gownd* and *shorl* as any lady in Portland wore. And finally he insisted upon my going to work to mend his old footings, and patch his coat. I told him they were too much worn to be worth mending; but he guessed they'd hold on till he got to Washington, and when he got his six thousand dollars a year, he'd have some new ones, and send the old suit home to cousin Ephraim.

I laughed right out, and led him to the glass to see what an elegant looking object he would be to stand before the President of the United States. Jack could not help laughing himself, but said the looks would make no difference; all President Jackson wanted was a good man, and one who had been firm in support of him.

I went to work, but with no very good will I assure you; and though Jack fretted and coaxed, I had no disposition to hurry, and once when he went out to get the toes of his shoes mended, I ventured to pick out all I had done. It was of no use, for he was so eagerly determined to go, that if I had not finished his coat, he would certainly have started without it, for he said he could *swop* his watch on the road any time for a new coat, or any one would be willing to trust him for one till he procured his salary, when he told his name. He says the President must be aware of his integrity and high-minded patriotism, and will undoubtedly reserve one of the salaries for him, as a compensation for his arduous public services. The public papers, he says, will give him a lift in his pretensions, and there is no doubt but that he shall be successful. One thing is certain, the same town will never hold Jack and me. He is always coming to me for advice when he gets what he calls the ' agitations,' and I have talked myself almost into a consumption to infuse a little common sense into him; but all to no purpose, he will ask advice and then do as he is a mind to.

Your loving cousin,

SARAH DOWNING.

LETTER XXXIII.

In which Mr Downing tells about the talk he had with the Boston Editors on his way to Washington.

City of New York, May 4, 1831.

DEAR UNCLE JOSHUA, — I have got so fur at last, and a pretty hard run I've had of it to get here, I can tell ye. This running after offices is pretty tuff work for poor folks. Sometimes I think there aint much profit in it after all, any more than there is in buying lottery tickets, where you pay a dollar and sometimes get four shillings back, and sometimes nothing. Howsomever I dont mean to be discouraged yet, for if I should give out now and go back again, them are sassy chaps in Portland would laugh at me worse than they did afore. What makes me feel kind of down hearted about it, is because I've seen in the newspapers that tu of them are good offices at Washington are gone a ready. One Mr Livingston's got one of 'em, and Mr Woodbury that lives up in New-Hampshire's got tother, and I'm considerable afraid the others will be gone before I get there.

I want you to be sure and get my recommendation into the post-office as soon as you can, so it may get there as soon as I do. It's a week to day since I started from Portland, and if I have good luck I'm in hopes to get there in about a week more. Any how, I shall worry along as fast as I can. I have to foot it more than three quarters of the way, because the stage folks ask so much to ride, and my money's pretty near gone. But if I can only jest get there before the offices are gone I think I shall get one of 'em, for I got a good string of recommendations in Boston as I come along. I never thought of getting any recommendations of strangers, till a man I was travelling with, kind of talked round and round, and found out what I was after. And then says he, if you want to make out, you must get the newspaper folks to give you a lift, for they manage these matters. And he told me I better get some of the Boston editors to recommend me, or it would be no use for me to go.

I thought the man was more than half right, so when I got into Boston I called round to see the editors. They all seemed very glad to see me, when I told 'em who I was; and I never see a better set of true republicans any where in the State of Maine. And when I told 'em that I was always a true republican, and my father and grandfather were republicans before me, they all talked so clever about patriotism, and our republican institutions, and the good of the people, that I could n't help thinking it was a plaguy shame there should be any such wicked parties as Federalists, or Huntonites, or Jacksonites, to try to tare the country to pieces and plague the republicans so.

This dont include President Jackson. He is n't a Jacksonite, you know; he 's a true republican as there is in Downingville. I had a talk with the Boston Patriot man first. He said he would give me a recommendation with a good deal of pleasure; and when I got my office at Washington I must stick to the good old republican cause like wax; and if all true republicans were only faithful to the country, Henry Clay, the republican candidate, will come in all hollow.

He'll be next President, says he, jest as sure as your name is Jack Downing. Then I went to see the editor of the Boston Gazette. He said he certainly should be very happy to give me a recommendation; and he trusted when I got to Washington where I should have considerable influence, I should look well to the interests of the republican party. He said there was an immense sight of intrigue and underhand work going on by the enemies of the country to ruin Mr Calhoun, the republican candidate for President. But he said they would'nt make out; Mr Calhoun had found out their tricks, and the republicans of old Virginny and South Carolina were all up in arms about it, and if we republicans in the northern states would only take hold and fight for the good cause, Mr Calhoun would be elected as true as the sun will rise to-morrow.

The next I went to see was the editor of the Boston Statesman. He seemed to be a little shy of me at first,

and was afraid I want a true republican ; and wanted to
know if I did n't run against Governor Smith last year
down there in Maine.   I told him I had seen Governor
Smith a number of times in Portland, but I was sure I
never run against him in my life, and did n't think I
ever come within a rod of him.   Well he wanted to
know if I was n't a candidate for Governor in opposition
to Mr Smith.   I told him no, I was a candidate on the
same side.   Was n't you, said he, looking mighty sharp
at me, *was n't you one of the federal candidates for governor ?*   My stars, uncle Joshua, I never felt my hair
curl quicker than it did then.   My hand kind of draw'd
back and my fingers clinched as if I was jest agoing to
up fist and knock him down.   To think that he should
charge me with being a *federal candidate !* it was too
much for flesh and blood to bear.   But I cooled down
as quick as I could, for fear it might hurt me about getting my office.   I told him I never was a federal candidate, and there never was a drop of federal blood in
me ; and I would run from a federalist if I should meet
one as quick as I would from *poison*.   That's right, says
he, I like that, that's good stuff, and he catched hold of
my hand and gave it such a shake, I did n't know but
he'd a pull'd it off.

He said he would give me the best recommendation
he could write, and when I got to Washington I must
stick to the old Gineral like the tooth ache, for the
federalists were intriguing desperately to root him out
of his office and upset the republican party.   If the republicans could only be kept together, he said President
Jackson, the republican candidate, could be elected as
easy as a cat could lick her ear ; but if we suffered ourselves to be divided it would be gone goose with us, and
the country would be ruined.   So you must stick to the
re-election of Gineral Jackson, said he, *at all events ;* and
then he kind of whispered in my ear, and says he, in
case any thing should happen, if Gineral Jackson should

be sick or any thing, you must remember that Mr Van Buren is the *republican candidate*.

I told him he never need to fear me; I should stick to the republican party thro' thick and thin. So I took my recommendation and trudged along. I have n't time to-day to tell you how I got along with the rest of the editors, and a thousand other things that I met with along by the way, and all the fine things in this great city, and so on. But I shall write to you again soon.

Your loving neffu,

JACK DOWNING.

To Uncle Joshua Downing, Downingville, State of Maine.

———

LETTER XXXIV.

In which Mr Downing relates his interview with Major Noah.

Washington City, May 30, 1831.

To the Portland Courier, if it ever gets there, away down east ni the State of Maine, to be sent to Uncle Joshua Downing, up in Downingvllle, with care and speed.

DEAR UNCLE JOSH, — I've got here at last, to this great city where they make offices, and I'm determined not to leave it till I get one. It is n't sich a great city after all as New York, though they do a great deal more business here than they do at New York. I dont mean vessel business and trade, for there's no end to that in New York, but in making offices and sich like; and they say its the most profitable business in the country. If a man can get hold of a pretty good office, he can get rich enough by it in three or four years, and not have to work very hard neither. I tell you what, uncle, if I

make out to my mind here, I shall come back again one
of these days in a rather guess way than what I come
on. I dont have to foot it again I'll warrant you, and
guess poor cousin Sally wont have to set up all night to
mend my coat and darn my stockings. You'll see me
coming dressed up like a lawyer, with a fine carriage
and three or four hosses. And then them are chaps in
Portland that used to laugh at me so about being Governor, may sneeze at me if they dare to, and if they
dont keep out of my way I'll ride right over 'em. I had
a pretty tuff time coming on here. Its a long tiresome
road through the Jarseys. I had to stop twice to get
my shoes tapt, and once to get an old lady to sow up a
rip in my coat while I chopped wood for her at the door
to pay for it. But I shant mind all the hard work I've
had of it, if I can make out to come home rich.

I got a pretty good boost in Boston, as I writ you in
my last, by the editors giving me recommendations. But
it was nothing at all hardly to what I got in New York,
for they gave me a *public dinner* there. I cant think
what's the matter that it hasn't been published yet. Major Noah promised me he'd have it all put into the New
York Courier and Enquirer the very next day after I
left New York, so that it should get to Washington as
soon as I did ; and now I've been here about a week
and it hasn't come yet. If it does'nt come soon, I shall
write an account of the dinner myself, and send it home
and get it put in the Portland Courier. It was a most
capital dinner, uncle ; I dont know as I ever eat hartier
in my life, for being pretty short of money I had pinch-
ed rather close a day or two, and to tell the truth I was
as hungry as a bear. We had toasts and speeches and a
great many good things. I dont mean sich toast as they
put butter on to eat, but toast to drink. — And they dont
exactly drink 'em neither ; but they drink the punch
and speak the toasts.

I cant think Major Noah meant to deceive me about

publishing the proceedings of the dinner, for he appeared to be a very clever man, though he was the funniest chap that ever I see. There wasn't a man in New York that befriended me more than he did ; and he talked to me very candidly, and advised me all about how to get an office. In the first place, says he, Mr Downing, you cant get any kind of an office at Washington, unless you are a true blue genuine democratic republican. I told him I had recommendations coming to prove that I was all that. They are very strict, says he, in regard to that at Washington. If James Madison should apply for an office at Washington, says he, he couldn't get it. What, says I, him that was President! for it kind of startled me a little if such an old republican as he was couldn't get an office. It's true, says he, if James Madison should apply for an office he couldn't get it. -- Why not, says I ? Because, says he, *he has turned federalist*. It's melancholy to think, says he, how many good old republicans at the south are turning federalists lately. He said he was afraid there wasn't more than one true genuine old democratic republican left in Virginny, and that was old Mr Ritchie of the Richmond Enquirer ; and even he seemed to be a little wavering since Mr Calhoun and some others had gone over.

Well there's Mr Clay, says I, of Kentucky, I dont think he'll ever flinch from the republican cause. Henry Clay, says he, turning up his nose, why he's been a federalist this six years. No, no, Mr Downing, if you think of going that gate, you may as well turn about and go home again before you go any further. What gate, says I ? Why to join the Clay party, says he. I told him I never had sich a thought in my life ; I always belonged to the republican party, and always meant to. He looked rather good natured again when he heard that ; and says he, do you know what the true republican doctrine is? I told him I had always had some kind of an idea of it, but I didn't know as I could ex-

plain it exactly. Well, says he, I'll tell you; it is to
support General Jackson for re-election, through thick
and thin. That is the only thing that will save the country from ruin. And if general Jackson should be unwell or any thing jest before election, so he could not
be a candidate, the true republican doctrine is to support Mr Van Buren. I told him, very well, he might
depend upon my sticking to the republican party, all
weathers. Upon that he set down and wrote me a recommendation to the President for an office, and it almost made me blush to see what a master substantial
genuine republican he made me. I had a number more
capital recommendations at New York, but I havn't time
to tell you about 'em in this letter. Some were to Mr
Clay, and some to Mr Van Buren, and some to Mr Calhoun. I took 'em all, for I thought it was kind of un-
certain whose hands I might fall into hereafter, and it
might be well enough to have two or three strings to
my bow.

I havn't called on the President yet, though I've been
here about a week. My clothes had got so shabby, I
thought I better hire out a few days and get slicked up
a little. Three of the offices that I come after are gone
slick enough, and the other one's been given away to
a Mr White, but he wouldn't take it; so I'm in hopes
I shall be able to get it. And if I dont get that, there's
some chance for me to get in to be Vice President, for
they had a great Jackson meeting here 'tother day, and
they kicked Mr Calhoun right out doors, and said they
wouldn't have him for Vice President no longer. Now
some say they think I shall get it, and some think Mr
Van Buren 'll get it.

Howsomever, I feel pretty safe, for Maj. Noah told
me if I couldn't get any thing else, the President could
easily make a foreign mission for me. I shall call on
the good old Gineral in two or three days and find out
what my luck is, and then I shall let you know. Give

my love to ant and cousin Nabby, and all of 'em. It makes me feel kind of bad when I think how fur I've got from home.   Your loving neffu,

JACK DOWNING.

LETTER XXXV.

In which Mr Downing tells how he stript up his sleeves and defended Mr Ingham on his front door-steps during the after-clap that followed the blow-up of the Cabinet.

Washington City, June 21, 1831.

To the Portland Courier again away down there in the State of Maine, to be sent to Uncle Joshua Downing, up in Downingville, or else to Cousin Nabby, it is n't much matter which, being that some of it is about the ladies.

DEAR UNCLE JOSH. — It's pretty trying times here. They carry on so like the old smoker, I dont hardly know what to make of it. If I had n't said I would n't leave Washington till I got an office, I dont know but I should come back to Downingville and go to planting potatoes. Them are Huntonites and Jacksonites down there in Maine last winter were pretty clever sort of folks to what these chaps are here. Cause down there if they got ever so mad, they did n't do nothing but talk and jaw one another ; but here if any body does n't do to suit 'em, fact they 'll up and shoot him in a minute. I did n't think getting an office was such dangerous kind of business, or I dont know as I should have tried it. How-somever, it's neck or nothing with me now, and I must do something to try to get some money here, for I about as lieves die as to undertake to foot it away back again clear to the State of Maine. And as the folks have to go armed here, I want you to put my old fowling piece into the stage and send it on here as quick as possible. I

hope you'll be as quick as you can about it, for if I get
an office I shant dare to take it till I get my gun. They
come pretty near having a shooting scrape here yesterday. The Telegraph paper said something about Mr
Eaton's wife. It was nothing that I should think they
need to make such a fuss about; it only said that some
of the ladies here refused to visit her. But some how or
other it made Mr Eaton as mad as a March hair. He
declared he'd fight somebody, he did n't care who.

The first man he happened to come at was Mr Ingham.
So he dared Mr Ingham out to fight. Not to box, as
they do sometimes up in Downingville, but to stand and
shoot at each other. But Mr Ingham would n't touch to,
and told him he was crazy. That made Mr Eaton ten
times more mad than he was before; and he declared
he'd flog him any how, whether he was willing or not.
So he got a gang of gentlemen yesterday to go with him
to the Treasury office where Mr Ingham does his writing, and waited there and in a grog shop close by as
much as two hours for a chance to catch him and give it
to him. Mr Ingham was out a visiting in the city, and
when he got home his folks told him what was going on,
and begged him not to go to the office for he would certainly be killed. Poh, says he, do you think I'm afraid
of them are blustering chaps? There's more smoke than
fire there, I can tell ye; give me my pistols, it is time for
me to go to the office. Some of the ladies cried, and some
almost fainted away. But he pacified 'em as well as he
could, and then set out for the office, and three or four
men went with him, and I guess they carried something
under their arms that would make daylight shine through
a feller pretty quick. And I guess the gang of gentlemen waiting for him begun to smell a rat, for they cleared out pretty soon and never touched him. But their
courage came again in the evening, and this same gang
of gentlemen turned out and marched up to Mr Ingham's
house, and threatened to burst the doors open and drag

him out by the hair of the head and skin him alive. I
thought this was carrying the joke rather too far, so I
tho't I'd put in my oar; for when I see any body run
upon too hard I cant help taking their part.

So I stepped up on to Mr Ingham's front door steps,
and threw my hat down, and rolled up my sleeves, and
spit on my hands; and by that time the chaps began to
stare at me a little. And now, says I, Major Eaton, this
is quite too bad. A man's house is his castle. Here's
Mr Ingham in his house as peaceable as a lamb; he is
n't a meddling with nobody, and you need n't think to
drag him out here to-night, I can tell ye. If you really
want to take a bit of a box, just throw away your powder and ball, and here's the boy for you. I'll take a fist
or two with you and glad of the chance. You impudent
scoundrel, says he, who are you? what business is it to
you what I *done?* Clear out, or I'll send you where you
ought to been long ago. Well, then, you'll send me into
some good office, says I, for there's where I ought to
have been more than two years ago. Well, says he,
clear out, and up he come blustering along towards the
steps. But I jest put my foot down, and doubled up my
fist, and now, says I, Major Eaton, it wont be healthy for
you to come on to these steps to-night.

Says he, I'm going through that door whether or no.
Says I, you dont go through this door to-night, without
you pass over the dead body of *Jack Downing* of the State
of Maine. My stars, when they heard that, they dropt
their heads as quick as though they had been cut off, for
they did n't know who I was before. Major Eaton and
the whole gang of gentlemen with him turned right about
and marched away as still as a pack of whipped puppies.
They were afraid I should have 'em all up before the
President to-day, and have 'em turned out of office; for
it's got whispered round the city that the President sets
a great deal by me, and that I have a good deal of influence with him.

12*

This morning Mr Ingham started for Philadelphy. Before he left, he thanked me a thousand times for defending his house so well last night, and he wrote a letter to the President, telling him all about the scrape. I went a piece with him to see him safe out of the city on the great road towards Baltimore.

About my prospects for an office, I cant tell you yet. how I shall come out. I've been in to see the President a number of times, and he talks very favorable. I have some chance to get in to be Secretary of War, if old Judge White dont take it; and if I dont get that the President says he 'll do the best he can for me.

I never had to be so strict a republican before in my life as I've had to be since I've been here in order to get the right side of the President. I'll tell you something about it in my next, and about my visits to the President, and a good many other famous things here.

P. S. Be sure and send the old gun as quick as possible.   Your loving neffu,

JACK DOWNING.

––––

LETTER XXXVI.

In which Cousin Ephraim tells about the persecution of poor Mrs No-tea.

TROUBLE IN DOWNINGVILLE.

To cousin Jack Downing, down to Portland, if he's got back, if he hasn't I want the Portland Courier to send this on to Washington.

DEAR COUSIN JACK. — Your uncle Joshua has been turned out of General Combs' employ only jest because your cousin Naby, Mrs Inkhorn, and Mrs Thimblebury, and a few other of the topping-folks, wouldn't invite

poor Mrs No-tea to their husking and quilting parties.
I had a long talk with the General t'other day — he was
hopping mad, and declared he would turn every man
and woman off of his farm and out of his mills rather
than that good woman should be treated in the manner
she had been. She was as good as the best of 'em any
day, and he could prove it. He didn't care so much
about her going to their afternoon visits when they went
sociable without stays, and took their knitting-work and
got home again before milking time; but when there
was a grand husking or quilting, he thought it pesky
hard and lonely for her to stay at home, while every
body else in Downingville was trying the double shuffle
and the cutting out jigg. I tho't so too; but I told the
General it was no use for him to make such a fuss about
it; that he had better attack old Ticonderogue in front
and rear than undertake to make women haw or jee
if they want a mind to — they always would have their
own way in spite of every body and Tom Walker besides, and the less he had to do with them the better.
With that he up and smashed his pipe into the fire-place
and stompt like fury and bedlame.

I scampered off in less than no time to inform you
how matters were going. You had better come up and
try to put things to rights.

As you have no wife nor children, I think you can
manage affairs more to your own and the General's
liking than any one else of the family.

Your luvin cousin,

EPHRAIM.

LETTER XXXVII.

Mr Downing receives a Captain's Commission in the United States Army with orders to go and protect the inhabitants of Madawaska.

Washington City, the 20th day of Oct. 1831.

To the Portland Courier away down in the State of Maine, to be sent to Uncle Joshua Downing up in Downingville, this with care and speed, and dont let any body see it.

DEAR UNCLE JOSH,— I've got it at last as true as you're alive, and now I dont keer a snap for the fattest of 'em. I'll teach them are young chaps down to Portland that used to poke fun at me so because I did n't get in to be Governor, that they must carry a better tongue in their heads, or they 'll find out who they are talking to. I guess they'll find out by and by it wont be healthy for 'em to poke fun at an officer of my rank. And as for Jemime Parsons that married the school master winter before last, when she had promised as fair as could be that she would have me, she may go to grass for what I keer ; I would n't have her now no more than I'd have a Virginny nigger. And I guess when she comes to see me with my regimentals on she'll feel sorry enough, and wish her cake was dough again. Now she's tied down to that clodpole of a school master, that was 'nt fit for a school master neither, for he has had to go to hoeing potatoes for a living, and much as ever he can get potatoes enough to keep 'em from starving, when if she had only done as she had promised, she might now be the wife of Capt. Jack Downing of the United States Army. But let her go ; as I said afore, I dont care a snap for her or all old White's cattle. I'll tell you what 'tis uncle, I feel about right now. It seems to me I could foot it home in two days, for my feet never felt half so light before.

There's nothing like trying, in this world, uncle; any body that tries can be something or other, if he dont get discouraged too soon. When I came on here, you know, I expected to get one of the great Secretaries' offices; but the good old President told me they had got him into such a hobble about them are offices that he could n't give me one of 'em if he was to die. But he treated me like a gentleman, and I shall always vote for him as long as I live, and I told him so. And when he found out that I was a true genuine republican, says he, Mr Downing, you must be patient, and I'll bear you in mind, and do something for you the very first chance. And you may depend upon it Mr Downing, he added with a good deal of earnestness, I never desert my friends, let that lying Stephen Simpson of Philadelphy say what he will about it, a good for nothing ungrateful dog. And he fetched a stomp with his foot and his eyes kind of flashed so fiery, that I could n't help starting back, for I did n't know but he was going to knock me over. But he look'd pleasant again in a minute, and took me by the hand, and now, says he, Mr Downing, I give you my honor that I'll do something for you as soon as I possibly can. I told him I hoped he would be as spry as he could about it, for I had but jest ninepence left, and I did n't know how I should get along very well, in a strange place too. But he told me never to mind that at all; I might come and eat my meals at his house whenever I'd a mind to, or he would be bondsman for my board where I put up. So I've worked along from that time to this, nearly four months, as well as I could, sometimes getting a little job of garden-work, and some-times getting a little wood to saw, and so on, nearly enough to pay my expenses. I used to call and see the President once in a while, and he always told me I must be patient and keep up a good heart, the world was n't made in one day, and something would turn up for me by and by. But fact, after digging, and sawing, and

waiting four months, my patience got most wore out,
and I was jest upon the point of giving up the chase,
and starting off for Downingville with the intention of
retiring to private life ; when last night, about seven
o'clock, as I sot eating a bowl of bread and milk for my
supper, a boy knocked at the door and wanted to see
Mr Downing.   So they brought him into the room where
I was, and says he, Mr Downing, the President wants to
see you for something very particular, right away this
evening.   My heart almost jump'd right up in my mouth.
My spoon dropt out of my hand, and to eat another
mouthful I could n't if I was to starve.   I flew round,
and washed my face and hands, and combed my head,
and brushed up as well as I could, and should have looked tolerable spruce if it had n't been for an unlucky hole
in the knee of my trouses.   What to do I did not know.
It made me feel bad enough I can tell you.   The woman
where I boarded said she would mend them for me if I
would take them off, but it would take her till about nine
o'clock, and the President was waiting for me, and there
'twas.   Such a hobble I never was in before.   But this
woman is a kind good creature as ever was ; she boards
me for four and sixpence a week, considering that I
split wood for her, and bring water, and do all sich kind
of chores.   And she always had some contrivance to get
out of every difficulty ; and so she handed me a neat
little pocket handkerchief and told me to tie that round
my knee.   Being thus rigged out at last, I started off as
fast as I could go for the President's.

When I went into his room, the old gentleman was
setting by a table with his spectacles on, and two great
lamps burning before him, and a bundle of letters and
papers in his hand.   He started up and took me by the
hand, and says he, good evening Mr Downing, I 'm very
glad to see you ; you are the very man I want now,
above all others in the world.   But how is this, said he ?
looking at my knee.   Not lame, I hope ?   That would

be a most unfortunate thing in this critical moment. It would knock my plan in the head at once. I felt kind of blue, and I guess I blushed a little; but I turned it off as well as I could; I told him I was n't lame at all, it was nothing but a slight scratch, and by to-morrow morning I should be as well as ever I was in my life. Well then says he, Mr Downing, set down here and see what I 've got to tell you. The old gentleman set himself back in his chair and pushed his spectacles up on his forehead and held up the letter in his hand, and says he, Mr Downing, here is a letter from Governor Smith of Maine, and now Sir, I 've got something for you to do. You see now that I was sincere when I told you if you would be patient and stick to the republican text, I would look out for you one of these days. I 'm always true to my friends; that lying Stephen Simpson might have had an office before now if he had behaved himself.

Well, dear sir, said I, for I felt in such a pucker to know what I was going to get that I could n't stand it any longer, so says I, what sort of business is it you 've got for me to do ? Says he, Mr Downing, I take it you are a man of courage; I have always thought so ever since you faced Mr. Eaton so boldly on Mr. Ingham's door steps. Tho' I was sorry your courage was not displayed in a better cause, for that Ingham is a rascal after all. I told him as for courage I believed I had some of the stuff about me when there was any occasion for it, and that I never would stand by and see any body abused. Well, says, he, we must come to the point, for the business requires haste.

Governor Smith writes me that there are four of your fellow citizens of Maine in a British jail at Fredericton, who have been taken from their farms by British constables and sheriffs and other officers and carried off by force to prison. By this time my very hair begun to curl, I felt so mad, and I could n't help jumping up and smiting my fists together, and saying pretty hard things

about the British.   Well, says the President, I like your
spunk Mr Downing ; you 're jest the man I want in this
business.   I 'm going to give you a captain's commission
in the United States' army, and you must go down there
and set that business right at Madawaska.

   You must go to Maine and raise a company of volunteers, as quick as possible, tell 'em I 'll see 'em paid,
and you must march down to Fredericton and demand
the prisoners, and if they are not given up you must
force the jail, and if the British make any resistance
you must fire upon them and bring the prisoners off at
some rate or other.   Then write me and let me know
how affairs stand, and I 'll give you further orders.   At
any rate you must see that the rights of Maine are well
protected, for that state has come round so in my favor
since last year I 'm determined to do every thing I can
for them ; I tell you Mr Downing, I never desert my
friends.   So after he gave me the rest of my orders, and
my commission, and a pocket full of money, and told
me to be brave and if I wanted any thing to let him
know, he bid me good night, and I went home.   But I
could n't sleep a wink all night.   I was up before day
light this morning, and I 've got two women to work for
me to day fixing up my clothes, and I shall be ready to
start to morrow morning.   I want you to keep this matter pretty still till I get there, except that you my let
cousin Ephraim know it and get him to volunteer some
of the Downingville boys for my company.   I want to
get them pretty much all there if I can, for I know what
sort of stuff the Downingville boys are made of, and
shall know what I 've got to depend upon.

      In haste, your loving neffu,
                    CAPT. JACK DOWNING.

LETTER XXXVIII.

In which Captain Downing describes his return to Down-ingville, after an absence of two years.

Downingville, Nov. 8, 1831.

To the Editor of the Portland Courier.

My DEAR OLD FRIEND, YOU. — I got home to Downing-ville last night after an absence of nearly two years. I meant to stop at Portland as I come on from Washington, but some how or other, I got into the wrong stage somewhere in New Hampshire, and come the upper road before I knew it. So the first thing I knew, when I thought I had got almost to Portland, I found myself plump in Downingville. But the dear folks were all so glad to see me, I didn't feel much sorry. Cousin Nabby hopped right up and down, like a mouse treed in a flour barrel ; and Ephraim snapped his thumb and finger, and spit on his hands as though he had a cord of wood to chop ; and poor ant Keziah set down and cried as much as two hours steady. Uncle Joshua catched down his pipe, and made the smoke roll out well ; I never saw him smoke so fast before in my life ; he finished two pipes full of tobacco in less than five minutes. I felt almost like a fool myself, and had to keep winking and swallowing, or I should have cried as hard as any of 'em. But you know it wouldn't do for a captain to cry, especially when he was going to enlisting soldiers.

Well, I must hurry along with my letter, for I haven't got much time to write to-day. I have been round among the folks in Downingville this forenoon to see how they felt about the Madawaska business, and whether any of 'em would go a sogering down there with me. I find some of 'em are right up about it, and ready

13

to shoulder their guns and march to-morrow if I say the word, and others are a little offish.

I guess I shall get about half enough for a company here pretty easy, and if I find it hard dragging to pick up the rest, I shall come right down to Portland to fill up my company there. For uncle Joshua tells me he has had some letters from Portland within a few days, and he says there are a number of chaps down there as warm as mustard about going to war down to Mada-waska, and are only waiting for a good chance to list, and some of 'em he thinks will make capital sargents and corporals. I should be glad if you would send me word whether you think I could pick up some good lusty fellows there in case I should want 'em. I pay a month's wages cash down. But there is one subject that I feel rather uneasy about, and that is the greatest reason of my writing you to-day, to see if you can tell me any thing about it. Last night uncle Joshua and I sot up talking politicks pretty late, after all the rest of the folks had gone to bed. I told him all about one thing another at Washington, and then we talked about the affairs of this State.

I found uncle Joshua didn't stand jest where he used to. You know once he was a little might in favor of Mr Huntoon ; and then, when I was up for Governor, he was altogether in favor of me ; and then he was pretty near equally balanced between Mr Smith and Mr Goode-now ; but now, when I come to talk with him, I found he was all plump over on the democratic republican side. You know I've been leaning that way tu, ever since I got in to be good friends long with President Jackson. So says I, Well, uncle, our party is strong enough now to carry all afore 'em in this State. I guess governor Smith will have more than three quarters of the votes next time. At which uncle turned round to-wards me, and rolled up his great eyes over his specta-cles, and took his pipe out of his mouth and put on a mighty knowing look, and says he, Jack, jest between you and me, *a much better man and a much greater republican than Gov. Smith, will be Governor of the State of Maine after another election.*

I was kind of struck with a dunderment. I sot and looked at him as much as two minutes, and he all the time looked as knowing as a fox. At last, says I, Uncle, what do you mean? Didn't all the democratic republican papers in the State, when Gov. Smith was elected, say he was the very best republican there was in the State for Governor? Well, well, Jack, said he, mark my words, that's all. But, said I, uncle, what makes you think so? O, said he, I have read the Argus and the Bangor Republican, and I have had a letter from a man that knows all about it, and when the time comes you'll see. And that was all I could get out of him. Now I wish you would let me know what this mystery means. And I remain your old friend,

CAPT. JACK DOWNING.

LETTER XXXIX.

Captain Downing's first Military Report to the President.

Madawaska, Nov. 15, 1831.

To his Excellency, Gineral Jackson, President of the United States, &c.

MY GOOD OLD SIR. — The prisoners are out and no blood spilt yet. I had prepared to give the British a most terrible battle, if they hadn't let 'em out. I guess I should made 'em think old Bonapart had got back among 'em again, for a keener set of fellows than my company is made up of never shouldered a musket or trod shoe-leather. I was pesky sorry they let 'em out quite so soon, for I really longed to have a brush with 'em ; and how they come to let 'em go I dont know, unless it was because they heard I was coming. And I expect that was the case, for the prisoners told me the British Minister at Washington, sent on some kind of word to governor Campbell, and I suppose he told him how I had got a commission, and was coming down upon New Brunswick like a harrycane.

If I could only got down there a little sooner and fit sich a great battle as you did at New Orleans, my fortune would have been made for this world. I should have stood a good chance then to be President of the United States, one of these days. And that's as high as ever I should want to get. I got home to Downingville in little more than a week after I left you at Washington, for having a pretty good pocket full of money, and knowing that my business was very important I rid in the stage most all the way. I spose I needn't stop to tell you how tickled all my folks were to see me. I did'nt know for awhile but they'd eat me up. But I spose that's neither here nor there in making military reports, so I'll go on. I found no difficulty in getting volunteers. I believe I could have got nearly half the State of Maine to march if I had wanted 'em. But as I only had orders to list one good stout company, I took 'em all in Downingville, for I rather trust myself with one hundred genuine Downingville boys, than five hundred of your common run. I took one supernumerary however, when I got to Bangor. The editor of the Bangor Republican was so zealous to go, and said he'd fight so to the last drop of his blood, that I could'nt help taking him, so I appointed him supernumerary corporal. Poor fellow, he was so disappointed when he found the prisoners were out that he fairly cried for vexation. He's for having me go right on now and give all New Brunswick a real thrashing.

But I know what belongs to gineralship better than that ; I haven't had my orders yet. Well, after we

left Bangor we had a dreadful rough and tumble sort of
a journey, over rocks and mountains and rivers and
swamps and bogs and meadows, and through long pieces
of woods that I did n't know as we should find the way
out. But we got through at last, and arrived here at
Madawaska day before yesterday. I thought I better
come this way and make a little stop at Madawaska to
see if the prisoners' wives and little ones were in want
of any thing and then go down to Fredericton and blow
the British ski high.

When our company first came out in [sight in Madawaska, they thought it was the British coming to catch
some more of 'em; and such a scattering and scamper-
ing I guess you never see. The men flew into the
woods like a flock of sheep with forty dogs after 'em,
and the women catched their babies up in their arms
and run from one house to another screeching and
screaming enough to make the woods ring again. But
when they found out we were United States troops come
to help 'em, you never see any body so glad. They all
cried for joy then. The women run into the woods and
called for their husbands to come back again, for there
was nobody there that would hurt them, and back they
came and treated us with the best they had in their
houses. And while we sot chatting, before the women
hardly got their tears wiped up, one of 'em looked up
towards the woods and screamed out *there comes the prisoners.* Some turned pale a little, thinking it might be
their ghosts, but in a minute in they come, as good flesh
and blood as any of us, and then the women had another good crying spell.

I asked one of the prisoners how they got away, for
I thought you would want to know all about it; and
says he we come away on our legs. Did you break out
of jail, said I? I guess there was no need of that, said
he, for we want locked in half the time. Did you knock
down the guard, said I, and fight your way out?

13*

Humph! said he, I guess we might have hunted one while before we could find a guard to knock down. Nobody seemed to take any care of us, if we wanted a drop of grog we had to go out and buy it ourselves. Well but, said I, if you were left in such a loose state as that, why did you not run away before? Tut, said he, shrugging up his shoulders, I guess we knew what we were about; the longer we staid there the more land the state of Maine would give us to pay us for being put in jail, but when they turned us out of jail, and would'nt keep us any longer, we thought we might as well come home.

And now, my good old sir, since matters are as they are, I shall take up my head quarters here at Madawaska for the present, and wait for further orders. I shall take good care of the people here, and keep every thing in good order, and not allow a single New Brunswicker to come any where within gun-shot. As for that Leftenant Governor, Mr Archibald Campbell, he better keep himself scarce; if he shows his head here again, I shall jest put him into a meal bag and send him to Washington. I shall expect to hear from you soon, and as I shall have to be here sometime, I dont know but you had better send me on a little more money. My uniform got rather shattered coming through the woods, and it will cost me something to get it fixt up again.

This from your old friend and humble servant,

                 CAPT. JACK DOWNING.

LETTER XL.

Capt. Downing visits the Legislature of Maine again.

Augusta, State of Maine, Jan. 4, 1832.

To the Editor of the Portland Courier.

MY DEAR OLD FRIEND, — Here I am right among the Legislater folks, jest as I used to be down there to Portland. I got here last night after a pretty hard journey from Madawaska, rather lame, and my feet and ears froze pretty bad. I hope I shant lose any one of 'em, for if I should lose my feet I should n't stand much of a fag with the British down there to Fredericton in case we should have a brush with 'em. And all my hopes about ever being President of the United States depends on the woful whipping I 'm going to give the British. And I 'm afraid I should n't be much better off if I should lose my ears, for a President without ears would cut rather a sorry figure there to Washington. I sent on to the old President to see if he would let me have a furlough to come up to Augusta, while the Legislaters were here, for I thought I could n't stan it without being here to see how they get along. The President said he did n't think there would be any fighting down to Madawaska before the spring opens, so he did n't care if I went. I jest hobbled into the Legislater to-day to see 'em chuse officers; but I have n't any time to tell you what a great fine house they 've got into. I believe it 's vastly better than the one they had to Portland though. And I guess there 'll be no stopping the wheels of government this year, for I believe they have got the house fixed so as to carry the wheels by *steam*.*

---

* *Note.* The State House being new and the walls not dried, when fires came to be made in the rooms, it filled them with thick vapor for several days, which led Capt. Downing to suppose the Legislature was going by steam.

They got the steam up before I went in, and it was so thick sometimes, that I should think the wheels might go like a buzz.

They told me there was a good many new members, and a good many more of 'em, than there was last year; so I did n't know as I should see hardly any body that I knew. But I never was more agreeably disappointed in my life than I was by the first voice I heard calling the members to order.

I knew it as quick as I could tell the fife and drum of my own company at Madawaska. And if I should hear that fife and drum this very minute it would n't give a pleasanter thrill to my feelings. 1 look'd round and sure enough there was the sandy honest look, and the large fleshy figure, of my old friend Mr. Knowlton of Montville, holding a broad brimmed hat in his hand, and calling upon the great jam of folks to come to order. I could n't hardly help crowding right in among 'em to shake hands with him, I was so glad to see him. But as I was only a lobby member I thout it would n't do.

But I 'll tell you what 't is, you may depend upon the business going off glibb here this winter; for having a building go by steam and Mr Knowlton here too to drive it, it aint all the Jacksonites and Huntonites in the state that can stop it. And besides I cant find out as yet that there is any more than one party here; if there should be hereafter, I 'll let you know. I was glad they chose Mr White to be speaker, for he 's always so good natured and uses every body so well, I cant help liking him. I have n't been in the Sinnet yet, but they say Mr Dunlap is President. I was in hopes to see Elder Hall here this winter, but I believe he has n't come.

Your old Friend,
CAPT. JACK DOWNING.

LETTER XLI.

Progress of proceedings in the Legislature.

Augusta, State of Maine, Jan. 19, 1832.

To the Editor of the Portland Courier.

MY DEAR OLD FRIEND. — If I could n't write to you once in a while, I don't know but I should die. When any thing has kept me from writing two or three weeks, I get in such a taking it seems as though I should split, and the only way I can get relief is to take my pen and go at it. The reason why you have n't heard from me this fortnight past, is this dreadful furenza. We've all got it here, and it's nothing but cough, cough, the whole time. If a member gets up to speak, they all cough at him. If he says any thing that they like, they cough at it ; and if he says any thing that they dont like, they cough at it. So let him say what he will they keep a steady stream of coughing. I've been amost sick for a week. Some days I want hardly able to set up. But I'm getting cleverly now, and I hope I shall be able to let you hear from me once or twice a week during the session.

The wheels of government go pretty well this winter. Some say that some folks have tried to trig 'em two or three times, but I dont hardly think that is the case, for they havn't been stopt once. And, as I said in my last letter, if my friend Mr Knowlton stands as foreman, and keeps his broad shoulders to the wheels, I dont believe they will stop this winter. By the way, I made a little small mistake about Mr Knowlton's hat. I should n't have thought it worth while to mention it again, if the Augusta Courier of this morning had n't spoke of it as though I did n't mean to tell the truth. Now you know Mr Editor, I would n't be guilty of tellng a falsehood for my

right hand.   When Mr Knowlton called the members to
order the first day of the session, I certainly thought I
saw him holding in his hand a broad brimmed white hat.
It might be my imagination, remembering how he used
to look, or it might possibly be the hat of the member
standing by the side of him, for I was some ways off.

I'm pesky fraid the general government may settle that
hash down there to Madawaska as Mr Netherlands that
they left out to, recommended. If they should I'm afraid
my jig would be up about fighting a battle very soon, or
getting in to be President.

Our party's got into a dreadful kind of a stew here
about who shall be next Senator to Congress and one
thing another. We've got into such a snarl about it,
I'm afraid we never shall get unravelled again without
cutting off the tangles, and that would divide us so we
never should hold together in the world. I wrote to the
Argus yesterday, to be sure not to reply to the Age for
its ungentlemanly remarks about Judge Preble, and hope
it will be prudent enough to follow my recommendation.
We must try to hush these matters up, or it 'll be the
death of the party. I've had a serious talk with friend
Ruggles, and am in hopes he'll put his hand over the
Thomaston paper and not let it belch out any thing that
our enemies can make a handle of. And I guess we
shall have a caucus and try to put a cooler on the Bangor Republican and the Age.

The Legislaters like Augusta considerable well, if it
did n't cost 'em so much more than it did in Portland for
a living. Such as had to pay two dollars and a half in
Portland for board have to pay three and four dollars
here. When I was in Portland, I used to get boarded
for seven and six pence a week, and here the cheapest
I could get boarded any where, was ten and sixpence.
The Augusta Courier last week said something about the
folks here giving me a public dinner. I should like it
pretty well, for I have rather slim dinners where I
board,

If you see cousin Sally, I wish you'd jest ask her if she has time before and after school, if she'll knit me a pair of footings and send 'em up by the stage-driver, for mine have got pretty full of holes, and I have n't any body here to mend 'em.

Your old friend,

CAPT. JACK DOWNING.

————

LETTER XLII.

Capt. Downing is suddenly called to his company at Mad-awaska.

Augusta, State of Maine, Jan. 23, 1832.

To the Editor of the Portland Courier, again.

DEAR FRIEND,—The more I write to you, it seems to me the better I like you. I believe there is n't but one person that I set so much by, and that is Gineral Jackson, who was so kind as to give me a commission, and let me have spending money besides. I 'm pretty much out of money now, and the man that I board with keeps dunning me for pay; so I wish you would be so kind as to send me four or five dollars till I get some more from the President. I writ for it last week, and I think I shall get it in a few days. I told you in my last letter, if I got over the furenza, you should hear from me pretty often. I 'm getting nicely again now. I dont cough more than once in five minutes or so, and my toes and ears that were froze so bad coming up from Madawaska are nearly healed over. All I have to do to 'em now is jest to grease 'em a little when I go to bed at night and in the morning when I get up. I have to keep a handkerchief over my ears yet when I go out, but my toes are so well I dont limp hardly a mite.   As to our legislater business we get along middling well, but not quite so fast as I thought we should considerin it goes by steam.   One reason I suppose is because Mr Knowlton has been a good deal unwell and could n't take hold and drive it right in end as he used to.   But he 's got better now, so I hope the wheels will begin to buzz again.

About the quarrel that our party's got into, I 'm pesky fraid it 'll blow us up yet ; and I don't know what we shall do to stop it.   We 've had a caucus as I told you we should in my last letter, and tried to hush matters up as well as we could.   But some of 'em are so grouty, I expect nothing but what they 'll belch out again.

I was glad the Argus took my advice and kept back the reply to the Age.

We had a little bit of a tussle here to see who should be appointed agent to go to Washington to tell the President to hold on to the territory down to Madawaska. Mr Preble and Mr Deane and I were the three principal candidates. — Some thought Mr Preble ought to go because it would be for the interest of the republican party ; and some thought Mr Deane ought to go because he had been down there a good deal and knew all about the Madawaska country ; and some thought I ought to go because I had been down there the last of any body, and because I was such good friends with the President I should be likely to do better than any body else could.   I thought my claims were the strongest, and the Governor said he thought so too.   But he said as affairs now stood it would n't do to appoint any body but Mr Preble.

And besides I dont know as I ought to go off jest now, for I had a letter yesterday from one of my subalterns down to Madawaska, that there 's some trouble with my company there : some of the Sarjents been breaking orders, &c, and I dont know but I shall have to go down and Court Martial 'em.

Your friend,
CAPT. JACK DOWNING.

LETTER XLIII.

Capt. Downing returns to Augusta. Is saved from freezing by a bear-skin.

Augusta, State of Maine, Feb. 8, 1832.

To the Editor of the Portland Courier.

HERE I be again, my dear friend, right back on the old spot, poking about the Legislater to see what's going on, and to help take care the interests of our party. I got down there to Madawaska jest in the nick of time; for I got a hoss and rid day and night; and it was well I did, for Sargant Joel had got so outrageous mad, I raly believe if I had n't got there the day I did, he would have strung one or two of 'em right up by the neck. But I quashed matters at once and sot 'em to studying that are little court martial book, and told 'em when they had any more fuss they must try all their cases by that, and they would n't find any law for hanging in it.

It's dreadful cold down there to Madawaska, I froze my toes and ears again a little, but not so bad as I did afore, for I took care to rop up in a great bear skin. I see the Legislater's been disputing about passing a law to kill off all the bears and wolves and sich kind of critters.

I dont know whether that's a good plan or not. There's a good deal might be said on both sides. Them are bears are pesky mischievous. I heard a story while I was gone, but I dont know how true 'tis, how a great bear chased the Councillor that the Governor sent down to Fredickton to carry provisions to our prisoners in jail there. Some reckoned the bear smelt the bread and cheese that he had in his saddle bags, and so took after him to get some of it. However, the

14

Councillor got back safe. But I think this is a great argument in favor of killing off the bears. And on the other hand I believe the bear skin was all that kept me from freezing to death going to Madawaska tother day. So it seems we ought not to kill 'em quite all off, but raise enough to keep us in bear-skins; for I suppose my life would be worth as much to the State as the Councillor's.

I feel a little put out with Dr Burnham for an unhansome running he gave me 'tother day in the Senate. He called me an ' old rogue.' I cant swallow that very well; for that's a character I never bore in Downingville nor Washington, nor any where else. He was disputing about paying Mr Deane and Cavano for going to Madawaska. He said they had n't ought to pay so much, for if they went at this rate, next thing that old rogue, Capt. Jack Downing, would be sending in his bill.

But he need n't trouble himself about that, for as long as I have President Jackson to look to for paymaster, I dont care a snap about sending in any bills to the Legislater. But as for being called an old rogue, I wont. I dont mean to make a great fuss about it in the papers, as the Argus and Age did, so as to break up the harmony of the republican party. But if Dr Burnham dont give me satisfaction, I'll call a caucus of the party and have him over the coals and du him over.

Your loving friend,
CAPT. JACK DOWNING.

LETTER XLIV.

In which Captain Downing tells about the Legislature's
making Lawyers.

Augusta, State of Maine, March 1st, 1832.

To the Editor of the Portland Courier.

My Dear Old Friend, — I begin to feel as uneasy
as a fish out of water, because I havn't writ to you for
most two weeks. Now, old March has come, and found
us digging here yet; and sometimes I'm most afraid we
shall be found digging here, when we ought to be at
home digging potatoes, or planting of 'em at least. I've
been waiting now above a week for the Legislater to *do*
something, that I could write to you about; but they
dont seem to get along very smart lately. Sometimes
the wheels almost stop ; and then they start and rumble
along a little ways, and then they drag again. I dont
think we shall get through before sometime next week,
if we do before week arter. These secret sessions take
up a good deal of time. I dont see what in natur they
have so many of 'em for. I tried to get into some of
'em, but they wouldn't let me ; they said lobby members
had no business there, and shot the door right in my
face. There's one kind of business though that they
carry on here pretty brisk lately, and that is, *making
lawyers.* Some days they make 'em almost as fast as
uncle Ephraim used to make sap-troughs ; and I've
known him to chop off and hew out two in fifteen minutes.

But for all the Legislater can make 'em so fast, it is
as much as ever they can get along with all that come
and want to be made over into lawyers. And 'tother
day, when the law committee got pretty well stuck, having so many of 'em on hand, a new batch come up, and

Mr Hall of your town moved to refer them to the committee on *manufactures*. This is a capital committee to make things, and I havn't heard any complaint since, but what they can turn 'em out as fast as they come. It rather puzzled me at first to know what made every body want to be worked over into lawyers; so I asked one of 'em that stood waiting round here a day or two, to be put into the hopper and ground over, what he wanted to be made into a lawyer for? And he kind of looked up one side at me, and give me a knowing wink, and says he, don't you know that the lawyers get all the fat things of the land, and eat out the insides of the oisters, and give the shels to other folks? And if a man wants to have any kind of an office, he can't get it unless he's a lawyer; if he wants to go to the Legislater, he can't be elected without he's a lawyer; and if he wants to get to Congress, he cant go without he's a lawyer; and any man that don't get made into a lawyer as fast as possible, I say, is a fool. The whole truth come across my mind then, as quick as a look, why it was that I spent two or three years trying to get an office, and couldn't get one. It was because I wasn't a lawyer. And I dont believe I should have got an office to this day, if my good friend President Jackson hadn't found out I was a brave two fisted chap, and jest the boy to go down to Madawaska and flog the British.

We've agreed *unanimously* to support Governor Smith for re-election; and he'll come in all hollow, let the Jacksonites and Huntonites say what they will about it. Our party know too well which side their bread is buttered, to think of being split up this heat. I should write you more to day, but I feel so kind of agitated about these secret sessions,* that I cant hardly hold my pen still. I'm a little afraid they are intriguing to send

* The Legislature about this time held several secret sessions on the subject of the North-Eastern Boundary.

on to the President to take my commission away from me. It has been thrown out to me that I ought to be down to Madawaska, instead of being here all winter. Some have hinted to me that Mr Clifford has taken a miff against me, because the other day when he was chosen Speaker pro. tem. one of my friends voted for me ; and he thinks I was a rival candidate, and means to have me turned out of office if he can.

I am your loving friend,

CAPT. JACK DOWNING.

LETTER XLV.

Capt. Downing is in a peck of trouble about the Legisla-
ture's selling Madawaska to the General Government to
be given up to the British, and sits down and figures up
the price.

Madawaska, State of Maine, *or else Great Britain,* I dont know
which, March 12, 1832.

To the Editor of the Portland Courier — this with care and speed.

MY DEAR OLD FRIEND, — I cleared out from Augusta in such a kind of a whirlwind, that I hadn't time to write you a single word before I left. And I feel so kind of crazy now, I dont know hardly which end I stand upon. I've had a good many head-flaws and worriments in my life time, and been in a great many hobbles, but I never, in all my born days, met with any thing that puzzled me quite so bad as this ere *selling out* down here. I fit in the Legislater as long as fighting would do any good, that is, I mean in the caucus, for they wouldn't let me go right into the Legislater in the day time and talk to 'em there, because I was only a lobby member. But

14*

jest let them know it, lobby members can do as much as
any of 'em on sich kind of business as this. I laid it
down to 'em in the caucus as well as I could. I asked
'em if they didn't think I should look like a pretty fool,
after marching my company down there, and standing
ready all winter to flog the whole British nation the
moment any of 'em stept a foot on to our land, if I
should now have to march back again and give up the
land and all without flogging a single son-of-a-gun of
'em. But they said it was no use, it couldn't be helped:
Mr Netherlands had given the land away to the British,
and the President had agreed to do jest as Mr Netherlands said about it, and all we could do now was to get
as much pay for it as we could.

So I set down and figured it up a little to see how
much it would come to, for I used to cypher to the rule
of three when I went to school, and I found it would
come to a pretty round sum. There was, in the first
place, about two millions of acres of land. This, considerin the timber there was on it, would certainly be
worth a dollar an acre, and that would be two millions
of dollars. Then there was two or three thousand inhabitants, say twenty-five hundred; we must be paid for
them too, and how much are they worth? I've read in
the newspapers that black slaves, at the south, sell for
three or four hundred dollars apiece. I should think,
then, that white ones ought to fetch eight hundred.
This, according to the rule of three, would be two hundred thousand dollars. Then there's the pretty little
town of Madawaska that our Legislater made last winter, already cut and dried with town officers all chosen,
and every thing ready for the British to use without any
more trouble. We ought to have pay for this too, and I
should think it was worth ten thousand dollars.

And then the town of Madawasca has chosen Mr
Lizote to be a representative in the Legislater, and as
the British can take him right into the Parliament with-

out choosing him over again, they ought to pay us for that too. Now I have read in the newspapers that it sometimes costs, in England, two hundred thousand dollars to choose a representative to Parliament, reckoning all the grog they drink and all the money they pay for votes. But I wouldn't be screwing about it, so I put Mr Lizote down at one hundred thousand dollars. And then I footed up, and found it to be, —

For land, including timber, two millions of dollars,	$2,000,000
For inhabitants, including women and children, two hundred thousand dollars,	200,000
For the town of Madawaska, officers and all, ten thousand dollars,	10,000
For Mr Lizote, all ready to go to Parliament, one hundred thousand dollars,	100,000
Total,	$2,310,000

This was a pretty round sum, and I begun to think, come to divide it out, it would be a slice a-piece worth having; especially if we didn't give the Feds any of it, and I supposed we shouldn't, as there wasn't any of 'em there in the caucus to help see about it.

'In this view of the subject,' I almost made up my mind that we ought to be patriotic enough to give it up, and help the general government out of the hobble they had got into. And I was jest a-going to get up and make a speech and tell 'em so, when Mr McCrate of Nobleborough, and Capt. Smith of Westbrook, two of the best fellers in our party, came along and see what I was figuring about, and, says they, Capt. Downing, *are you going to sell your country?* In a minute I felt something rise right up in my throat, that felt as big as an ox-yoke. As soon as I got so I could speak, says I, *No, never*, while my name is Jack Downing, or my old rifle can carry a bullet. They declared too, that they wouldn't *sell out* to the general government, nor the

British, nor nobody else. And we stuck it out most of the evening, till we found out how it was going, and then we cleared out, and as soon as the matter was fairly settled, I started off for Madawaska; for I was afraid if my company should hear of it before I got there, it would make a blow up among 'em, and I should have to court-martial 'em.

When I first told 'em how the jig was up with us, that the British were going to have the land, without any fighting about it, I never see fellows so mad before in my life, unless it was Major Eaton at Washington when he sot out to flog Mr Ingham. They said if they could only have had one good battle, they wouldn't care a snap about it, but to be played tom-fool with in this way they wouldn't bear it. They were so mad, they hopped right up and down, and declared they never would go back till they had been over to Fredericton and pulled the jail down, or thrashed some of the New Brunswick boys. But, after a while, I pacified 'em by telling 'em if we didn't get a chance to fight here, I rather thought we might away off to Georgia, for there was something of a bobbery kicking up, and if the President should want troops to go on there, I was very sure my company would be one of the first he would send for.

So here we are, lying upon our arms, not knowing what to do. I have written to the President, and hope to hear from him soon. If the land is to go, I want to know it in season to get off before it's all over ; for I'll be hanged if ever I'll belong to the British.

Your distrest friend,
CAPT. JACK DOWNING.

LETTER XLVI.

Capt. Downing declines the office of Mayor of Portland.

Portland, State of Maine, April 10, 1832.

To the citizens of Portland.

WHEN I arrived in this city, last night, from Mada-waska, jest after the hubbub was over about the election, I was informed some of my friends in Ward No. 7, had voted for me for Mayor. I believe the votes are put in the papers long with the scattering votes, as I see they dont publish my name.

Now the upshot ont is, I cant take that are office, I've got so much other business to attend to. And so I take this opportunity to declare that *I absolutely decline being a candidate.* I have a great regard for the citizens of Portland, for it was they that first gave me a boost up towards an office, and I should be very glad to do any thing for 'em that I could ; but I must beg to be excused from being Mayor this year.

I am with respect,

CAPT. JACK DOWNING,

LETTER XLVII.

In which Captain Downing relates a confidential conversa-
tion with President Jackson while on a journey to Ten-
nessee.

Washington City, October 20, 1832.

To the Editor of the Portland Courier, away down east in the State
of Maine : [*O dear, seems to me I never shall get there again.*]

MY DEAR OLD FRIEND, — I have n't done any thing
this three months that seemed so natural as to set down
and write to you.   To write the name of the *Portland*
Courier raises my sperits right up.   It makes me feel as
if I was again talking with you, and uncle Joshua, and
cousin Ephraim, and cousin Nabby, and ant Sally, and
all of 'em.   I and President Jackson got back here yesterday from Tennessee, where we've been gone most all
summer.   And a long journey we've had of it too.   I
thought that from here to Portland was a dreadful ways,
but it's a great deal further to Tennessee.   I did n't
think before that our country was half so large as I find
it is.   It seems as if there was no end to it ; for when
we got clear to Tennessee the President said we want
half way acrost it.   I could n't hardly believe him, but
he stood tu it we want.   Why, says he, Jack, I've got
the largest country in the world, and the hardest to govern tu.   Say what you will of free governments, where
folks will act pretty much as they are a mind to, it's the
hardest work to administer it that ever I did.   I had
rather fight forty New Orleans battles than to govern
this everlasting great country one year.   There are so
many, you see, want to have a finger in the pye, it's the
most difficult business you can imagine.   You thought
you had a tough time of it, Jack, to take care of them
are small matters down to Madawaska last winter, with

your brave company of Downingville boys. But that's no more than a drop in the bucket to being President one month. I tell you, Jack, there is n't a monarch in Europe who has so hard a time of it as I have. There are so many cooks, the broth most always comes out rather bad. If I have to write a message, one must put in a sentence, and another a sentence, and another, till it gets so at last I can't hardly tell whether I've written any of it myself or not. And sometimes I have a good mind to throw it all in the fire and say nothing at all. But then again that wont do, for since I've undertaken to be President, I must go through with it. And then there was such a pulling and hauling for offices along in the outset, it seemed as though they would pull me to pieces. If I gave an office to one, Mr Ingham or Mr Branch would be mad, and if I gave it to another Mr Van Buren would n't like it, and if I gave it to another, perhaps Mrs Eaton would make a plaguy fuss about it. One wanted me to do this thing and another wanted me to do that; and it was nothing but quarrel the whole time. At last Mr Van Buren said he'd resign, if I would turn the rest out. So I made a scattering among 'em and turned 'em all out in a heap. All but Mr Lewis and Mr Kendall who staid to give me their friendly advice and help me through my trying difficulties.

And then again to be so slandered as I have been in the papers, it is enough to wear the patience of Job out. And if I got a little angry at the contrariness of the Senate, they must needs call me a 'roaring lion,' the rascals. But that Senate did use me shamefully. The very best nominations I made, they always rejected. To think the stupid heads should reject Mr Van Buren, decidedly the greatest man in the country, it was too provoking. Yes, Mr Van Buren is the first man in this country, and jest between you and me, Jack, he's the only man in it that is well qualified to succeed me in the government of this great nation of twenty-four republics.

And he must come in too, or the country wont be worth a stiver, much longer. There's Clay, he would make pretty work of it, if he should come in. Why, Jack, he would gamble one half of the country away in two years, and spend the other half in digging Canals and building rail-roads ; and when the funds in the Treasury failed he would go to the United States Bank and get more.

Calhoun would break the Union to pieces in three months if he was President. He's trying all he can now to tear off something of a slice from it at the south. And as for Wirt, he's a fiddling away with the Anti-masons. Letting Anti-masonry alone, he's a pretty good sort of a man ; but he has n't energy enough to steer our crazy ship of state in these stormy times. I would sooner trust it in the hands of Mrs Eaton than him. There's no one fit for it but Mr Van Buren ; and if it was not for getting him in I would n't have consented to stand for another term.

But, my dear friend, by stopping to tell you some of the conversation I and the President had along the road, I have almost forgot to tell you any thing about myself and the thousand things I met with on my journey. But I can't write any more to-day. I expect to start from here Monday on my way to Portland. You may hear from me a few times before I get there, as I shall stop along by the way some to see how matters go in Pennsylvany and New York.

If you have a chance, send my love to all my folks up at Downingville, and tell 'em old Jack is alive and hearty.

I remain your loving friend,
                    CAPT. JACK DOWNING.

LETTER XLVIII.

*In which Capt. Downing runs an Express from Baltimore
to Washington, and foots it through Pennsylvany Avenue to the President's house.*

Washington City, Nov. 5, 1832.

To the editor of the Portland Courier, in the Mariners' Church
building, 2d story, eastern end, Fore Street, Portland, away down
east, in the State of Maine.

MY DEAR OLD FRIEND. — Here I am back again to
Washington, though I've been as far as Baltimore on my
way down east to see you and the rest of my uncles and
aunts and couzins. And what do you think I posted
back to Washington for? I can tell you. When I got
to Baltimore I met an *express* coming on full chisel from
Philadelphia, to carry the news to Washington that
Pennsylvania had gone all hollow for old Hickory's
second election. The poor fellow that was carrying it
had got so out of breath, that he declared he couldn't go
no further if the President never heard of it.

Well, thinks I, it will be worth a journey back to
Washington, jest to see the old gineral's eyes strike fire
when he hears of it. So says I, I'll take it and carry it
on for you if you are a mind to. He kind of hesitated
at first, and was afraid I might play a trick upon him;
but when he found out my name was Jack Downing, he
jumped off his horse quick enough; I'll trust it with you,
says he, as quick as I would with the President himself.
So I jumped on and whipped up. And sure enough, as
true as you are alive, I did get to Washington before
dark, though I had but three hours to go it in, and its
nearly forty miles. It was the smartest horse that ever
I backed, except one that belongs to the President. But,
poor fellow, he's so done tu I guess he'll never run another express. Jest before I got to Washington, say

15

about two miles from the city, the poor fellow keeled
up and could n't go another step. I had lost my hat on
the way and was too much in a hurry to pick it up, and
he had thrown me off twice and torn my coat pretty bad,
so that I did n't look very trig to go through the city or
go to the President's fine house. But notwithstanding,
I knew the President would overlook it, considerin the
business I was coming upon; so I catched the express
and pulled foot, right through Pennsylvany Avenue,
without any hat, and torn coat sleeves and coat tail flying. The stage offered to carry me, but I thought I
wouldn't stop for it.

Almost the first person I met was Mr Duff Green.
Says he, Capt. Downing, what's the matter? I held up
the express and shook it at him, but never answered him
a word, and pulled on. He turned and walked as fast
as he could without running, and followed me. Pretty
soon I met Mr Gales of the Intelligencer, and says he,
for mercy sake, Captain Downing, what's the matter?
Have you been chased by a wolf, or Governor Houston,
or have you got news from Pennsylvania? I did n't turn
to the right nor left, but shook the express at him and
run like wild-fire.

When I came up to the President's house, the old
gentleman was standing in the door. He stepped quicker than I ever see him before, and met me at the gate.
Says he, my dear friend Downing, what's the matter?
Has the United States Bank been trying to bribe you,
and you are trying to run away from 'em? They may
buy over Webster and Clay and such trash, but I knew
if they touched you they would get the wrong pig by the
ear. As he said this, Duff Green hove in sight, puffing
and blowing, full speed.

Oh, said the President, Duff Green wants to have a
lick at you, does he? Well dont retreat another step,
Mr Downing, I'll stand between you and harm. Upon
that he called his boy and told him to bring his pistols in

'Stop Major! I'll give you a ride.' —
'Cant stop; got an express for the Gineral.'

a moment. By this time I made out to get breath enough jest to say Pennsylvany, and to shake the express at him. The old man's color changed in a minute. Says he, come in, Mr Downing, come in, set down, dont say a word to Duff. So in we went, and shut the door. Now, says the President, looking as though he would route a regiment in five minutes, now speak and let me know whether I am a dead man or alive.

Gineral, says, I, its all over with —— I wont hear a word of it, says he, stomping his foot. His eyes flashed fire so that I trembled and almost fell backwards. But I see he did n't understand me. Dear gineral, says I, its all over with Clay and the Bank — at that he clapt his hands and jumpt up like a boy. I never see the President jump before, as much as I've been acquainted with him. In less than a minute he looked entirely like another man. His eyes were as calm and as bright as the moon jest coming out from behind a black thunder cloud.

He clenched my hand and gave it such a shake, I did n't know but he would pull it off. Says he, Jack, I knew Pennsylvany never would desert me, and if she has gone for me I'm safe. And now if I dont make them are Bank chaps hug it, my name is n't Andrew Jackson. And after all, Jack, I aint so glad on my own account, that I'm re-elected, as I am for the country and Mr Van Buren. This election has all been on Mr Van Buren's account; and we shall get him in now to be President after me. And you know, Jack, that he's the only man after me, that's fit to govern this country.

The President has made me promise to stop and spend the night with him, and help him rejoice over the victory. But I have n't time to write any more before the mail goes.

Your loving friend,
CAPT. JACK DOWNING.

LETTER XLIX.

In which Capt. Downing receives a Major's commission,
and is appointed to march against the Nullifiers.

Washington City, Dec. 8, 1832.

To the Editor of the Portland Courier, in the Mariners' Church
building, second story, eastern end, Fore Street, Portland, away
down east, in the State of Maine.

MY DEAR OLD FRIEND. — I believe the last time I
wrote to you, was when I come back with the express
from Baltimore, and Duff Green chased me so through
the street to find out what I was bringing, and the President thought he was running to get a lick at me, and
called for his pistols to stand between me and harm, you
know.   Well, I intended to turn right about again after
I had made the old gentleman's heart jump up by telling him that he had got Pennsylvany and would be
elected as sure as eggs was bacon, and make the best of
my way towards Portland.   For you cant think how I
long to see you and uncle Joshua and ant Kesiah and
cousin Ephraim and cousin Nabby and all the rest of
the dear souls up in Downingville.   It seems as though
it was six years instead of six months since I left that
part of the country, and when I shall be able to get back
again is more than I can tell now ; for I find when a
man once gets into public life he never can say his time
is his own ; he must always stand ready to go where his
country calls.   The long and the short of it is, the President has got so many other fish for me to fry, it's no use
for me to think of going home yet.   That evening after
I got back with the express, the President said we must
honor this victory in Pennsylvany with a glass of wine.
I am sure, said he, Capt. Downing, you will have no ob-
jection to take a glass with me on this joyful occasion.

I told him as for that matter, I supposed I could take a glass of wine upon a pinch, even if the occasion was not half so joyful. So he had two or three bottles full brought in, and filled up the glasses. And now, says the President, I will give you a toast. The State of Pennsylvania, the most patriotic State in the Union; for though I go against all her great public interests, still she votes for me by an overwhelming majority.

He then called for my toast. And what could I give but my dear native Downingville; the most genuine unwavering democratic republican town in New England.

Good, said the President; and that Downingville has never been rewarded yet. You shall have a Post Office established there, and name to me which of your friends you would like should be Post Master, and he shall be appointed.

The President then gave his second toast; Martin Van Buren, the next President of the United States, and the only man in the country that is fit for it. Capt. Downing, your toast if you please. So I gave Uncle Joshua Downing, the most thorough going republican in Downingville.

Good, said the President, I understand you, Captain Downing; your uncle Joshua shall have the Post Office.

His third toast was the editor of the Washington Globe; and mine was the editor of the Portland Courier. But I told him he mustn't ask me for any more toasts, for that was as fur as I could go.

The President toasted several more of his friends, sich as Major Eaton, and Mr Kendall, and Mr Lewis, and the Hon. Isaac Hill, and so on, till it got to be pretty late in the evening, and I told the President I would be glad if he would excuse me, for I wanted to start early in the morning on my way down east, and I thought I should feel better if I could get a little nap first. And besides I had got to go and get the old lady that used to do my washing and mending, to patch up my coat

15*

that got such a terrible shipwreck by being thrown off the horse with the express.

Start down east to-morrow morning, Capt. Downing, said he, you must not think of it. I have an important and delicate job on hand which I cant get along with very well without your assistance. There's that miserable ambitious Calhoun has been trying this dozen years to be President of the United States; but he can't make out, so now he is determined to lop off a few of the southern States and make himself President of them. But if he don't find himself mistaken my name is n't Andrew Jackson. As he said this he started up on his feet, and begun to march across the floor with a very soldier-like step, and his eyes fairly flashed fire. No, said he, Capt. Downing, he must wait till somebody else is President besides me before he can do that. Let him move an inch by force in this business, if he dares. I'll chase him as far beyond Tennessee as it is from here there, but what I'll catch him and string him up by the neck to the first tree I can find.

I must send some troops out there to South Carolina to reconnoitre and keep matters strait, and your gallant defence of Madawaska last winter points you out as the most suitable man to take the command. — I shall give you a Major's commission to-morrow, and wish you to enlist two or three companies of brave volunteers and hold yourself in readiness to obey orders. In case we should have to come to a real brush, said the President, I shall take command myself, and make you Lieutenant General. But I wish you to bear in mind, let what will come, never to shoot that Calhoun. Shooting is too good for him. He must dance upon nothing with a rope round his neck.

As for your coat, Capt. Downing, dont trouble the old lady with it. It looks as though it had seen service enough already. I'll give you one of mine to wear till you have time to get a suit of regimentals made. I told

him I felt a little uneasy about taking the command
among strangers, unless I could have my Downingville
company with me. Send for them, said the President,
by all means, send for them. There are no troops equal
to them except it is some of the boys from Tennessee.
So I shall forthwith send orders to Sargeant Joel to
march 'em on here. As I am to have my commission
to-morrow, I shall venture to subscribe myself your friend,

MAJOR JACK DOWNING.

LETTER L.

*In which uncle Joshua tells what a tussle they had in Dow-
ningville to keep the Federalists from praising the
President's Proclamation against the Nullifiers.*

Downingville, State of Maine, Dec. 27, 1832.

To Major Jack Downing, at Washington City, or if he is gone to
South Carolina I want President Jackson to send this along tu
him.

MY DEAR NEFFU, — We had almost gin you up for
dead, you had been gone so long, before we got your
letter in the Portland Courier telling how you had been
away to Tennessee along with President Jackson.
Your poor mother had pined away so that she had
nothing left, seemingly, but skin and bones, and your
cousin Nabby had cried her eyes half out of her head,
poor girl. But when the Portland Courier came bringing that are letter of yourn, Downingville was in a complete uproar all day. Sargent Joel had come home
from Madawaska and dismissed your company, and gone
to work in the woods chopping wood. But as soon as
he heard your letter had come, he dropped his ax, and I
dont think he 's touched it since ; and he put on his
regimentals and scoured up the old piece of a scythe

that he used to have for a sword, and stuck it into his waistband, and strutted about as big as a major gineral. Your mother begun to pick up her crums immediately, and has been growing fat ever since. And Nabby run about from house to house like a crazy bed-bug, telling 'em Jack was alive and was agoing to build up Downingville and make something of it yet.

We got your last letter and the President's Proclamation both together, though I see your letter was written two days first. That Proclamation is a capital thing. You know I 've made politics my study for forty years, and I must say it 's the most ginuine republican thing I ever come acrost. But what was most provoking about it, was, all the old federalists in town undertook to praise it tu. Squire Dudley, you know, was always a federalist, and an Adams man tu. I met him the next day after the Proclamation come, and he was chock full of the matter. Says he, Mr. Downing, that Proclamation is jest the thing. It 's the true constitutional doctrine. We all support the President in this business through thick and thin.

My dander began to rise, and I could not hold in any longer. Says I, squire Dudley, shut up your clack, or I 'll knock your clam-shells together pretty quick. It 's got to be a pretty time of day indeed, if after we 've worked so hard to get President Jackson in, you Federalists are going to undertake to praise his proclamation as much as though he was your own President. You 've a right to grumble and fine fault with it as much as you like ; but dont let me hear you say another word in favor of it, if you do I 'll make daylight shine through you. The old man hauled in his horns and meeched off looking shamed enough.

The next day we concluded to have a public meeting to pass resolutions in favor of the Proclamation. I was appointed chairman. The federal party all come flocking round and wanted to come in and help praise the

President. We told 'em no; it was our President, and our Proclamation, and they must keep their distance. So we shut the doors and went on with our resolutions. By and by the federal party begun to hurra for Jackson outside the house. At that I told Sargent Joel and your cousin Ephraim and two or three more of the young democrats to go out and clear the coast of them are fellers. And they went out and Sargent Joel drew his piece of a scythe and went at 'em and the federalists run like a flock of sheep with a dog after 'em. So we finished our resolutions without getting a drop of federalism mixed with 'em, and sent 'em on to the President by Sargent Joel. He got his company together last week and they filled their knapsacks with bread and sasages and doe-nuts, and started for Washington according to your orders.

I was glad to see that hint in your letter about a post office here. We need one very much. And if the President should think I ought to have it, being I've always been such a good friend to him, why you know, Jack, I'm always ready to serve my country.

So I remain your loving Uncle,

JOSHUA DOWNING.

P. S. If the President should n't say any thing more about the post office, I think you had better name it to him again before you go to South Carolina; for if any thing should happen to you there, he might never do any more about it.

LETTER LI.

In which Major Downing describes the arrival of Sargent Joel with the Company at Washington.

Washington City, Jan. 4, 1833.

To my dear Cousin Ephraim Downing, what watches the Legislater at Augusta, away down east, in the State of Maine, while I stay here and look arter Congress and the President.

DEAR COUSIN, — Sargent Joel got here day before yesterday with my hearty old company of Downingville boys, that went down to Madawaska with me last winter. They cut rather a curious figure marching through Pensilvany Avenu. One half of 'em had worn their shoes out so that their toes stuck out like the heads of so many young turtles, and t'other half had holes through their knees or elbows, and Sargent Joel marched ahead of 'em swinging his piece of an old scythe for a sword, and inquiring of every one he met for Major Jack Downing. They all told him to keep along till he got to the President's house, which was the biggest house in the city except the Congress house, and there he would find me. I and the President were setting by the window in the great east room, looking out and talking about Mr Calhoun and so on, when the President begun to stare as though he saw a catamount.

He started up on his feet, and says he, Major Downing, if my eyes dont deceive me there 's Nullification now coming up Pensilvany Avenu. He begun to call for his pistols, and to tell his men to fasten up the doors, when I looked out, and I knew Joel's strut in a minute. Says I, dear Ginneral, that's no nullification, but its what 'll put a stopper on nullification pretty quick if it once gets to South Carolina. It 's my Downingville Company commanded by Sargent Joel. At that the President looked more pleased than I 've seen him before since he got the news of the vote of Pensilvany. He ordered 'em into the east room and gave 'em as much as they could eat and drink of the best the house affords. He has found quarters for 'em in the neighborhood, and says we must be ready to march for South Carolina whenever he says the word.

But I 'll tell you what 't is, cousin Ephraim, I begin to grow a little kind of wamble-cropt about going to South Carolina, arter all. If they 've got many such fellers there as one Ginneral Blair there is here from that State, I 'd sooner take my chance in the woods forty miles above Downingville, fighting bears and wolves and catamounts, than come within gun-shot of one of these Carolina giants. He 's a whaler of a feller, as big as any two men in Downingville. They say he weighs over three hundred pounds. About a week ago he met Ginneral Duff Green in the street and he fell afoul of him with a great club and knocked him down, and broke his arm and beat him almost to death, jest because he got mad at something Mr Green said in his paper. And what makes me feel more skittish about getting into the hands of such chaps, is, because he says he could n't help it. He says all his friends persuaded him not to meddle with Ginneral Green, and he tried as hard as he could to let him alone, but he ' found himself unequal to the effort.' So Green like to got killed.

The folks here sot out to carry him to court about it, but he said he would n't go, and so he armed himself with four pistols and two dirks and a great knife, and said he 'd shoot the first man that touched him. Last night he went to the Theatre with all his arms and coutrements about him. And after he sot there a spell, and all 'the folks were looking to see the play go on, he draws out one of his pistols and fires it at the players. Then there was a dreadful uproar. They told him he must clear out about the quickest. But he said if they 'd let him alone he 'd behave like a gentleman. So they went on with the play again.

By and by he draws out another pistol and points it towards the players. At that there was a whole parcel of 'em seized him and dragged him out into another room, big as he was. But pretty soon he got upon his feet, and begun to rave like a mad ox. He pulled off his coat and threw it down, and declared he 'd fight the whole boodle of 'em. The constables were all so frightened they cut and run, and nobody dared to go a near him, till he got cooled down a little, when some of his friends coaxed him away to a tavern. Now as for going to South Carolina to fight such chaps as these, I 'd sooner let nullification go to grass and eat mullen.

Sargent Joel told me when he left Downingville you had jest got loaded up with apples and one thing another to go down to Augusta to peddle 'em out; and that you was a going to stay there while the Legislater folks were there. So I thought it would be a good plan for you and I to write to one another about once a week or so, how matters get along.

Give my love to the folks up in Downingville whenever you see 'em.

So I remain your loving Cousin,

MAJOR JACK DOWNING.

LETTER LII.

In which Major Downing gives his opinion about NULLIFI-
CATION, *and illustrates it with a lucid example.*

Washington City, Jan. 17, 1833.

To the editor of the Portland Courier, in the Mariners' Church
Building, second story, eastern end, Fore street, away down east
in the State of Maine.

MY KIND AND DEAR OLD FRIEND,— The President's
Message to Congress makes cracking work here. Mr
Calhoun shows his teeth like a lion. Mr McDuffie is
cool as a cowcumber, though they say he's got a terrible
tempest inside of him, that he'll let out before long. For
my part I think the President's Message is about right.
I was setting with the President in the east room last
night, chatting about one thing and another, and the
President says he, Major Downing, have you read my
message that I sent to Congress to day. I told him I
had n't. Well, says he, I should like to have you read
it and give me your opinion upon it. So he handed it
to me and I sot down and read it through.

And when I got through, now says I Gineral I'll tell
you jest what I think of this ere business. When I was
a youngster some of us Downingville boys used to go
down to Sebago Pond every spring and hire out a month
or two rafting logs across the Pond. And one time I
and cousin Ephraim, and Joel, and Bill Johnson, and
two or three more of us had each a whapping great log
to carry across the Pond. It was rather a windy day
and the waves kept the logs bobbing up and down pretty
considerable bad, so we agreed to bring 'em along side
and side and lash 'em together and drive some thole-pins
in the outermost logs and row 'em over together. We
went along two or three miles pretty well. But by and

16

by Bill Johnson begun to complain. He was always an uneasy harumscarum sort of a chap. Always thought every body else had an easier time than he had, and when he was a boy, always used to be complaining that the other boys had more butter on their bread than he had. Well, Bill was rowing on the leward side, and he begun to fret and said his side went the hardest, and he would n't give us any peace till one of us changed sides with him.

Well Bill had n't rowed but a little ways on the windward side before he began to fret again, and declared that side went harder than 'tother, and he wouldn't touch to row on that side any longer. We told him he had his choice, and he should n't keep changing so. But he only freted the more and begun to get mad. At last he declared if we did n't change with him in five minutes, he'd cut the lashings and take his log and paddle off alone. And before we had hardly time to turn round, he declared the five minutes were out, and up hatchet and cut the lashings, and away went Bill on his own log, bobbing and rolling about, and dancing like a monkey to try to keep on the upper side. The rest of us scrabbled to as well as we could, and fastened our logs together again, though we had a tuff match for it, the wind blew so hard. Bill had n't gone but a little ways before his log begun to role more and more, and by and by in he went splash, head and ears. He came up puffing and blowing, and got hold of the log and tried to climb up on to it, but the more he tried the more the log rolled ; and finding it would be gone goose with him pretty soon if he staid there, he begun to sing out like a loon for us to come and take him. We asked him which side he would row if we would take his log into the raft again. O, says Bill, I'll row on either side or both sides if you want me to, if you'll only come and help me before I sink.

But, said the President, I hope you did n't help the

foolish rascal out till he got a pretty good soaking. He got soaked enough before we got to him, says I, for he was jest ready to sink for the last time, and our logs come pesky near getting scattered, and if they had, we should all gone to the bottom together. And now Gineral, this is jest what I think : if you let South Carolina cut the lashings you'll see such a log-rolling in this country as you never see yet. The old Gineral started up and marched across the floor like a boy. Says he, Major Downing, she sha'nt cut the lashings while my name is Andrew Jackson. Tell Sargent Joel to have his company sleep on their arms every night. I told him they should be ready at a moment's warning.

I wish you would jest give cousin Ephraim up to Augusta a jog to know why he dont write to me and let me know how the Legislater is getting along.

I remain your loving friend,
MAJOR JACK DOWNING.

LETTER LIII.

In which cousin Ephraim tells the Major how matters get along at Augusta, and gives a specimen of the value of political promises.

Augusta, State of Maine, Jan. 30, 1833.

To the Editor of the Portland Courier, that we take up in Downingville : dear sir, I want you to send this on to cousin Jack to Washington City, 'cause he told me you would send it and not charge any postage.

To Major Jack Downing.

DEAR COUSIN JACK, — I got your letter some time ago; but I had n't time to answer it afore now, because I had to go back up to Downingville to get another load of apples. These Legislater folks cronch apples down by

the wholesale between speeches, and sometimes in the
middle of speeches tu. That arternoon that Mr Clark
spoke all day, I guess I sold nigh upon a half a bushel
for cash, and trusted out most three pecks besides. The
folks up to Downingville are all pretty well, only your
poor old mother; she 's got the reumatics pretty bad
this winter. She says she wishes with all her heart
Jack would come home, and not think of going to South
Carolina. Ever since she heard about Ginneral Blair
she cant hardly sleep nights, she 's so afraid you 'll get
shot. I tell her there 's no danger of you as long as you
have President Jackson one side of you and Sargent
Joel 'tother.

The Legislater is jogging along here pretty well; I
guess they 'll get through about the first of March, if
they dont have too many boundary questions come along.
We made some Major Ginnerals here 'tother day, and I
tried to get you elected. Not because I thought you
cared much about the office now, but jest for the honor
of Downingville. I tried most all the members, and
thought to be sure you would come in as slick as greese.
For about forty of 'em told me they thought it *belonged*
to you. They said it was against their principles to
pledge their votes to any body ; but they whispered in
my ear that they would *do what they could*, and they had
n't *scarcely* a doubt but what you 'd be elected. Sixty-
eight of 'em told me you was the *best man for it*, and
would undoubtedly be chosen as a matter of course.
And twenty five of 'em promised me right up and down
by the crook of the elbow, that they *would vote* for
you.

Well Jack, after all this, you did n't get but *two votes*.
By that time I begun to think it was n't so strange that
it took you two years hard fishing before you could get
an office.

This is the most democratic Legislater that they have
ever had in this state yet. They are most all real gin-

uine democrats, and they have give Mr Holmes and Mr Sprague a terrible basting for being federalists, and they have turned Mr Holmes out and put Mr Shepley in.

The Legislater is talking of moving the seat of government back to Portland again. They say it will be better all round. They wont have to go so fur through the snow-drifts to their boarding houses, and wont have to pay much more than half so much for their board. And here they have to pay four pence apiece every time they are shaved; but in Portland they can get shaved by the half dozen for three cents apiece. I hope they will go, for I can get more for my apples in Portland than I can here.

P. S. Bill Johnson was married last week, and he quarrelled with his wife the very next day. So you see he is the same old sixpence he used to be. He says he 'll send a petition to the Legislater to be divorced, and he declares if they don't grant it, he 'll cut the lashings as he did once on the raft on Sebago Pond, sink or swim.

N. B. Uncle Joshua wished me to ask you to ask the President about that post office again, as his commission has n't come yet.

I remain your loving Cousin,
EPHRAIM DOWNING.

16*

LETTER LIV.

*In which Major Downing goes up top the Congress house
and listens to see if he can hear the guns in South Carolina, and also has a talk with the President, about the
slander of the newspapers.*

[*Note.* The first of February, 1833, was the day appointed by
South Carolina for putting in force her nullifying Ordinance.]

Washington City, Feb. 1, 1833.

To the editor of the Portland Courier, in Mariners' Church Building, second story, eastern end, Fore Street away down east, in the
State of Maine.

MY DEAR FRIEND. — This is nullification day, and it's
most night, and I aint dead yet, and hant been shot at
once to-day. I got up this morning as soon as it was
light, and went out and looked away towards South Carolina, and listened as hard as I could to see if I could
hear the guns crackin and the cannons roarin. But it
was all still as a mouse. And I've been up top the Congress house five or six times to-day, and listened and
listened, but all the firing I could hear was inside the
Congress house itself, where the members were shooting
their speeches at each other. I had my company all
ready this morning with their dinners in their napsacks,
to start as quick as we heard a single gun. We shant
go till we hear something from these nullifiers, for the
President says he aint agoing to begin the scrape, but if
the nullifiers begin it, then the hardest must fend off.

Yesterday a friend handed me a couple of papers
printed at Hallowell away down pretty near to Augusta
in the State of Maine, called the American Advocate,
and I found something in 'em that made me as mad as a
March hair. The first one mentioned that Capt. Dow
was chosen Mayor of Portland, and then said, he is the

reputed author of the Jack Downing letters that have been published in the Portland Courier. The other paper that was printed two or three days afterwards, said Mr. Dow the new Mayor of Portland is not the author of Jack Downing's letters; they are written by Mr Seba Smith, the Editor of the Portland Courier. Now, Mr Editor, my good old friend, is n't this too bad? I have n't come acrost any thing that made me feel so wamble-cropt this good while. Jest as if Major Jack Downing could n't write his own letters.

I've been to school, put it altogether, off and on, more than six months; and though I say it myself, I always used to be called the best scholar among all the boys in Downingville, and most always used to stand at the head of my class. I'd been through Webster's spelling book before I was fifteen, and before I was twenty I could cypher to the rule of three. And now to have it said that I dont write my own letters, is too bad. It's what I call a rascally shame. I was so boiling over with it last night, that I could'nt hold in; and so I took the papers and went in and showed them to the President. I always go to the President when I have any difficulty, and when he has any he comes to me; so we help one another along as well as we can. When the President had read it, says he, Major Downing, it's strange to see how this world is given to lying. The public papers are beginning to slander you jest as they always do me. I have n't written scarcely a public document since I've been President, but what it's been laid off to Mr Van Buren, or Mr McLane, or Mr Livingston, or Mr Taney, or somebody or other. And how to help this slanderous business I dont know. But it's too provoking, Major, that's certain. Sometimes I've a good mind to make Congress pass a law that every editor who says I dont write my proclamations and messages, or that you dont write your letters, shall forfeit his press and types; and if that dont stop him, that he shall be strung up by the neck without Judge or Jury.

And now, Mr Editor, I wish you would jest give that Hallowell man a hint to mind his own p's and q's in future, and look out for his neck. And as you know very well that I do write my own letters, I would thank you jest to tell the public so.

I remain your sincere and loving friend,
MAJOR JACK DOWNING.

LETTER LV.

In which Cousin Ephraim explains the science of Land-speculation.

Augusta, State of Maine, March 4, 1833.

To Major Jack Downing, at President Jackson's house in Washington City.

DEAR COUSIN JACK, — The Legislater folks have all cleared out to-day one arter t'other jest like a flock of sheep; and some of 'em have left me in the lurch tu, for they cleared out without paying me for my apples. Some of 'em went off in my debt as much as twenty cents, and some ninepence, and a shilling, and so on. They all kept telling me when they got paid off, they'd settle up with me. And so I waited with patience till they adjourned, and thought I was as sure of my money as though it was in the Bank.

But, my patience, when they did adjourn, such a hubbub I guess you never see. They were flying about from one room to another, like so many pigeons shot in the head. They run into Mr Harris' room and clawed the money off of his table, hand over fist. I brustled up to some of 'em, and tried to settle. I come to one man that owed me twelve cents, and he had a ninepence in change, but he wouldn't let me have that, because he should lose a half cent. So, while we were bothering about it, trying to get it changed, the first I knew the rest of 'em had got their money in their pockets and were off like a shot, some of 'em in stages, and some in sleighs, and some footing it. I out and followed after 'em, but 'twas no use; I couldn't catch one of 'em. And as for my money, and apples tu, I guess I shall have to whistle for 'em now. Its pesky hard, for I owe four and sixpence here yet for my board, and I've paid away every cent I've got for my apples, and dont know but I shall have to come down with another load to clear out my expenses. Howsomever, you know uncle Joshua always told us never to cry for spilt milk, so I mean to hold my head up yet.

I dont know but I shall have to give up retailing apples, I meet with so many head-flaws about it. I was thinking that, soon as the Legislater adjourned, I'd take a load of apples and apple-sass, and a few sassages, and come on to Washington, and go long with your company to South Carolina. But they say Mr Clay has put a stopper on that nullification business, so that its ten chances to one you wont have to go.

I dont care so much about the apple business after all; for I've found out a way to get rich forty times as fast as I can by retailing apples, or as you can by hunting after an office. And I advise you to come right home, as quick as you can come. Here's a business going on here that you can get rich by, ten times as quick as you can in any office, even if you should get to be President. The President dont have but twenty-five thousand dollars a year; but in this ere business that's going on here, a man can make twenty-five thousand dollars in a wee if he's a mind to, and not work hard neither.

I spose by this time you begin to feel rather in a pucker to know what this business is. I'll tell you: but you must keep it to yourself, for if all them are

Washington folks and Congress folks should come on here and go to dipping into it, I'm afraid they'd cut us all out. But between you and me, its only jest buying and selling land. Why, Jack, its forty times more profitable than money digging, or any other business that you ever see. I knew a man here t'other day from Bangor, that made ten thousand dollars, and I guess he want more than an hour about it. Most all the folks here and down to Portland and Bangor have got their fortunes made, and now we are beginning to take hold of it up in the country.

They've got a slice up in Downingville, and I missed it by being down here selling apples, or I should had a finger in the pie. Uncle Joshua Downing, you know he's an old fox, and always knows where to jump; well, he see how every body was getting rich, so he went and bought a piece of a township up back of Downingville, and give his note for a thousand dollars for it. And then he sold it to uncle Jacob and took his note for two thousand dollars; and uncle Jacob sold it to uncle Zackary and took his note for three thousand dollars; and uncle Zackary sold it to uncle Jim, and took his note for four thousand dollars; and uncle Jim sold it to cousin Sam, and took his note for five thousand dollars; and cousin Sam sold it to Bill Johnson, and took his note for six thousand dollars. So you see there's five of 'em that want worth ninepence apiece before, have now got a thousand dollars apiece clear, when their notes are paid. And Bill Johnson's going to logging off of it, and they say he'll make more than any of 'em.

Come home, Jack, come home by all means, if you want to get rich. Give up your commission, and think no more about being President, or any thing else, but come home and buy land before its all gone.

Your loving cousin,
EPHRAIM DOWNING.

P. S.   Didn't Mr Holmes and Mr Sprague look rather blue when they got the resolutions that our Legislater passed, giving them such a mortal whipping ?

———

LETTER LVI.

In which Major Downing tells how Mr Clay put a stop to that fuss in South Carolina, besides hushing up some other quarrels.

Washington City, March 10, 1833.

To the editor of the Portland Courier, in the Mariners' Church building, 2nd story, eastern end, Fore street, away down east, in the State of Maine, to be sent to Cousin Ephraim Downing, up in Downingville, cause I spose he 's gone home before this time from Augusta.

DEAR COUSIN EPHRAIM, — I got your letter this morning.   It was a shame for them are Legislater folks to skulk off without paying you for your apples.   But they are the worst folks about standing to their word that I know of.   They've promised me an office more than twenty times, but some how or other, come to the case in hand, their votes always went for somebody else.   But I dont care a fig for 'em as long as I've got the President on my side, for his offices are as fat again as the Legislater offices are.   The President's offices will support a man pretty well if he does n't do any thing at all.   As soon as Mr Clay's Tariff Bill passed, the President called me into his room, and says he, Major Downing, the nullification jig is up.   There'll be no fun for you in South Carolina now, and I guess you may as well let Sargent Joel march the company back to Downingville, and wait till somebody kicks up another bobbery some where and then I'll send for 'em, for they are the likeliest company I've seen since I went with my Tennesse   rangers to

New Orleans. And as for you Major Downing, you shall still hold your commission and be under half pay, holding yourself in readiness to march at a moment's warning and to fight whenever called for.

So you see, Cousin Ephraim, I am pretty well to live in the world, without any of your land speculations or apple selling down east. I cant seem to see how 'tis they all make money so fast in that land business down there that you tell about. How could all our folks and Bill Johnson and all of 'em there in Downingville make a thousand dollars apiece, jest a trading round among themselves, when there aint fifty dollars in money, put it all together, in the whole town. It rather puzzles me a little. As soon as I see 'em all get their thousand dollars cash in hand, I guess I'll give up my commission and come home and buy some land tu.

But at present I think I rather have a bird in the hand than one in the bush. Our Congress folks here cleared out about the same time that your Legislater folks did, and I and the President have been rather lonesome a few days. The old gentleman says I must n't leave him on any account; but I guess I shall start Joel and the company off for Downingville in a day or two. They 've got their clothes pretty much mended up, and they look quite tidy. I should'nt feel ashamed to see 'em marched through any city in the United States.

It is n't likely I shall have any thing to do under my commission very soon. For some say there 'll be no more fighting in the country while Mr Clay lives, if it should be a thousand years. He's got a master knack of pacifying folks and hushing up quarrels as you ever see. He's stopt all that fuss in South Carolina, that you know was jest ready to blow the whole country sky high. He stept up to 'em in Congress and told 'em what sort of a Bill to pass, and they passed it without hardly any jaw about it. And South Carolina has hauled in her horns, and they say she'll be as calm as a clock now.

And that is n't the only quarrel Mr Clay has stopt. Two of the Senators, Mr Webster and Mr Poindexter, got as mad as March hairs at each other. They called each other some pesky hard names, and looked cross enough for a week to bite a board nail off. Well, after Mr Clay got through with South Carolina, he took them in hand. He jest talked to 'em about five minutes, and they got up and went and shook hands with each other, and looked as loving as two brothers.

Then Mr Holmes got up and went to Mr Clay, and almost with tears in his eyes asked him if he would n't be so kind as to settle a little difficulty there was between him and his constituents, so they might elect him to come to Congress again. And I believe some of the other Senators asked for the same favor.

So as there is likely to be peace now all round the house for some time to come, I'm in a kind of a quandary what course to steer this summer. The President talks of taking a journey down east this summer, and he wants me to go with him, because I'm acquainted there, and can show him all about it. He has a great desire to go as fur as Downingville, and get acquainted with Uncle Joshua, who has always stuck by him in all weathers through thick and thin. The President thinks uncle Joshua is one of the republican pillars of New-England, and says he shall always have the post office as long as he lives, and his children after him.

I rather guess on the whole I shall come on that way this summer with the President. But wherever I go, I shall remain your loving cousin,

MAJOR JACK DOWNING.

17

LETTER LVII.

*In which Major Downing gives the result of a consultation
amongst the government on the question, whether the
President should shake hands with the Federalists during his journey down East.*

Washington City, April 20, 1833.

To the Editor of the Portland Courier, in the Mariners' Church
building, second story eastern end, Fore Street, away down East
in the State of Maine.

My Dear Old Friend, — Bein I hant writ to you
for some time, I'm afraid you and our folks up in Downingville will begin to feel a little uneasy by and by, so
I'll jest write you a little if it aint but two lines, to let
you know how we get on here. I and the President
seem to enjoy ourselves pretty well together, though its
getting to be a little lonesome since the Congress folks
went off, and Sargeant Joel cleared out with my Downingville Company. Poor souls, I wonder if they have
got home yet; I have n't heard a word from 'em since
they left here. I wish you would send up word to Sargeant Joel to write to me and let me know how they got
along. He can send his letter in your Currier, or get
uncle Joshua to frank it; either way it wont cost me any
thing. Now I think of it, I wish you would jest ask
cousin Nabby to ask uncle Joshua to frank me on two
or three pair of stockings, for mine have got terribly out
at the heels. He can do it jest as well as not; they
make nothing here of franking a bushel basket full of great
books to the western States. And they say some of the
members of Congress used to frank their clothes home
by mail to be washed.

I and the President are getting ready to come on that
way this summer. We shall come as far as Portland,

and I expect we shall go up to Downingville ; for the
President says he must shake hands with uncle Joshua
before he comes back, that faithful old republican who
has stood by him through thick and thin ever since he
found he was going to be elected President. He will
either go up to Downingville, or send for Uncle Joshua
to meet him at Portland.

There is some trouble amongst us here a little, to know
how we shall get along among the federalists when we
come that way. They say the federalists in Massachusetts want to keep the President all to themselves when
he comes there. But Mr Van Buren says that 'll never
do ; he must stick to the democratic party ; he may
shake hands with a federalist once in a while if the democrats dont see him, but whenever there's any democrats round he mustn't look at a federalist. Mr Mc-
Lane and Mr Livingston advise him tother way. They
tell him he'd better treat the federalists pretty civil, and
shake hands with Mr Webster as quick as he would with
uncle Joshua Downing. And when they give this advice
Mr Lewis and Mr Kendle hop right up as mad as
march hairs, and tell him if he shakes hands with a single federalist while he is gone, the democratic party will
be ruined. And then the President turns to me and
asks me what he had better do. And I tell him I guess
he better go straight ahead, and keep a stiff upper lip,
and shake hands with whoever he is a mind to.

Mr Van Buren staid with us awhile at the President's,
but he's moved into a house now on Pennsylvany Avenue. He's a fine slick man I can tell you, and the
President says he's the greatest man in America. He's
got the beat'em-est tongue that ever I see. If you had
a black hat on, he could go to talking to you and in ten
minutes he could make you think it was white.

Give my love to our folks up in Downingville when
you have a chance to send it to 'em, and believe me
your old friend,

                              MAJOR JACK DOWNING,

LETTER LVIII.

*In which Major Downing defends the President from the
assault of Lieut. Randolph on board the Steam-boat
Cygnet.*

On board the Steam-boat Cygnet, near the city of Alexandria,
down a little ways below Washington, May the 6th, 1833.

To the Editor of the Portland Courier in the Mariners' Church
Building, 2d story, Eastern end, Fore-street, away down East, in
the State of Maine.

My dear old Friend. — We've had a kind of a hurly
burly time here to-day. I did n't know but we should
burst the biler one spell; and some of us, as it was, got
scalding hot. You see, I and the President and a few
more gentlemen got into the steam-boat this morning to
go round into old Virginny to help lay the foundation of
a monument, so they should n't forget who Washington's mother was.

When we got down along to Alexandria, the boat
hauled up to the side of the wharf awhile to let some
more folks get in, and while she lay there, I and the
President and a few more of 'em sot in the cabin reading and chatting with one another. The President had
jest got through reading a letter from uncle Joshua
Downing, urging him very strongly to come up as fur as
Downingville when he comes on that way. And says
he, Major Downing, this uncle Joshua of yours is a real
true blue republican as I know of any where. I would
n't miss seeing him when I go down east for a whole
year's salary.

Says I, your honor, Downingville is the most thorough
going republican town there is any where in the eastern
country; and you ought not to come back till you have
visited it. Jest as I said that there was a stranger came
into the cabin and stept along up to the President, and

begun to pull off his glove. I thought there was some mischief bruing, for his lips were kind of quivery, and I did n't like the looks of his eyes a bit. But the President thought he was trying to get his gloves off to shake hands with him, and the good old man is always ready to shake hands with a friend; so he reached out his hand to him and smiled, and told him never to stand for the gloves, and the words want hardly out of his mouth when dab went one of the fellow's hands slap into the President's face.

In a moment I levelled my umbrella at the villain's head, and came pesky near fetching him to the floor. Two more gentlemen then clenched him by the collar and had him down as quick as ever you see a beef ox knocked down with an ax. In a minute there was a crowd round him as thick as a swarm of bees.

But, my stars, I wish you could have seen the President jest at that minute. If you ever see a lion lying down asleep and a man come along with a great club and hit him a polt with all his might, and then see that lion spring on his feet, and see the fire flash in his eyes, and hear him roar and gnash his teeth, you might give some sort of a guess what kind of a harrycane we had of it.

The old Gineral no sooner felt the fellow's paw in his face than he sprung like a steel-trap, and catched his cane and went at him. But there was such a crowd of men there in an instant, that it as was much impossible to get through 'em as it was for the British to get through his pile of cotton wool bags at New-Orleans. If it had n't been for that, I dont think but he would have kicked the feller through the side of the steam-boat in two minutes.

However, somehow or other the rascal got hussled out of the boat on to the wharf, and fled like a dog that had been stealing sheep. They have sent some officers after him, but where they will overtake him nobody knows.

The President has got cleverly cooled down again,

and we are going on to lay the foundation of the monument.

My love to all the good folks up in Downingville.

In haste your old friend,

MAJOR JACK DOWNING.

LETTER LIX.

In which Major Downing shakes hands for the President at Philadelphia, while on the grand tour down East.

To Uncle Joshua Downing, Post Master, up in Downingville, in the State of Maine. This to be sent by my old friend, the Editor of the Portland Courier, with *care and speed*.

Philadelphia, June 10, 1833.

DEAR UNCLE JOSHUA, — We are coming on full chisel. I've been trying, ever since we started, to get a chance to write a little to you; but when we've been on the road I couldn't catch my breath hardly long enough to write my name, we kept flying so fast; and when we made any stop, there was such a jam round us there wasn't elbow room enough for a miskeeter to turn round without knocking his wings off.

I'm most afraid now we shall get to Downingville before this letter does, so that we shall be likely to catch you all in the suds before you think of it. But I understand there is a *fast mail* goes on that way, and I mean to send it by that, so I'm in hopes you'll get it time enough to have the children's faces washed and their heads combed, and the gals get on their clean gowns. And if Sargent Joel *could* have time enough to call out my old Downingville Company and get their uniform brushed up a little, and come down the road as fur as your new barn to meet us, there's nothing that would please the President better. As for victuals, most any thing wont come amiss; we are as hungry as bears after travelling a hundred miles a day. A little fried pork and eggs, or a pot of baked beans and an Indian pudding would suit us much better than the soft stuff they give us here in these great cities.

The President wouldn't miss of seeing you for any thing in the world, and he will go to Downingville if he has legs and arms enough left when he goes to Portland to carry him there. But for fear any thing should happen that he shouldn't be able to come, you had better meet us in Portland, say about the 22d, and then you can go up to Downingville with us, you know.

This travelling with the President is capital fun after all, if it wasn't so plaguy tiresome. We come into Baltimore on a Rail Road, and we flew over the ground like a harrycane. There isn't a horse in this country that could keep up with us, if he should go upon the clean clip. When we got to Baltimore, the streets were filled with folks as thick as the spruce trees down in your swamp. There we found Black Hawk, a little, old, dried up Indian king. — And I thought the folks looked at him and the prophet about as much as they did at me and the President. I gave the President a wink that this Indian fellow was taking the shine off of us a little, so we concluded we wouldn't have him in our company any more, and shall go on without him.

I cant stop to tell you in this letter how we got along to Philadelphy, though we had a pretty easy time some of the way in the steam-boats. And I cant stop to tell you of half of the fine things I have seen here. They took us up into a great hall this morning as big as a meeting-house, and then the folks begun to pour in by thousands to shake hands with the President; federalists and all, it made no difference. There was such a stream of 'em coming in that the hall was full in a few minutes, and it was so jammed up round the door that they couldn't get out again if they were to die. So they had to knock out some of the windows and go out t'other way.

The President shook hands with all his might an hour or two, till he got so tired he couldn't hardly stand it. I took hold and shook for him once in awhile to help him along, but at last he got so tired he had to lay down on a soft bench covered with cloth and shake as well as he could, and when he couldn't shake he'd nod to 'em as they come along. And at last he got so beat out, he couldn't only wrinkle his forward and wink. Then I kind of stood behind him and reached my arm round under his, and shook for him for about a half an hour as tight as I could spring. Then we concluded it was best to adjourn for to-day.

And I've made out to get away up into the garret in the tavern long enough to write this letter. We shall be off to-morrow or next day for York, and if I can possibly get breathing time enough there, I shall write to you again.

Give my love to all the folks in Downingville, and believe me your loving neffu,

MAJOR JACK DOWNING.

———

LETTER LX.

In which the President and Major Downing have a very narrow escape at the breaking down of the bridge in New York.

To uncle Joshua Downing, Post Master up in Downingville, State of Maine, to be sent in the Portland Courier with care and speed.

NEW YORK CITY, Friday evening, June 14, 1833.

DEAR UNCLE JOSHUA, — Here we are amongst an ocean of folks, and cutting up capers as high as a cat's

'Then I took hold and shook hands for him about half an hour as tight as I could spring.'

back. I spose you will see by the papers how we all like to got drowned yesterday going across a little bridge between the castle and the garden.

It was a pesky narrow squeak for me and the President. He was riding over on a great fine hoss, and I was walking along by the side of him and trying to clear the way a little, for they crowded upon us so, there was no getting along, and hardly a chance to breathe. When we got under the arch we stopped a little bit for the crowd to clear away, when all at once I thought I heard something crack. Says I, Gineral, you better go ahead, I'm afraid there's mischief bruing here. At that he give his hoss a lick and pushed through the crowd, but we had n't got more than a rod, before crash went the bridge behind us, all down in a heap, and two toll-houses on top of it and as many as a hundred folks splashed into the water, all mixed up together one top of 'tother. The President looked over his shoulder, and seeing I was safe behind him, called out for Mr Van Buren, and asked me to run and see if he was hurt. I told him he had forgot himself, for Mr Van Buren was n't in the company; but Mr Woodbury and Mr Cass were in for it, for I could see them floundering about in the water now. Run, Major, said the President, run and give them a lift. Take Mr Woodbury first, you know I can't spare him at any rate.

So there was a parcel of us took hold and went to hauling of 'em out of the water like so many drownded rats. But we got 'em all out alive, except a few young things they called dandies; they looked so after they got wet all over that we could n't make out whether they were alive or dead. So we laid 'em up to dry and left 'em; and I went on to help the President review the troops on the battery, as they call it; and a grand place it is tu. I've seen more fine shows here, it seems to me, than ever I see before in my life. Such a sight of folks, and fine ladies, and fine houses, and vessels, and steamboats, and flags a flying, and cannons firing, and fire works a whisking about, I never see the beat of it. I didn't think there was so much fun in this world before, for all I've been about so much at Madawaska and among the nullifiers and all round.

But I cant tell you much about it till we get there, for I cant find any time to write. I've only catched a few minutes this evening while the President is gone into Mr Niblo's garden. One of the master sights that I've seen yet was that balloon that went up this afternoon, carrying a man with it. Poor fellow, I dont much think he'll ever get back again, for he looked to me the last I see of him as though he would land in England, or the moon, or some other country.

All these sights keep us back a little longer than we expected. I dont think now we shall be in Portland before the 28th or 29th of this month. So I thought I'd jest write you a line that you might be down there about that time.

In haste your loving neffu,
                    MAJOR JACK DOWNING,

LETTER LXI.

In which Major Downing describes the visit of the President at Boston, and also complains of the rascally counterfeiters that write letters in his name for the newspapers.

[*Note by the Editor.* It will be recollected that the President while in Boston, was for a few days seriously ill.]

Boston, Tuesday, June 25, 1833.

To the Editor of the Portland Courier.

MY DEAR OLD FRIEND, — I'm keeping house with the President to day, and bein he's getting considerable better, I thought I'd catch a chance when he was taking a knap, and write a little to let you know how we get along. This ere sickness of the President has been a bad pull-back to us. He hasn't been able to go out since Sunday afternoon, and I've been watchin with him this two nights, and if I wasn't as tough as a halter, I should be half dead by this time.

And if the President want tougher than a catamount, he'd kick the bucket before he'd been round to see one half the notions there is in Boston. Poor man, he has a hard time of it ; you've no idea how much he has to go through. It's worse than being dragged through forty knot holes.

To be bamboozled about from four o'clock in the morning till midnight, rain or shine, jammed into one great house to eat a breakfast, and into another great house to eat a dinner, and into another to eat supper, and into two or three others between meals, to eat cooliations, and to have to go out and review three or four rigiments of troops, and then to be jammed into Funnel Hall two hours, and shake hands with three or four thousand folks, and then to go into the State House and stand there two or three hours and see all Boston streaming through it like a river through a sawmill, and then to ride about the city awhile in a fine painted covered waggon with four or five horses to draw it, and then ride awhile in one without any cover to it, finney-fined off to the top notch, and then get on to the horses and ride awhile a horseback, and then run into a great picture room and see more fine pictures than you could shake a stick at in a week, and then go into some grand gentleman's house, and shake hands a half an hour with a flock of ladies, and then after supper go and have a little still kind of a hubbub all alone with three or four hundred particular friends, and talk an hour or two, and take another cooliation, and then go home, and about midnight get ready to go to bed, and up again at four o'clock the next morning and at it. — If this aint enough to tucker a feller out I dont know what is. The President wouldn't have stood it till this time if he hadn't sent me and Mr Van Buren and the rest of us to some of the parties, while he staid to home to rest.

The President's got so much better I think we shall be able to start for Salem to-morrow, for we must go through with it now we've begun, as hard work as 'tis. I think we shall get to Portland about the 4th of July ; so if you get your guns and things all ready you can kill two birds with one stone. I hope you'll be pretty careful there how you point your guns. They pointed 'em so careless at New York that one of the wads come within six inches of making daylight shine through the President.

Now I think ont, there is the most rascally set of fellers skulking about somewhere in this part of the country that ever I heard of, and I wish you would blow 'em up. They are worse than the pick-pockets. I mean them are fellers that's got to writing letters and putting my name to 'em, and sending of 'em to the printers. And I heard there was one sassy feller last Saturday down to Newburyport that got on to a horse, and rid about town calling himself Major Jack Downing, and all the soldiers and the folks marched up and shook hands with him, and thought it was me. — Now, my dear old friend, isn't this too bad ? What would you do if you was in my case ? I say again they are worse than the pick-pockets. Isn't it Mr Shakespeare that says something about ' he that steals my munny-pus steals trash, but he that steals my name ought to have his head broke ?' I wish you would find that story and print it.

There, the President's jest waked up, so I must subscribe myself, in haste,   Your friend,
                                        MAJOR JACK DOWNING.

LETTER LXII.

In which the President and the rest of 'em turn a short Corner at Concord and set their faces towards Washington.

CONCORD, Nu Hamsheer, June 30, 1833.
To the Editor of the Portland Courier.

MY DEAR OLD FRIEND,—The jig is all up about our going to Portland and Downingville. I've battled the watch with the President this two days about it, and told him he must go there if he had the breath of life in him; and he kept telling me he certainly would if horses could carry him there.

But the President is n't very well, and that aint the worst of it; there 's been a little difficulty bruin among us, and the President's got so riled about it, that he's finally concluded to start on his way back to morrow. I cant help it; but I feel bad enough about it. If I wasn't a military man I could cry a barrel of tears.

I dont know how they will stan it in Downingville when they come to get the news. I'm afraid there will be a master uproar there, for you know they are all full-blooded democrats.

But the stage is jest agoing to start, and I've only time to write you this line, in haste from your friend,

MAJOR JACK DOWNING.

18

LETTER LXIII.

In which cousin Nabby describes the unutterable disappointment at Downingville because the President did n't come, and tells what a terrible pucker ant Keziah was in about it.

GREAT UPROAR IN DOWNINGVILLE.

Letter from Major Downing's Cousin Nabby to the editor of the Portland Courier.

RESPECTABLE SIR:—As cousin Jack is always so mity budge in writing letters to you, and as he and the President has showed us a most provoking trick and run off like a stream of chalk back to Washington without coming here, after they had promised over and over again that they would come, and we had got all slicked up and our clean gownds on, and more good victuals cooked, than there ever was in all Downingville before, I say, Mr Editor, I declare it's tu bad; we are all as mad as blazes about it, and I mean to write and tell you all about it if I live, and if cousin Jack dont like it he may lump it, so there now.

Ye see cousin Jack writ to us that he and the President and some more gentlemen should be here the 4th of July, and we must spring to it and brush up and see how smart we could look and how many fine things we could show to the President. This was a Saturday before the 4th of July come a Thursday. The letter was to Uncle Joshua, the Post Master. Most all the folks in Downingville were at the Post Office waiting when the mail come in, for we expected to hear from Jack.

Uncle Joshua put on his spettacles and opened the mail and hauled out the papers and letters in a bunch. In a minute I see one to Uncle Joshua with the President's name on the outside; so I knew it was from Jack,

for the President always puts his name on Jack's letters. We all cried out to Uncle Joshua to open it and
let us know what was in it. But he's such a provoking
odd old man he would n't touch it till he got every one
of the papers and letters sorted and put up in their
places. And then he took it and set down in his arm
chair, and took out his tobacker box and took a chaw
of tobacker, and then he broke open the seal and sot
and chawed and read to himself. We all stood tiptoe
with our hearts in our mouths, and he must needs read
it over to himself three times, chawing his old quid and
once in awhile giving us a knowing wink, before he
would tell us what was in it. — And he would n't tell
us arter all, but, says he, you must all be ready to put
the best side out Thursday morning ; there'll be business
to attend to, such as Downingville never see before.

At that we all cut and run, and such a hubbub as we
were in from that time till Thursday morning I guess
you never see. Such a washing and scrubbing and
making new clothes and mending old ones and baking
and cooking. Every thing seemed to be in a clutter all
over the neighborhood. Sargent Joel flew round like a
ravin-distracted rooster. He called out his company
every morning before sun-rise and marched 'em up and
down the road three hours every day. He sent to the
store and got a whole new set of buttons and had 'em
sowed on to his regimental coat, and had a new piece of
red put round the collar. And had his trowses washed
and his boots greesed, and looked as though he might
take the shine off of most any thing. But the greatest
rumpus was at uncle Joshua's ; for they said the President must stay there all night. And ant Keziah was in
such a pucker to have every thing nice, I did n't know
but she would fly off the handle.

She had every part of the house washed from garret
to cellar, and the floors all sanded, and a bunch of green
bushes put into all the fire places. And she baked three

ovens full of dried punkin pies, besides a few dried
huckleberry pies, and cake, and a great pot of pork and
beans. But the worst trouble was to fix up the bed so
as to look nice; for ant Keziah declared the President
should have as good a night's lodging in her house as he
had in New York or Boston. So she put on two feather
beds on top the straw bed, and a bran new calico quilt
that she made the first summer after she was married
and never put it on a bed before. And to make it look as
nice as the New York beds, she took her red silk gown
and ripped it up and made a blanket to spread over the
top. And then she hung up some sheets all round the
bed-room, and the gals brought in a whole handful of
roses and pinks and pinned 'em up round as thick as flies
in August.

After we got things pretty much fixed, uncle Joshua
started off to meet cousin Jack and the President, and
left Sargent Joel to put matters to rights, and told us
we must all be ready and be paraded in the road by
nine o'clock Thursday morning. Well Thursday morning come, and we all mustered as soon as it was daylight and dressed up. The children were all washed
and had their clean aprons on and their heads combed
and were put under the care of the schoolmarm to be
paraded along with her scholers.

About eight o'clock all the village got together down
the road as fur as uncle Joshua's new barn; and Sargent Joel told us how to stand, as he said, in militery
order. He placed Bill Johnson and cousin Ephraim
out a little ways in front with each of 'em a great long
fowling piece with a smart charge in to fire a salute, and
told 'em as soon as the President hove in sight to let
drive, only be careful and pint their guns up so as not
to hurt any body. Then come Sargent Joel and his
company; and then come the schoolmarm and the
children; and then come all the women and gals over
sixteen with ant Keziah at their head; and then come

all the men in town that owned horses riding on horseback; and all the boys that Sargent Joel did n't think
was large enough to walk in the profession got up and
sot on the fences along by the side of the road.

There we stood till about nine o'clock, when sure
enough we saw somebody come riding out of the woods
down the hill. The boys all screamed ready to split
their throats hoorah for Jackson, and Bill Johnson fired
off his gun. Cousin Ephraim, who aint so easy flut-
tered, held on to his and did n't fire, for he could n't
see any body but uncle Joshua on his old grey horse.
Along come uncle Joshua on a slow trot, and we looked
and looked, but could n't see any body coming behind
him.

Then they all begun to look at one another as wild as
hawks and turn all manner of colors. When uncle
Joshua got up so we could see him pretty plain he looked as cross as a thunder cloud. He rid up to Sargent
Joel, and says he, you may all go home about your
business, and put away your knick-nacks, for Jack and
the President are half way to Washington by this time.

My stars! what a time there was then. I never see
so many folks boiling over mad before. Bill Johnson
threw his gun over into the field as much as ten rods,
and hopped up and down and struck his fists together
like all possessed. Sargent Joel marched back and
forth across the road two or three times, growing redder and redder, till at last he drew out his sword and
fetched a blow across a hemlock stump and snapped it
off like a pipe stem. Ant Keziah fell down in a conniption fit; and it was an hour before we could bring
her tu and get her into the house.—And when she come
to go round the house and see the victuals she had cooked up, and go into the bed-room and see her gown all
cut up, she went into conniption fits again and had 'em
half the night. But she's better to day, and has gone to
work to try to patch up her gown again.

18*

I thought I would jest let. you know about these
things, and if you are a mind to send word on to cousin
Jack and the President, I'm willing. You may tell 'em
there aint five folks in Downingville that would hoorah
for Jackson now, and I dont believe there's one that
would vote for him unless 'tis uncle Joshua, and he
would n't if he was n't afraid of losing the post office.

But there, uncle Joshua has called to me and says he
wont keep the mail open another minute for my letter,
so I must prescribe myself your respected friend,

NABBY DOWNING.

—

NOMINATION FOR THE PRESIDENCY.

From the National Intelligencer.

We do not know whether it be necessary, in copying
the subjoined effusion, to enter into a protest against
misinterpretation of our motives. We should be sorry
to be understood, whilst humoring a jest, as meaning
to burlesque so serious an action as the choice of President of the United States. We copy the following for
the sake of its moral, as well as its wit, and we do not
like the moral the less for being taught with a smiling
countenance.

From the Mauch Chunk Courier.

Our next President.

Many of the papers in the United States have already
manifested a disposition to agitate the subject of the next
Presidency, and several distinguished individuals have
been informally named for that office, among whom are
Mr Van Buren, Mr M'Lean, Mr Cass, Mr Clay and Mr
Webster. As we are opposed to a premature discussion
of this ticklish question, we have not hitherto committed
ourself in favour of either of these individuals. Indeed,
we have considered it very imprudent in these times, for

any one who wishes to be an orthodox politician, to "come out" for any body until he can ascertain who will be most likely to succeed. Accordingly we have stood upon our "reserved rights" of neutrality, to watch the signs of the times, and see who would probably be the most *popular* candidate. Recent indications have satisfactorily convinced us on that point, and as we wish to be considered among the "originals"— the *real Simon Pures*, we would lose no time in nominating

For President,

MAJOR JACK DOWNING,

Of Downingville.

In recommending this distinguished personage to our fellow citizens, it will be scarcely necessary to enumerate his various claims to their suffrages. Suffice it to say, his military renown, his valuable public services in assisting President Jackson to put down the Nullifiers, especially in shaking hands with the Yankees "down east," and last though not least, the fidelity with which he and his uncle Joshua stuck to the Old Hero after he found he was going to be President, eminently qualify him for that exalted station.

———

LETTER LXIV.

In which Major Downing tells about going to Cambridge and making the President a Doctor of Laws.

On board the Steam-boat, going from Providence to York, July 2, 1833.

To my old friend, the Editor of the Portland Courier, in the Mariners' Church building, second story, eastern end, Fore street, away down east in the State of Maine.

MY DEAR FRIEND. — We are driving back again full chisel, as fast as we come on when we were on the Rail

Road between Washington and Baltimore. And we 've been drivin so fast on a round turn in all the places where we've been, and have had so much shaking hands and eating and one thing another to do, that I could n't get time to write to you at half the places where I wanted to, so I thought I'd set down now, while the President's laid down to rest him awhile, and tell you something about Cambridge and Lowell. Ye see when we were at Boston they sent word to us to come out to Cambridge, for they wanted to make the President a Doctor of Laws. What upon arth a Doctor of Laws was, or why they wanted to make the President one, I could n't think. So when we come to go up to bed I asked the Gineral about it. And says I, Gineral, what is it they want to do to you out to Cambridge ? Says he they want to make a Doctor of Laws of me. Well, says I, but what good will that do ? Why, says he, you know Major Downing, there's a pesky many of them are laws passed by Congress, that are rickety things. Some of 'em have very poor constitutions, and some of 'em have n't no constitutions at all. So that it is necessary to have somebody there to Doctor 'em up a little, and not let 'em go out into the world where they would stan a chance to catch cold and be sick, without they had good constitutions to bear it. You know, says he, I have had to doctor the Laws considerable ever since I've been at Washington, although I was n't a regular bred Doctor. And I made out so well about it, that these Cambridge folks think I better be made into a regular Doctor at once, and then there 'll be no grumbling and disputing about my practice. Says he, Major, what do you think of it ? I told him I thought it was an excellent plan ; and asked him if he did n't think they would be willing, bein I'd been round in the military business considerable for a year or two past, to make me a Doctor of War. He said he did n't know, but he thought it would be no harm to try 'em. But says he, Major, I feel a little kind of streaked about it after all ; for they say they will go to talking to me in Latin, and although I studied it a little once, I dont know any more about it now than the man in the moon. And how I can get along in that case I dont know. I told him my way, when any body talked to me in a lingo that I did'nt understand, was jest to say nothing, but look as knowing as any of 'em, and then they ginerally thought I knew a pesky sight more than any of 'em. At that the Gineral fetched me a slap on my shoulder, and haw hawed right out. Says he, Major Downing, you are the boy for me ; I dont know how I should get along in this world if it was n't for you.

So when we got ready we went right to Cambridge as bold as could be. And that are Cambridge is a real pretty place; it seems to me I should like to live in them Colleges as well as any place I've ssen. We went into the Libry, and I guess I stared a little, for I did n't think before there was half so many books in the world. I should think there was near about enough to fill a meetin house. I dont believe they was ever all read or ever will be to all ages.

When we come to go in to be made Doctors of, there was a terrible crowding round ; but they give us a good place, and then sure enough they did begin to talk in Latin or some other gibberish ; but whether they were talking to the Gineral, or who 'twas, I could n't tell. I guess the Gineral was a little puzzled. But he never said a word, only once in a while bowed a little. And I spose he happened sometimes to put in the bows in the wrong place, for I could see some of the sassy students look up one side once in a while, and snicker out of one corner of their mouths. Howsomever the Gineral stood it out like a hero, and got through very well. And when 'twas over, I stept up to Mr Quincy and asked him if he would n't be so good as to make me a Doctor of War, and hinted to him a little about my services down to Madawasca and among the nullifiers. At that he made

me a very polite bow, and says he, Major Downing, we
should be very happy to oblige you if we could, but we
never give any degrees of war here ; all our degrees are
degrees of peace. So I find I shall have to practise war
in the natural way, let nullification, or what will, come.
After 'twas all over we went to Mr Quincy's and had a
capital dinner. And on the whole had about as good a
visit to Cambridge as most any where.

I meant to a told you considerable about Lowell, but
the steamboat goes so fast, I shant have time to. We
went all over the Factories ; and there ! I wont try to
say one word about 'em, for I've been filled with such a
wonderment ever since, that my ideas are all as big as
hay stacks, and if I should try to get one of 'em out of
my head, it would tear it all to pieces. It beat all that
ever I heard of before, and the Gineral said it beat all
that ever he heard of. But what made the Gineral hold
his head up and feel more like a soldier, than he had
before since he was at New Orleans, was when we
marched along the street by them are five thousand gals,
all dressd up and looking as pretty as a million of but-
terflies. The Gineral marched along as light as a boy,
and seems to me I never see his eyes shine so bright
afore. After we got along about to the middle of 'em,
he whispered to me, and says he, Major Downing, is
your Cousin Nabby here among 'em ; if she is, I must
be introduced to her. I told him she was not ; as they
were expecting us to come to Downingville, she staid
to home to help get ready. Well, says he, if any thing
should happen that we can't go to Downingville, you
must send for your Cousin Nabby and Uncle Joshua to
come on to Washington to see me. I will bear all the
expenses, if they will only come, says he ; these northern gals are as much afore our southern and western
gals as can be, and I've thought of your Cousin Nabby
a great deal lately — he looked as though he was going
to say something more, but Mr Van Buren and the rest

of 'em crowded along up so near that it broke it off, and
we had to go along.

I see we've got most to York, and shall have to go ashore
in a few minutes, so I can't write any more now, but
remain your sincere and loving friend,

MAJOR JACK DOWNING.

———

LETTER LXV.

*In which Major Downing tells about the quarrel that he and
Mr Van Buren had at Concord after they went up cham-
ber to bed ; and also declares his intention to run for the
Presidency.*

Washington City, July 20, 1833.

To my old friend, the editor of the Portland Courier, away down
east in the State of Maine.

MY DEAR OLD FRIEND, YOU. — I dont know but you
might think strange on 't, that I should be back here to
Washington more than a fortnight, and not write to you.
But I hant forgot you. You need n't never be afraid of
that. We aint very apt to forget our best friends ; and
you may depend upon it Jack Downing will never forget
the editor of the Portland Courier any more than Andrew
Jackson will forget Jack Downing. You was the first
person that ever give me a lift into public life, and you
've been a boosting me along ever since. And jest between you and me I think I 'm getting into a way now
where I shall be able by and by to do something to pay you
for it. The reason that I have n't writ to you before, is,
that we have had pretty serious business to attend to since
we got back. But we 've jest got through with it, and
Mr Van Buren has cleared out and gone back about the
quickest to New York, and I guess with a bed-bug in his

ear.   Now jest between you and me in confidence, I 'll
tell you how 't is; but pray dont let on about it to any
body else for the world.   Did n't you think plaguy
strange what made us cut back so quick from Concord
without going to Portland or Portsmouth or Downingville ?   You know the papers have said it was because
the President want very well, and the President had to
make that excuse himself in some of his letters; but it
was no such thing.   The President could a marched on
foot twenty miles a day then, and only let him been at
the head of my Downingville company and he 'd a
made a whole British regiment scamper like a flock of
sheep.

But you see the trouble ont was, there was some difficulty between I and Mr Van Buren.   Some how or other
Mr Van Buren always looked kind of jealous at me all
the time after he met us at New York ; and I could n't
help minding every time the folks hollered ' hoorah for
Major Downing' he would turn as red as a blaze of fire.

And wherever we stopped to take a bite or to have a
chat, he would always work it, if he could, somehow or
other so as to crowd in between me and the President.
Well, ye see, I wouldn't mind much about it, but would
jest step round 'tother side.   And though I say it myself, the folks would look at me, let me be on which side
I would ; and after they'd cried hoorah for the President,
they'd most always sing out ' hoorah for Major Downing.'   Mr Van Buren kept growing more and more fidg-
ety till we got to Concord.   And there we had a room
full of sturdy old democrats of New Hampshire, and
after they had all flocked round the old President and
shook hands with him, he happened to introduce me to
some of 'em before he did Mr Van Buren.   At that the
fat was all in the fire.   Mr Van Buren wheeled about
and marched out of the room looking as though he could
bite a board nail off.   The President had to send for
him three times before he could get him back into the

We got so high at last, the President hopped off of the bed like a boy.

room again. And when he did come, he didn't speak
to me for the whole evening. However we kept it from
the company pretty much; but when we come to go up
to bed that night, we had a real quarrel. It was nothing but jaw, jaw, the whole night. Mr Woodbury and
Mr Cass tried to pacify us all they could, but it was all
in vain, we didn't one of us get a wink of sleep, and
shouldn't if the night had lasted a fortnight. Mr Van
Buren said the President had dishonored the country by
placing a military Major on half pay before the second
officer of the government. The President begged him
to consider that I was a very particular friend of his;
that I had been a great help to him at both ends of the
country; that I had kept the British out of Madawaska
away down in Maine, and had marched my company
clear from Downingville to Washington, on my way to
South Carolina, to put down the nullifiers; and he
thought I was entitled to as much respect as any man
in the country.

This nettled Mr Van Buren peskily. —He said he
thought it was a fine time of day if a raw jockey from
an obscure village away down east, jest because he had
a Major's commission, was going to throw the Vice
President of the United States and the heads of Departments into the back ground. At this my dander began
to rise, and I stepped right up to him; and says I, Mr
Van Buren, you are the last man that ought to call me
a jockey. And if you'll go to Downingville and stand
up before my company with Sarjeant Joel at their head,
and call Downingville an obscure village, I'll let you use
my head for a foot-ball as long as you live afterwards.
For if they wouldn't blow you into ten thousand atoms,
I'll never guess again. We got so high at last that the
old President hopt off the bed like a boy; for he had
laid down to rest him, bein it was near daylight, though
he couldn't get to sleep. And says he, Mr Donaldson,
set down and write Mr Anderson at Portland, and my

19

friend Joshua Downing at Downingville, that I can't come. I'm going to start for Washington this morning. What, says Mr Cass, and not go to Portsmouth and Exeter and round there! I tell you, says the President, I'm going to start for Washington this morning, and in three days I'll be there. What, says Mr Woodbury, and not go to Portland, where they have spent so much money to get ready for us! I tell you, says the President, my foot is down : I go not a step further, but turn about this morning for Washington. What, says I, and not go to Downingville, what will Uncle Joshua say ? At this the President looked a little hurt ; and says he, Major Downing, I can't help it. As for going any further with such a din as this about my ears, I cannot, and will not, and I am resolved not to budge another inch. And sure enough the President was as good as his word, and we were all packed up by sunrise, and in three days we were in Washington.

And here we've been ever since, battling the watch about the next Presidency. Mr Van Buren says the President promised it to him, and now he charges me and the President with a plot to work myself into it and leave him out. It's true I've been nominated in a good many papers, in the National Intelligencer, and in the Munch Chunk Courier printed away off among the coal diggers in Pennsylvany, and a good many more. And them are Pennsylvany chaps are real pealers for electing folks when they take hold ; and that's what makes Mr Van Buren so uneasy. The President tells him as he has promised to help him, he shall do what he can for him ; but if the folks *will* vote for me he can't help it. Mr Van Buren wanted I should come out in the National Intelligencer and resign, and so be put up for Vice President under him. But I told him no ; bein it had gone so fur I wouldn't do nothing about it. I hadn't asked for the office, and if the folks had a mind to give it to me I wouldn't refuse it. So after we had battled it about a fortnight, Mr Van Buren found it was no use to try to dicker with me, and he's cleared out and gone to New York to see what he can do there.

I never thought of getting in to be President so soon, though I've had a kind of hankering for it this two years. But now, seeing it's turned out as it has, I'm determined to make a bold push, and if I *can* get in by the free votes of the people, I mean to. The President says he rather I should have it than any body else, and if he hadn't promised Mr Van Buren beforehand, he would use his influence for me.

I remember when I was a boy about a dozen years old, there was an old woman come to our house to tell fortunes. And after she'd told the rest of 'em, father says he, here's Jack, you haven't told his fortune yet, and I dont spose it's worth a telling, for he's a real mutton-headed boy. At that the old woman catched hold of my hair, and pulled my head back and looked into my face, and I never shall forget how she looked right through me, as long as I live. At last, says she, and she gin me a shove that sent me almost through the side of the house, Jack will beat the whole of you. He 'll be a famous climber in his day, and wherever he sets out to climb, you may depend upon it, he will go to the top of the ladder. Now, putting all these things to- gether, and the nominations in the papers, and the 'hoorahs for Major Downing,' I dont know what it means, unless it means that I must be President. So, as I said afore, I'm determined to make a bold push. I've writ to Col. Crocket to see if I can get the support of the western States, and his reply is, '*go ahead.*' I shall depend upon you and uncle Joshua to carry the State of Maine for me ; and, in order to secure the other States, I spose it will be necessary to publish my life and writings. President Jackson had his life published be- fore he was elected, and when Mr Clay was a candidate he had hisn published. I've talked with the President about it, and he says, publish it by all means, and set the printer of the Portland Courier right about it.

So I want you to go to work as soon as you get this, and pick up my letters, and begin to print 'em in a book ; and I'll set down and write a history of my life to put into it, and send it along as fast as I can get it done. But I want you to be very careful not to get any of them are confounded counterfict letters, that the rascally fellers have been sending to the printers, mixed in long with mine. It would be as bad as breaking a rotten egg in long with the good ones ; it would spile the whole pudding. You can tell all my letters, for they were all sent to you first.

The President says I must have a picter of me made and put into the book. — He says he had one put into his, and Mr Clay had one put into his. So I believe I shall write to Mr Thatcher that prints the little Journal paper in Boston, and get him to go to some of the best picter-makers there, and get them to do me up some as slick as they can. These things, you know, will all help get the free votes of the people ; and that's all I want. For I tell you now, right up and down, I never will take any office that doesn't come by the free votes of the people. I'm a genuine democratic republican, and always was, and so was my father before me, and uncle Joshua besides.

There's a few more things that I want to speak to you about in this letter, but I'm afraid it will get to be too lengthy. That are story that they got in the newspapers about my being married in Philadelphy is all a hoax. I aint married yet, nor I shant be till a little blue-eyed gal, that used to run about with me, and go to school and slide down hill in Downingville is the wife of President Downing. And that are other story, that the President give me a Curnel's commission jest before we started down east, isn't exactly true. The President did offer me one, but I thanked him, and told him if he would excuse me, I should rather not take it, for I had always noticed that Majors were more apt to rise in the world than Curnels.

I wish you would take a little pains to send up to Downingville and get uncle Joshua to call a public meeting, and have me nominated there. I'm so well known there, it would have a great effect in other places. And I want to have it particularly understood, and so stated in their resolutions, that I am the genuine democratic republican candidate. I know you will put your shoulder to the wheel in this business and do all you can for me, for you was always a good friend to me, and, jest between you and me, when I get in to be President you may depend upon it you shall have as good an office as you want.

But I see it's time for me to end this letter. The President is quite comfortable, and sends his respects to you and uncle Joshua. I remain your sincere friend.

MAJOR JACK DOWNING.

————

LETTER LXVI.

In which Cousin Ephraim describes the method of putting
' dimocrats' over on to the federal side.

Downingville, State of Maine, August 12, 1833.

To Cousin Major Jack Downing, at Washington city, or else gone long with the President down to the Rip Raps. To be sent privately in the Portland Courier.

DEAR COUSIN JACK. — I've got something pretty heavy on my mind that I want to tell ye about, and ask your advice, and may be I shall want you to lend me a hand a little. I've been watching politics pretty snug ever since I was a little boy, and that's near about forty years;

19*

and I believe I know most as much about it as uncle Joshua, although he's twenty years older than I be. Now about this republicanism and federalism, I've minded that it always keeps changing, and always has, ever since I can remember. And I've minded tu it most always keeps going round one way; that is, the young federalists keep turning dimocrats, and the old dimocrats keep turning federalists. What it's for I dont exactly know, but that's the way it goes. I spose a man, on the whole, is n't hardly fit to be a dimocrat after he gets to be fifty years old. And here is old uncle Joshua in the Post Office, he's got to be about sixty, and he's hanging on to the dimocratic side yet, like the tooth-ache; and it begins to worry me a good deal. I think it's high time he went over. You know Downingville has always been a genuine republican town, and I want it should always go according to the *usages* [I think that's what they call it] of the dimocratic party.

When it gets to be time for an old dimocrat to go over on the federal side, I believe the Argus always puts 'em over. You remember there was old Mr Insley in Port-land, and old Gineral Wingate in Bath, as much as a dozen years ago, were some as big republicans as there was any where about. Well, they got to be considerable old, and had been in office sometime, so the Argus took and clapt 'em right over on to the federal side. And you know there was Mr Holmes, he was a whapping great republican. But he begun to grow old, and so the Argus put him over. And there was Mr Sprague; he was such a nice dimocrat every one said it was a pitty to put him over. But bein he'd been to Congress some-time, the Argus would n't hear a word, but shoved him right over.

And this summer the Argus is putting of 'em over con-siderable younger on to the federal side. It has put Judge Preble over, and Judge Ware, and Mr Mitchell, the Post Master at Portland, and he isn't near so old as uncle Joshua, and it has put Mr Megquier over, only think, such a young man as Mr Megquier, that's only been in the Sinnet three or four years. Now dont you think, according to dimocratic usage, it is high time old uncle Joshua was put over? I wish you would jest write to the Argus and have it done, for I feel a good deal worried about it.

And as soon as it comes out in the Argus that he is fairly over, I want you to tell the President that uncle Joshua is a federalist, and have him removed from the Post Office, for it would be an everlasting shame to have the Post Office in Downingville kept by a federalist.

N. B. If uncle Joshua should be removed I wish you would use your influence to get the President to give the office to me; for next to Uncle Joshua I spose I've done more for the republican party than any man in Downingville. I can have a recommendation from Sargent Joel and all the company. By attending to this you will much oblige your friend and cousin,

EPHRAIM DOWNING.

LETTER LXVII.

In which the President begun to say something about ME *and* DANIEL.

Washington City, Sept. 14, 1833.

To the Editor of the Portland Courier, away down East, in the State of Maine.

MY DEAR OLD FRIEND,—Its got to be a pretty considerable long while now since I've writ to you, for I never like to write, you know, without I have something to say.—But I've got something on my mind now, that

keeps me all the time a thinking so much that I cant
hold in any longer. So jest between you and me I'll
tell you what 'tis. But I must begin a little ways beforehand, so you can see both sides of it, and I'll tell
you what 'tis as soon as I get along to it.

You see I and the President has been down to the
Rip Raps a few weeks to try to recruit up a little; for
that pesky tower away down East like to did the job for
the old Gineral. So, after we got things pretty much
to rights here, we jest stepped aboard the steamboat and
went down to the Rip Raps. That are Rip Raps is a
capital place; it is worth all the money we ever paid for
it, if it was for nothing else only jest to recruit up the
Government. It is one of the most coolest places in the
summer time that you ever see. Let a feller be all worn
out and wilted down as limpsy as a rag, so that the doctors would think he was jest ready to fly off the handle,
and let him go down to the Rip Raps and stay there a
fortnight, and he'd come up again as smart as a steel-
trap. The President got recruited up so nicely, while
we were down to the Rip Raps, that ever since we got
back till two or three days ago, he has been as good-
natured and sociable as ever I should wish to see a body.
And now I'm coming, pretty soon, to what I was going
to tell you about, that bears so heavy on my mind.

You see the President likes, every morning after the
breakfast is out of the way, to set down and read over
the newspapers, and see what is going on in the country, and who's elected and so on. So when we've done
breakfast, we take the letters and papers that come
from the Post-Office, and go away by ourselves into the
great East Room where we can say jest what we've
a mind to, and nobody not hear us, and the President
sets down in his great arm rocking-chair and smokes his
segar, and I set down by the table and read to him.
Last Monday morning, as I was reading over the papers
one arter another, I come to a Pennsylvany paper and

opened it, and, says I, hullow, gineral, here's a speech of Mr Webster at Pittsburg, as large as life. Ah, said he; well, let us hear what Daniel has been talking to them are Pennsylvany and Ohio chaps about. So I hitched back in my chair, and read on. And by and by I begun to get into the marrow of the story, where he told all about Nullification, and what a dark time we had of it last winter, and how the black clouds begun to rise and spread over the country, and the thunders of civil war begun to roll and rumble away off to the South, and by and by how the tempest was jest ready to burst over our heads and split the country all into shivers, and how, in the very nick of time, the President's Proclamation came out and spread over the whole country like a rain-bow, and how every body then took courage and said the danger was all over. While I had been reading this, the President had started up on his feet, and walked back and forth across the room pretty quick, puffing away and making the smoke roll out of his mouth like a house a fire; and by the time I had got through, he had thrown his segar out of the window, and come and sot down, leaning his elbow on the table and looking right in my face. I laid the paper down, and there he sot looking right at me as much as five minutes, and never said a word; but he seemed to keep a thinking as fast as a horse could run. At last, said he, Major Downing, were you ever told that you resembled Daniel Webster?

Why, Gineral, says I, how do you mean, in looks or what?

Why perhaps a little of both says he, but mostly in looks.

Bless my stars, says I, Gineral, you dont mean to say that I am quite so *dark* as he is.

Perhaps not, says he; but you have that sharp knowing look, as though you could see right through a mill-stone. I know, says he, that Mr Webster is rather a dark looking man, but there is n't another man in this country that can throw so much *light* on a dark subject as he can.

Why yes, says I, he has a remarkable faculty for that; he can see through most any thing, and he can make other folks see through it too. I guess, says I, if he 'd been born in old Virginny he 'd stood next to most any body.

A *leetle* afore 'em, says the Giniral, in my way of thinking. I 'll tell you what 't is Major, I begin to think your New Englanders aint the worst sort of fellows in the world after all.

Ah well says I, seeing is believing, and you 've been down that way now and can judge for yourself. But if you had only gone as fur as Downingville I guess you would have thought still better of 'em than you do now. Other folks may talk larger and bluster more, says I, but whenever you are in trouble, and want the real support in time of need, go to New England for it and you never need to be afraid but what it will come.

I believe you are right, says the Giniral; for notwithstanding all I could do with my proclamation against nullification, I believe I should have rubbed hard if there had been no such men in the country as Major Downing and Daniel Webster.

But this nullification business is n't killed yet. The tops are beat down, but the roots are alive as ever, and spreading under ground wider and wider, and one of these days when they begin to sprout up again there 'll be a tougher scrabble to keep 'em down than there has been yet; and I 've been thinking, says he, and he laid his hand on my shoulder and looked very anxious, I 've been thinking says he, *if you and Daniel* —— and here the door opened and in cometh Amos Kendil with a long letter from Mr Van Buren about the Bank and the safety fund and the Government deposites and I dont know what all; and the President's brow was clouded in a minute; for he always feels kind of pettish when they plague him about the safety fund. I have n't had any chance to talk with him since, there 's so many of 'em round him ; and I 'm as uneasy as a fish out of water, I feel so anxious to know what the President was going to say about me and Daniel.   I shall watch the first chance when I think it will do to talk with him, and find out what he was going to say.   I cant hardly sleep a nights, I think so much about it.   When I find out I 'll write to you again.

Send my love to the folks up in Downingville when you have a chance.

I remain your sincere friend,

MAJOR JACK DOWNING.

LETTER LXVIII.

In which the President finished what he was going to say about ME *and* DANIEL.

Washington City, Sept. 30, 1833.

To the Editor of the Portland Courier, away down east in the State of Maine.

MY DEAR FRIEND, — Havn't you been in a terrible kind of a pucker ever since my last letter to you, to know what the President was going to say about me and Daniel ?   If you havn't, I have.   I never felt so uneasy for a fortnight hardly in my life.   If I went to bed I couldn't sleep, and I've got up and walked the floor as much as half the night almost every night since. — I've wished the Bank to Guinea more than fifty times, for there's been such a hubbub here about the Bank this fortnight past, that I couldn't get a moment's chance to talk with the President about any thing else.   We'd have cabinet meetings once in awhile to see about mov-

ing the deposites, and Mr Duane and Mr Cass and Mr
McLane would talk up to the President so about it, that
he'd conclude to let 'em alone and do nothing about it,
and let Congress manage it jest as they'd amind to.
And then we'd go home and Mr Kendle would come in
and talk the matter over, and read some great long letters from Mr Van Buren, and get the President so con-
fused that he would lose all patience a most.

But Mr Kendle is the master feller to hang on that
ever I see ; he's equal to the tooth ache. And he talked and palavered with the President till he finally
brought him over, and then the President put his foot
down, and said the deposites should be moved whether
or no. And then the botheration was to see who should
move 'em. The President told Mr Duane to do it ; but
he said his conscience wouldn't let him. Then the
President told Mr Taney to take Mr Duane's place, and
see if his conscience would let him. Mr Taney tried it
and found his conscience went easy enough, so Mr Duane packed up and went home to Philadelphy. We
were all dreadful sorry to lose Mr Duane, for he was a
nice man as you will see one in a thousand. It's a pity
he had such a stiff conscience; he might have staid here
in the Treasury jest as well as not, if it hadn't been for
that.

But this storm about the Bank begins to blow over,
and the President's got in a manner cooled down again.
This morning after breakfast we took the papers and
letters jest as we used to, and went away into the east
room to read the news and chat awhile ; and it really
did my heart good to see the President set down once
more looking so good natured in his great arm chair
smoking his segar. After I had read over the news to
him awhile, and got him in pretty good humour, I made
bold to out with it, and says I Gineral, there's one question I want to ask you. — And says he, you know Major,
I always allow you to ask me any thing you're a mind

to, what is it? Well says I, when we had that talk here about a fortnight ago, you begun to say something about me and Daniel; and jest as you got into the middle of it, Mr Kendle came in and broke it right off short as a pipe stem. It's been running in my head ever since, and I've been half crazy to know what it was you was going to say. Well, let us see, says the Gineral, where was it I left off; for this everlasting fuss about the Bank has kept my head so full I can't seem to remember much about it.

Why says I, you was talking about nullification; how the tops were beat down a little, but the roots were all running about under ground as live as ever, and it would n't be long before they'd be sprouting up again all over the country, and there'd be a tougher scrabble to keep 'em down than ever there had been yet; and then you said *if I and Daniel* —— and there that plaguy Kendle came in, I've no patience with him now when I think of it, and broke it right off. Ah, now I remember, says the Gineral, how twas. Well, says he, Major Downing, it is a solemn fact, this country is to see a blacker storm of nullification before many years comes about than ever it has seen yet; the clouds are beginning to gather now; I've seen 'em rolling over South Carolina, and hanging about Georgia, and edging along into old Virginny, and I see the storm's a gathering; it must come, and if there is n't somebody at the helm that knows how to steer pretty well, the old ship must go down. I aint afraid, says he, but what I can keep her up while I have the command, but I'm getting to be old and must give up soon, and then what'll become of her I dont know. But what I was going to say was this; I've been thinking if you and Daniel, after I give up, would put your heads together and take charge of her till the storm has blown over, you might save her. And I dont know who else can.

But how do you mean, Gineral, says I? Why to speak

plain, says he, if nullification shows its head, Daniel must talk and you must fight. There's nothing else will do the job for it that I know of. Daniel must go into the Presidential chair, and you must take command of the army, and then things will go straight. At this I was a little struck up; and I looked him right in the eye, and, says I, Gineral, do you mean that Daniel Webster ought to be President after you give up? Certainly, says he, if you want to keep the country out of the jaws of nullification. But, says I, Gineral, Daniel is a federalist, a Hartford Convention federalist, and I should like to know which is worst, the jaws of nullification, or the jaws of federalism. The jaws of a fiddle-stick! said the President, starting up and throwing his segar out of the window as much as two rods; but how do you know, Major Downing, that Daniel is a federalist? Because, says I, I've heard him called so down east more than a hundred times. And that's jest all you know about it, says he. Now I tell you how 'tis, Major Downing, Daniel is as thorough a republican as you be, or as I be, and has been ever since my Proclamation came out against nullification. As soon as that Proclamation came out Daniel came right over on to the republican ground and took it upon his shoulder and carried it through thick and thin where no other man in the country could have carried it. Says I, Gineral, is that a fact? And says he yes, you may depend upon it, 'tis every word truth. Well says I, that alters the case a little, and I'll write to Uncle Joshua and the editor of the Portland Courier and see what they think of it, and if they think it's best to have Daniel for President we'll have him in, and I'll take my turn afterwards: for seeing the people are bent upon having me for President I wont decline, though if it is thought best that I should wait a little while, I wont be particular about that. I'm willing to do that which will be best for the country.

So I remain your loving friend,

MAJOR JACK DOWNING.

LETTER LXIX.

In which Cousin Nabby describes her visit to Mr Maelzel's Congregation of Moskow.

Portland, October 22, 1833.

To Cousin Sally Downing, up in Downingville, in the care of Uncle Joshua, Post Master.

DEAR COUSIN : — I got here about noon yesterday, muddy and wet enough. Such dreadful muddy roads for the time of year, seems to me there never was before. Butter fetches a grand price. They would n't offer but eighteen cents at first, but soon as they come to see it and taste of it, they give me twenty cents right off for all of yours and mine, and never said a word. — So much for keeping a neat churn and clean milk-pans. The yarn and footins sold pretty well too, but I wont stop to tell you about that till I get back.

I'm going to stop here with ant Sally till next week, and I want you to come down if you can any way in the world, for here's a sight here that would make you jump higher than the cat's back if you should see it. I'll jest tell you a little about it. When I got here yesterday, I found ant Sally all in a flutter about going to see the congregation of Moskow. She said she was going to carry the children, and nothing would do but I must go too. She said it would n't cost but two and thrippence, and she would pay it rather than not have me go, for she should n't mind the pay, as all that was paid that evening would be given to the societies what takes care of little orphan children and carries wood to poor freezing widows. When she said that, I felt as though I should be willing to give two pounds of butter myself. So we all fixed and off we went up to Union Hall about seven o'clock.

I cant stop to tell you much about the sights I see there, but you *must* come and see 'em without fail. I dont know but they 've nigh upon scared me out of a year's growth ; they showed us first a little feller they called a fidler. I dont know what he was made of but he acted jest as though he was alive. He was n't more than a foot long, and he sot down in a chair as pretty as a little man. And somebody played some music to him and that sot him all of a didder, and he made his little fiddle stick fly so I did n't know but he would shake his arm off. Then they brought out a little doll baby ; a sweet looking little creature, dressed up as neat as a pink. And they brought it along up to us, and as true as you are alive it spoke right out and said ma-ma. I could n't hardly believe my own ears at first, but it said ma-ma again, and pa-pa, more than twenty times.

Then they sot a couple of little fellers up on a rope, and they went to hopping and jumping and dancing about, and whirling over and over round the rope, till I thought they would fall and break their necks more than fifty times. The prettiest one would sit up so straight, and turn his head round and look at us, and hold his hands out to us, that I told ant Sally I knew he was alive and I'd go and take the dear little creature down before he fell and killed himself. But she held on to me and declared I should n't go, for he had n't any more life in him than an ax handle ; but I cant hardly believe it now.

Then they said they would show us the Congregation of Moskow. And presently I begun to hear a racket and drums and fifes agoing, and bells a dinging, and by and by they pulled away some great curtains, that hung clear across the Hall, and there was a sight that beat all I ever see before. I jumped and was going to run for the door at first, for I thought Portland was all afire ; but ant Sally held on to me till I got pacified a little, and then I sot down.

And, there, I must say it was the grandest sight that ever I did see. A thousand buildings and meeting houses all in a light flame, and the fire and smoke rolling up to the clouds, and thousands and thousands of soldiers marching and riding through the streets, and the drums and the fifes and the bugles and the bells and the guns; O Sally, you must come and see it, if you have to come afoot and alone as the gal went to be married. The man says in the papers he aint agoing to keep it here only till next Friday night; but I'll coax him as hard as I can to stay till next week, so you can have a chance to see it. In haste your loving Cousin,

NABBY DOWNING.

LETTER LXX.

In which Major Downing concludes it is best to put some of his poetry into his book.

Washington, Oct. 20, 1833.

To the Editor of the Portland Courier, away down east in the State of Maine.

MY DEAR OLD FRIEND, -- I am glad you have got Mr Lilly, Wait, and Company, in Boston to print my book, for they say they print about the prettiest books there is agoing now days, and as many of 'em too as most any body. I shall go on to Boston in a few days, so as to see to it, and have it well done. I've been a thinking it might help the matter along some towards my getting in to be President, if you would look up that are piece of poetry that I writ for you three or four years ago about Sam Patch, and put it into the book. I dont know as many of the Presidents have wrote much poetry; but they say Quincy Adams has considerable, and

20*

it's helped him along a good deal.   And as I dont want
to leave any stone unturned that would be likely to help
me in, I think it's best to put that in the book.

I remain your loving friend,

MAJOR JACK DOWNING.

MAJOR DOWNING'S BIOGRAPHY OF SAM PATCH, THE JUMPER.

NOTE, BY THE EDITOR. There are some striking parallels between the race run by the renowned Sam Patch, of jumping memory, who figured in this jumping world in the year, *(anno Domini)* one thousand eight hundred and twenty-nine, and the no less renowned Major Jack Downing, who is figuring away ' in the full tide of successful experiment' at this present era. We think it fortunate for the memory of the jumping hero, as well as for the world, that his wonderful achievements have been recorded by so illustrious a genius and accomplished writer as Major Downing. It is fitting that their memory should go down to posterity together. They were both humble in their origin, and both were aspiring and lofty in their ambition. Neither of them however ever stooped to run after popularity, for popularity always run after them. Sam commenced with taking small jumps, and Jack commenced with reaching after small offices. Sam's ambition soon led him to leap from high bridges and factory walls, and Jack began anon to think of a Governor's chair and a seat in the Cabinet at Washington. Sam at length would stop nothing short of jumping down the falls of Gennesee and Niagara, and Jack has fixed his eye upon the lofty mark and is pressing forward with full vigor for the Presidency of the United States. Sam's last jump was a fatal one, and we sincerely hope the parallel may not be carried out, but that the Major may yet see many good days, and continue to serve his country as faithfully as he has hitherto done.

But we must explain how Major Downing came to be the biographer of Sam Patch.

While Mr Downing (we say Mr, because it was before he received any office) was attending upon the Legislature of Maine in 1830, one day when the wheels of government were clogged and some of the Senators had run away and there was nothing doing, Mr Downing came into our room, and sat down and looked over a file of newspapers. He soon got upon the achievements of Sam Patch, whose career had a short time before closed, and he read his history through. Mr Downing's head was full of the matter. He never read any thing before that filled him with such intense interest. He had got upon the track of a kindred spirit, and he was all animation. He went home with us and spent the night; but he could talk of nothing and think of nothing but Sam Patch. He had got his story by heart, and he was talking it over in his sleep all night. In the morning he rose pale and nervous. Says he, 'I believe that story of Sam Patch has been ground over in my head more than forty times to-night, and its got so now it comes through my head in lines all about the same length, jest like rolls out of a carding machine; and if you 'll give me some paper and pen and ink, I 'll put it down.' We furnished him accordingly, and he sat down and wrote the following splendid piece of biography, which we published in the Courier at the time and now insert in the volume of his life and writings.

BIOGRAPHY OF SAM PATCH.

Pawtucket is a famous place,
　　Where cotton cloth is made,
And hundreds think it no disgrace
　　To labour at the trade.

Among the spinners there was one,
　　Whose name was Samuel Patch;
He moped about, and did his stent—
　　Folks thought him no great scratch.

But still a maggot, in his head,
    Told Sam he was a ninny,
To spend his life in twirling thread,
    Just like a spinning Jenney.

And if he would become renown'd,
    And live in song or story,
'Twas time he should be looking round
    For deeds of fame and glory.

' What shall I do?' quoth honest Sam,
    ' There is no war a-brewing;
' And duels are but dirty things,
    ' Scarce worth a body's doing.

' And if I would be President,
    ' I see I'm up a tree,
' For neither prints, nor Congress-men,
    ' Have nominated me.'

But still that maggot in his head
    Told Sam he was a gump,
For if he could do nothing else,
    Most surely he could *jump*.

Aye, right, quoth Sam, and out he went,
    And on the bridge he stood,
And down he jump'd full twenty feet,
    And plung'd into the flood.

And when he safely swam to land,
    He stood there like a stump,
And all the gaping crowd cried out,
    ' O what a glorious jump.'

New light now shone in Samuel's eyes,
    His heart went pit a pat;
' Go, bring a ladder here,' he cries;
    ' I'll jump you more than that.'

The longest ladder in the town
    Against the factory was rear'd,
And Sam clomb up, and then jump'd down,
    And loud and long the gapers cheer'd.

Besides the maggot in his head,
    Sam's ear now felt a flee ;
' I'll raise some greater breezes yet;
    ' What's this dull town to me ?'

And off he went on foot, full trot,
    High hopes of fame his bosom fired,
At Paterson, in Jarsay State,
    He stopt awhile, for Sam was tired ;

And there he mounted for a jump,
    And crowds came round to view it,
And all began to gape and stare,
    And cry, ' How dare you do it ?'

But Sam ne'er heeded what they said,
    His nerves want made to quiver,
And down he jump'd some fifty feet,
    And splash'd into the river.

' Hoo-rah,' the mob cried out amain,
    ' Hoo-rah,' from every throat was pouring,
And Echo cried, ' Hoo-rah' again,
    Like a thousand lions roaring.

Sam's fame now spread both far and wide,
    And brighter grew from day to day,
And wheresoe'er a crowd convened,
    Patch was the lion of the play.

From shipmasts he would jump in sport,
    And spring from highest factory walls;
And proclamation soon was made,
    That he would leap Niagara falls.

And Sam approached those awful Falls,
And leapt them like a frog.

'What for?' inquired an honest Hodge,
  'Why scare to death our wives and mothers?'
'To show that some things *can* be done,'
  Quoth Sam, 'as well as others.'

Ten thousand people thronged the shores,
  And stood there all agog,
While Sam approached those awful falls,
  And leapt them like a frog.

And when they saw his neck was safe,
  And he once more stood on his feet,
They set up such a deafening cheer,
  Niagara's roar was fairly beat.

Patch being but a scurvy name,
  They solemnly did there enact,
That he henceforward should be call'd
  'Squire Samuel O'Cataract.'

And here our hero should have stopt,
  And husbanded his brilliant fame;
But, ah, he took one leap too much,
  And most all heroes do the same.

Napoleon's last great battle prov'd
  His dreadful overthrow,
And Sam's last jump was a fearful one,
  And in death it laid him low.

'Twas at the falls of Genessee,
  He jump'd down six score feet and five,
And in the waters deep he sunk,
  And never rose again alive.

The crowd, with fingers in their mouths,
  Turn'd homeward, one by one,
And oft with sheepish looks they said,
  'Poor Sam's last job is done.'

APPENDIX.

In which are published some of Major Downing's letters,
that he never wrote.

Note by the Editor. The following paragraph from
Mr Walsh's National Gazette, published some two or
three months ago, comes in so pat upon the present occasion, that we cannot refrain from copying it.

'It has been the fate of all successful authors, to have
counterfeits who deal with their originals as Hamlet
says that some players imitate nature. The Rabelais,
the Swifts, the Voltaires suffered in their day by the
productions of interlopers of the sort ; — mere bunglers
attempted to personate them, and confounded the less
discriminating or critical part of the reading public.
Major Jack Downing has paid in like manner, the pen-
alty of genius and popularity ; and he has complained
of the hardship and injustice, in a characteristic vein.
We humbly advise him to write over the whole story of
President Jackson's late expedition. It might confidently be predicted that a full narrative from his pen, *duly
authenticated*, would obtain as much vogue in these
United States, as did Peter Plymley's Letters in Great
Britain.'

Major Downing's letters were commenced in the Portland Courier, in January 1830, and have been continued

in that paper regularly up to the present time, Nov. 1833. The *real* Major has never sent any letter to any other paper. Though counterfeit or imitation letters occasionally appeared in other papers, it was not till President Jackson's tour to New England, that they were published in any considerable numbers. At that time the counterfeiters took a new start. Roused by the Major's account of their ' coming on full chisel,' and of his shaking hands for the President at Philadelphia, every body betook themselves to writing Jack Downing, till their letters almost overshadowed the land. The great mass of them were about as much like the original letters, as a hawk is like a hand-saw. Most of them had nothing to recommend them but extreme bad spelling, without point, wit, or moral. Others, which were written with some ability, were often deformed by low blackguardism, indelicacy, or profanity, qualities which it is believed are not to be found in the writings of the genuine Major. A few of the best specimens of the imitations are copied in the following pages. We cannot but remark however, in passing, that it appears to us to be an unjustifiable invasion of the Major's rights, for others to assume his name. It is really as much a forgery in point of honour and equity, as it would be for them to affix to their letters the name of Andrew Jackson. If they choose to attempt to write in the Major's style, they are at liberty to do it, as they would be to attempt the style of any other author ; but we believe all honourable men will say, *they have no moral right to assume his name.*

No. I.

Being the genuine letter of old Mr Zophar Downing,
' amost eighty-three yere old.'

[*Note.* — The following letter, we believe, was sent originally in the New York Commercial Advertiser, though we are not sure but it was a Baltimore paper. We regard it as the best picture, ' drawd off from nater,' that we have seen among the numerous imitations of the true letters of the Downing family. One thing is certain about it, whether the Major has an uncle in the western States or not, this letter bears indubitable evidence of having been written by a person *eighty-three years old.*]

> Uppington, Western Resarve,
> Tuesday, June 5, A. D. 1833, N. S.

To MY NEFEW JOHN DOWNING : — I am got to be amost eighty three Yere old, and I'm in my eighty third Year now, and its so long since I have took any Pen in my hand to write any thing nor a Letter to any Boddy living for now going on a very long Time. And what makes it particular bad for me is that my Fingers is got stiff with Rhumatiz and cold, and is all Thums, as much as tho they was froze in the Winter. — Your Aunt is sick abed ; she ketch'd cold some Time in Aperil, and I don't know when she will ever git over it ; she is in her eighty second Year most as old as I be, we are both very old and prety much done with this World, so to speake. I did not ever expect to write any more Letters to my Frinds because I'm in my eighty third Year and am too old most to write Letters. But you writ a Letter to me from the Citty of Washington and it was throw'd out of the Stage Wensday as it drove by. And when I redd about your goin to take the President of These United States to Downingvil then I said to your Aunt my dear I must try and write an Answer to Jonny's Letter.

I was jeest about as old as you be John when the Great Washington died, 14 day of December, and was with him and spoke with him seventeen year before, when he left the Army and wisht I might live many yeares, and what you writ to me makes me think a good deal of that time. I shant forget it to my dyin day — but I hope you wont have Ardint Sperrits in your Town on the Occasion. I dont drink any more Flip nor Tody sence 17 August A. D. 1831 and am better fort, and hope Brother Joshua has stopped. Two of my Cows was lost last year by Destemper and one of Mr Doolittles who lives oposite, is a hard worken Man. Some Destemper was here this yere but I follerd what was said in the Temperance Almanick and they was cured in time to git over it. I desire that my Brother Joshua woud write a Letter to me to let me know whether he is going to make out as well with his Ternips as he did 3 year ago, he wrote to your Aunt about it. I tryde that Plan here, but it dont do in this Soil, it is to dry most of it. Your Aunt tells me she dont think Brother Joshua can be so strong of his Age as I be, seeing he hant writ any of us since that Account of his Garding Sauce turn-in out so remarkable good that year.

It is thirty-two years ago next month since I was in Downingville, how is Deacon Wiloby and his family and his daughter Sooky was uncommon humersome, but your aunt always used to say she thot Sooky was a little too fond of seeing peeple perlite and that she was to espirin for Downingvil when she was young and a come-ly child. I thank you John for some newspapers you sent to me last when so much was writ about the President and the Vice President, one spell I was afeard that the poor salvages in Georgia State was agoin to suffer till the great Proclamation to the Nuliphiers as they are called which you sent to me, but I hope they are not now, they are a sufferin Peeple certin. If you do take the President east I hope there is no boddy but what will treat him respect. You know John I dont know much about politix, but I know something of my bible, and I hope I shall alwais read in it while I continue to live, and it says in the 2nd Book of Samuel, about Absalom's setting by the gate and shakin hands and kissin every boddy that passed by, and whisperin in their ears what he would do if he was king, and you know mor about the Vice President, and I ask you if that man aint adoin so too, and if it is not some boddys duty to speak to the President about it. But my hand shakes some, writin so much, and give my love and aunts to all our relations and to the neighbours of yours that I used to know. I am your loving Uncle,

                    ZOPHAR DOWNING.

                    No. II.

                    BANK REPORT.

            To the Editor of the N. Y. Daily Advertiser.

Major Downing's Official Report on the United States Bank.   Published by ' authority.'

                    Rip Raps, August 4th, 1833.

DEAR SIR,—I have jest got here after examinin the Bank ; and it was the toughest job, ever I had in my life. The Gineral was so bent on my doing it, that I had to ' go ahead,' or I'd sneak'd out the first day. I was nigh upon a week about it, figerin and siferin all the while. Mr Biddle see quick enuf it was no fool's journey I come on ; and I made some of his folks scratch their heads, I tell you. I gin 'em no notice of my comin, and I jump'd right in the thickest on 'em there one day, when they were tumblin in and shellin out the mun-

ny like corn. ' Now,' says I, ' my boys, I advise all on
ye to brush up your multiplication tables, for I am down
upon you with aligation, and the rule of three, and vul-
gar fractions ; and if I find a penny out of place, the
Gineral shall know it. I'm no green horn, nor member
of Congress, nor Judge Clayton, nor Mr Cambreleng,
neither,' says I. As soon as Mr Biddle read the letter
the Gineral sent by me, says he, ' Major, I'm glad the
Gineral has sent some one at last that knows something,
and can give a strait account ;' and with that he called
all the Bank folks, and tell'd 'em to bring their books
together. ' Now,' says he, ' Major, which eend shall we
begin at first.' ' It makes no odds which,' says I, ' all
I care about is to see if both eends meet ; and if they
don't, Mr Biddle,' says I, ' i'ts all over with you and the
bank — you'll all go, hook and line,' — and then we off
coats and went at it. I found some of them are fellers
there plagy sharp at siferin. They'd do a sum by a
kinder short Dilworth quick as a flash. I always use a
slate — it comes kinder natural to me ; and I chalk'd
her off there the first day and figur'd out nigh upon 100
pretty considerable tuf sums. There was more than
three cart load of books about us, and every one on 'em
bigger than the Deacon's family Bible. And sich an
etarnal batch of figerin I never see, and there wasn't a
blot or scratch in the whole on 'em.

I put a good many questions to Mr Biddle, for the
Gineral gin me a long string on 'em ; and I thought
some would stagger him, but he answered them all jest
as glib as our boys in Downingville do the catakize,
from the chief ' eend of man,' clean through the peti-
tions — and he did it all in a mighty civil way too, ther
was only one he kinder tried to git round, and that was
— how he come to have so few of the Gineral's folks
among the Directors until very lately ? ' Why,' says he,
' Major, and Major,' says he (and then he got up and
took a pinch of snuff and offered me one) says he, ' Ma-

jor, the Bank knows no party; and in the first go off,
you know, the Gineral's friends were all above matters
of so little importance as Banks and Banking. If we
had put a branch in Downingville,' says he, 'the Gineral
would not have had occasion to ask such a question,' and
with that he made me a bow; and I went home and took
dinner with him. It is plagy curious to hear him talk
about millions and thousands; and I got as glib too at
it as he is; and how on earth I shall git back agin to
ninepences and four-pence-happenies, I can't tell.

Arter I had been figerin away there nigh upon a week,
and used up four or five slate pencils, and spit my mouth
as dry as a cob, rubbin out the sums as fast as I did
them, I writ to the Gineral, and tell'd him it was no
use; I could find no mistake; but so long as the Bank
was at work, it was pretty much like counting a flock
of sheep in a fall day when they are jest let into a new
stubble, for it was all the while crossing and mixing, and
the only way was, to lock up all the Banks, and as fast
as you can count 'em black their noses.

' Now,' says I one day to Squire Biddle, 'I'll jest take
a look at your money bags, for they tell the Gineral you
han't got stuff enuf in the Bank to make him a pair of
spectacles; none of your rags,' says I, 'but the real
grit;' and with that he call'd two or three chaps in
Quaker coats, and they opened a large place about as
big as the 'east room' and sich a sight I never see—
boxes, bags and kags, all full, and should say nigh upon
a hundred cord. Says I, 'Squire Biddle, what on earth
is all this? for I am stumped.' 'O,' says he, 'Major,
that s our Safety Fund.' 'How you talk!' says I.
'Now,' says I, 'is that all genwine?' 'Every dollar of
it,' says he. 'Will you count it, Major?' says he. 'Not
to-day,' says I; 'but as the Gineral wants me to be particular, I'll jest hussle some of 'em;' and at it I went,
hammer and file. It raly did me good, for I did not
think there was so much real chink in all creation. So

when I got tired, I set down on a pile, and took out my wallet, and begun to count over some of the ' safety fund' notes I got shaved with on the grand tower. ' Here,' says I, ' Squire Biddle, I have a small trifle I should like to barter with you ; it's all " safety fund," ' says I ; ' and Mr Van Buren's head is on most all on 'em.' But as soon as he put his eye on 'em, he shook his head. I see he had his eye teeth cut. ' Well,' says I, ' it's no matter ;' but it lifted my dander considerable.

' Now,' says I, ' Mr Biddle, I've got one more question to put to you, and then I'm through. You say your bills are better than the hard dollars ; this puzzles me, and the Gineral too. Now, how is this ?' ' Well,' says he, ' Major, I'll tell you : Suppose you had a bushel of potatoes in Downingville, and you wanted to send them to Washington, how much would it cost to get them there ?' ' Well,' says I, ' about two shillins lawful — for I sent a barrel there to the Gineral, last fall, and that cost me a dollar freight.' ' Well,' says he, ' suppose I've got potatoes in Washington jest as good as yours, and I take your potatoes in Downingville, and give you an order to receive a bushel of potatoes in Washington, wouldn't you save two shillins lawful by that ? We sometimes charge,' says he, ' a trifle for drafts, when the places are distant, but never as much as it would cost to carry the dollars ;' and with that we looked into the accounts agin, and there it was. Says I, ' Squire Biddle, I see it now as clear as a whistle.'

When I got back to Washington, I found the Gineral off to the ' Rip Raps,' and so I arter him. One feller there tell'd me I could'nt go to the Rip Raps — that the Gineral was there to keep off business ; but as soon as I told him who I was, he ordered a boat and I paddled off.

The Gineral and I have talked over all the Bank business ; he says it is not best to publish my report, as he wants it for the message ; and it would only set them *Stock fish* nibblin agin in Wall Street. I made him stare when I tell'd him about the dollars I saw there; and once and awhile he would rinkle his face up like a ball of ravilins; and when I tell'd him Biddle would n't give me any of his 'Safety Fund' for any of Mr Van Buren's that I had with me, the Gineral took out his wallet, and slung it more than five rods into the brakers.

We are now pretty busy, fitting and jointing the beams and rafters of the message; and if Mr Van Buren dont get back before we begin to shingle it, I guess that his Safety Fund will stand but a poor chance.

The Gineral don't care much about having his head for a sign board, but says he, 'Major, when they put my head on one eend of a Bank Bill, and Mr Van Buren's on tother eend, and "promise to pay Andrew Jackson," and then blow up, it's too bad — I won't allow it — it shant be.' The Gineral says, if he allows Amos Kendle to make his report about the State Banks, it is but fair to let me publish mine about Square Biddle's Bank. So I am getting mine ready.

We have a fine cool time here, and ain't bothered with Office seekers; we can see 'em in droves all along shore, waitin for a chance. One fellow swam off last night to get appointed to some office — the Gineral thinks of making him minister to the King of the Sandwich Islands, on account of their being all good swimmers there.   Yours,

      J. DOWNING, Major, Downingville
          Militia, 2d Brigade.

No. III.

Giving some account of Peleg Bissel's Churn.

Rip Raps, Aug. 17, 1833.

To the Editor of the New-York Daily Advertiser.

MY GOOD FRIEND. — " *The Government* " will leave here on Saturday, so you must tell all our friends to stop sending any more letters here. We go strait to Washington, to put things to rights there for winter.

I and the Gineral have got things now pretty considerable snug ; and it is raly curious to see how much more easy and simple all the public affairs go on than they did a spell ago, when Mr Adams was President. If it warnt for Congress meetin we cou'd jest go about pretty much where we pleased, and keep things strait too ; and I begin to think now with the Gineral, that ater all, there is no great shakes in managin the affairs of the nation. We have pretty much all on us ben joggin about now since last grass; and things are jest as strait and clear now as they was then. The Gineral has nigh upon made up his mind, that there is no use to have any more Congress. They only bother us — they wou'd do more good to stay at home, and write letters to us tellin what is goin on among 'em at home. It would save a considerable sum of money too ; and I'm also sartin that there is a plagy raft of fellows on wages that dont earn nothin. Howsoever, we are goin on makin things more simple every day, and we once and a while nock off a pretty considerable number of cogg wheels and trunnel heads.

The Gineral says he likes things simple as a mouse trap. But what I like most is, he wont have no one about him who outranks me, so there is me, and Major Barry, and Major Smith, and Major Earl, and Major

Donaldson, and Major Lewis, and Major Eaton; — and
the major part of a pretty considerable of a man to
do the printing, and tell the folks where we be, and
once and a while where the land sales and contracts
be too.   There is enuff on us to do all that's wanted.
Every day jest ater breakfast, the Gineral lights his
pipe, and begins to think pretty hard, and I and Major
Donaldson begin to open letters for him; and there is
more than three bushels every day, and all the while
coming.   We dont git through more than a bushel a
day; and never trouble long ones, unless they come
from Mr Van Buren, or Mr Kindle, or some other of
our great folks.   Then we sort 'em out, jest as Zekel
Bigelow does the mackerel at his Packin Yard, for tho'
there are plagy many more sorts than he finds among
fish, we ony make three sorts, and keep three big baskets, one marked ' *not red*,' another ' red, and worth
nothin,' and another ' red, and to be answered.'   And
then all the Gineral has to do is to say, ' Major, I
reckon we best say so and so to that,' and I say 'jest
so,' or not, as the notion takes me — and then we go
at it.

We keep all the Secretaries, and the Vice President,
and some District Attornys, and a good many more of
our folks, and Amos Kindle, moving about; and they
tell us jest how the cat jumps.   And as I said afore, if
it warnt for Congress meetin once a year, we'd put the
Government in a one horse wagon and go jest where
we liked.

The Gineral was amazingly tickled t'other day.   Peleg Bissel — (you know Peleg, who is all the while whit-
lin, and sawin, and makin clocks, and apple parers, and
churns, and lives nigh Seth Sprague's School house,
down to Downingville,) well, Peleg sent the Gineral a
new churn of his own invention; and he calls it the
' Jackson Churn,' he wants a patent for it.   The cute
critur says, in his letter to the Gineral, that that are

churn is jest like his government — its ony got one
wheel, and a smasher ; and that it will make more butter than any other churn, and out of eny most any thing.
The Gineral is so well pleased with it, he will set and
turn it nearly all day. Says he, ' Major, I like this ere
churn amazingly, that Bissel is a knowin fellow. If that
churn had been made by Congress, it would have more
than fifty wheels and springs, and make no more butter
ater all. Major,' says he, 'tell Peleg I thank him ; and
send him a patent.'

And so I did ; and I told him in the letter, that the
Gineral would keep his churn in the hall of the white
house, to let folks see that it did n't require as many cog
wheels to make butter as they think on, and then when
they come up chamber, in the Cabinet Room, and find
ony me and the President, they 'll understand it the better. When the Gineral come to sign this letter, ' well,'
says he, ' Major, that's just what I was thinkin on.
We get every day an everlastin bach of letters from Mr
Van Buren and Amos Kindle, and they are so plagy
jagged, that we cant make 'em fit exactly with some
others, eny most as jagged, from the South and West,
and all from our folks too. One wants one thing, and
one wants t'other. Some of our folks down South say,
if the Bank is put down, we shall all be split up into
splinters there. And jest so, ony t'other way, they say,
we shant find in a week any of our folks north if the
Bank is rechartered, and some talk of the Nullifiers in
Georgia going for Mr Van Buren, and that we must look
out sharp, and not do nothin agin 'em. And some say
that are tower of Mr Webster away West, and his
speeches, bother some on 'em plagily. I was a little
stumped for a spell myself; and I tell'd the Gineral,
says I ' Gineral, if you expect me to satisfy all these
folks, you're mistaken, we cant do it,' says I. ' Well
then,' says he, ' we must send for Mr Van Buren.' This
kinder nettled me, and says I, ' Gineral, you ha'nt for-

got that are churn already ' — 'no, no,' says he, 'we'll
stick to that Major.' 'Well then,' says I, 'do you think
that Mr Van Buren will use that are churn? he keeps
his bread buttered,' says I, 'by more wheels than that
are churn's got.' 'Well Major," says the Gineral, 'he
is a plagy curious critter, ater all — he'll make wheels
turn sometimes right agin one another, yet he gits along
— and when he lets his slice fall, or some one nocks it out
of his hand, it always somehow falls butter side up '—
'well,' says I, 'Gineral, dont you know why?' 'not exactly,' says he, 'Major' — 'well,' says I, — 'I'll tell you
— he butters both sides at once,' says I. The Gineral
drew his face all into a rumple for about a minute, and
then he snorted right out.

The Gineral talks of goin to the Hermitage next
spring — he says he thinks he has done enuf for the
country — and I think so too — he says I may go along
with him or stay and lend Mr Van Buren a hand — we'll
say something about this in the Message.

Yours as before,

J. DOWNING, Major.
Downingville Militia, 2d Brigade.

No. IV.

The Public Crib at Washington.

Washington, August 30, 1833.

To Mr Dwight — New-York Daily Advertiser.

MY GOOD OLD FRIEND — Ever since we got 'the Government' back here from the Rip Raps, we have been
as busy as if we was all on us cocking hay jist afore a
shower.

I tell'd you some time ago that I and the Gineral was

fittin and jointin the beams and rafters of the message,
but almost every day some plaguy new motion comes in
from Mr Van Buren, and some other of our folks, and
we have to chizzle new mortises, and run new braces
and string pieces, so that I begin to think it will look
curious enuf when its done. The Gineral says he
dont care how it fronts, only he is determined to show a
sharp corner to the Nullifiers. We shall have a good
deal to say about the *Grand Tower;* there is nothin since
the 8th of January at New-Orleans tickles the Gineral
half so much. Every time we talk about it, the Gineral
gits right up, and says he, ' Major, I ony wish I was fifty
years younger, and then,' says he, ' give me the yankees
east of Horse Neck, and I'd like no better sport than to
have nullification all over the rest of creation.'

When things dont go right, and the Gineral gits a little
wrathy, if I ony tell him the yankees are ready to back
him, he is as firm as granite. It would make you crawl
all over to read that letter we writ to France, when we
come to hear that the King there kinder shuffled round
that bill we drawed on him. ' He wont pay it, wont he?'
Says he — ' Major, what do you think of that ?'— 'why,'
says I, ' Gineral, I think its a nasty mean action — and a
rascally one too, says I.' ' Well,' says he, ' that's enuff,'
— and then we writ the letter,— its jest like Zekel Bigelow's speech — it cuts, shaves, and makes the hair fly —
and if it dont bring the money, I'm mistaken.

If Mr Livingston had stayd one week longer in York,
the Gineral was for sending me right out.

The most curious part of ' the Government ' here, is
to manage the office seekers. You see, things aint now
as they was afore Mr Van Buren's time, then it was
kinder divided round among the Departments.

The Post Master Gineral appointed all the Post Mas-
ters and their folks. The Secretary of the Treasury
appointed all the folks in the Custom Houses, and all
folks who collected money. These two had an ever-

lastin batch of fellers to appint, and made them feel
pretty considerable big, and then the War Secretary had
a good slice in appinting the cadets, and Ingen Agents,
and all the contracts was kinder sifted round among the
Departments; and so by the time a new President was
to be made, some of these Secretaries was a leetle bigger
than the President himself. Now this is the way they
kinder jockied Mr Adams, who got to be the smallest
man at Washington, by lettin other folks plant his corn,
and do his huskin; and afore he knowd it, his own field
was all in weeds — and theirs well howed, rich and clean
as a whistle.

But things aint so now, we've got ony one crib, and
that's a whappin one too, and ony one door to it; and
when we shell out our corn, we take good care and
know well who gets it, and where he is going to plant it;
and that aint all — we make 'em agree about the *Huskin
Frolic*,* for that's the best ont arter all.

The longer I am in 'the Government' the more I
larn. But I must allow that of all the inventions I've
hearn on of Mr Van Buren's, this is about the slickest.

There is ony one thing wantin, and that he is tryin
for pretty hard — and that is the Bank. If he can ony
get that in the crib too, Virginy fences would n't stop
our cattle.

Ony think what an everlastin raft of fellows we should
have — all the Presidents and Cashiers, and Clerks, and
Money Counters, about the crib, from Downingville to
New-Orleans! — and that aint the best ont; we would
have a branch alongside every post office to keep our
postages safe.

I should like this well enuf if I was sartin I and the
Gineral and Mr Van Buren was to be here all the while,
to keep a good look out on the crib door. But the

* The Major, we presume, means the Elections, or Hustings, by
this metaphor.

Gineral talks of going hum to put the Hermitage to rights; and I am in the notion that Congress is a leetle too strong for 'the Government' when the Gineral aint in it — and I shall go with him. I am eny most fag'd out myself, and I begin to think with the Gineral, I have done enuf for the country.

We are lookin for Amos Kindle now every hour. He writ the Gineral tother day, and teld him my 'Bank Report' warn't true, and that I must have got a loan of Squire Biddle. Now that's jist the way with some folks. What they dont know they guess at; and it's jist so with old Miss Crane, who keeps the tavern this side Downingville — jist as sure as any one goes by without stopping, the old critur says, 'There goes so and so, and has got no money, too, and he knows I would n't trust him.'

Howsumever, no one can make the Gineral rathy with me. He knows I am the best friend about him ; whenever they gets things in any kind of a twist or a snarl, says he, 'Major, do you unravel that. I'm the big wheel and you are the smasher,' says he; and then we jist give Peleg Bissel's churn a turn or two and all is right.

You don't print my letters right — you git some words wrong and spell 'em bad. Jist so the printers sarved the Gineral's letters too ; and folks thought he didn't know nothin, till we got to Cambridge, where they made a doctor on him.

Your friend,

J. DOWNING, Major,
Downingville Militia, 2d Brigade.

No. V.

Preparation of the Message.

Washington, 2d Nov. 1833.

To my old friend, Mr Dwight, of the New York Daily Advertiser.

The Congressmen are jest beginnin to arrive here, and I suppose in a short time we shall have them here as thick as huckleberries ; and the Gineral is brushin round now, and says the Message must be finished and painted off hand, and we are all as busy as bees in gittin it dove tailed together ; and after next week, the Gineral says, there cant be any more alterations. It is the first message I ever had any hand in ; and tho' I say it, I guess you will say it is about as complete a thing as ever was sent express any where.

I have been to work on it ever since we was at the Rip-Raps ; and tho' it has been sometimes all pulled to bits, to git in some notions we did n't think on, yet it will look pritty slick, I tell you when it 's done ; and we will lay on paint enuf to kiver up all the cracks and seams.

We shall give a pritty good lick at the Bank, and won't leave as much on 't standing as would make a good sized oven. It is curius now to see how easy it is to build up, or nock all to bits, any thing on paper. Now jest see about the Bank. There it stands in Chestnut street, with its hundred cord of specie, and its cart load of books ; and its branches here and there, and all busy and full of clarks, and directors, and folks in Europe, and all about creation dealin with it ; and the brokers in Wall street all busy about it ; and Biddle's bills goin about, and most folks thinkin they are better than hard dollars ; and all the old men and women holdin the stock, supposin it will go up agin as high as they paid for it ; and I and the Gineral, and Amos Kindle, and Mr Van Buren, talkin

over it ; and one line in the Message nocks it all into kin-
dlin wood. For you see when ' The Government' says
a thing must be jest so ! there is no help for it. We can't
stand to chat about trifles. The Giniral has smashed
three pipes the last time we talked about it. ' Biddle
and the Bank must be smashed,' says he, ' Major ;' —
and so smash they go, Congress or no Congress.

The next thing was the Ingins. Here the Giniral is
at home, and I don't pretend to say nothin for I never
did like an Ingin, and never can. The Cherokees give
us a good deal of trouble in Georgia last year ; but the
Giniral took sides with Georgia, because he had a good
many friends there, and Mr Van Buren had too ; for that
State was the ony one that nominated him Vice-President
a spell ago ; and if he had got in there, and Mr Craw-
ford President, who was ailin all over with some plagy
appleplexy — I and the Giniral would never have been
hearn on arterwards. But no matter—The Giniral says
he didn't make that treaty with the Cherokees ; and it
was made so long ago, he has enymost forgot it : and
treaties oughtent to last forever. But this treaty with
the Creeks in Alabama he did make, and he knows all
about it ; and he means to stand by it, and turn all the
squatters off the land in Alabama, jest as they wanted
him to do in Georgia ; but he would n't. There is trouble
enuf about it, I tell you ; and you dont know nothing
about it in York. But the Giniral is tickled to death
about it ; and as soon as he saw the Proclamation of the
Governor of Alabama, you never see a critur so spruced
up as the Giniral was. Major, says he, we shall have
another Nullification this Congress, arter all. You
need 'nt say much about it, says he, in the Message,—
we'll keep that for a Proclamation. Well, says I, Gineral, you are a master hand at gettin into trouble. But,
says he, Major, aint I a master one in gittin out of one,
says he ?

We've got an old trunk up chamber, full of troubles —

old Laws, and Treaties, and Contracts, and State
Claims; and whenever we want any powder, all we 've
got to do is to open that, and look among old papers and
get up a row in no time. The Gineral likes this a leetle
better than I do; for the most of the labor falls on me,
and the ony way I can git rid of it, is to make our folks
down stairs do it, if I see it gives any of 'em a boost with
his party — for I dont care nothin about any thing here
but the Gineral; and if I can git him threw this Congress, its pretty much all I care about, and he too; for
ater that I'm goin with him to the Hermitage, for I expect by that time there wont be much more left of us
than our beards and shoe strings.

> Your friend,
> **J. DOWNING,** Major,
> Downingville Militia, 2d Brigade.

No. VI.

Sir George Downing.

Some account of Sir George Downing of London, sup-
posed to be one of Major Downing's ancestors.

From the New York Daily Advertiser.

THE DOWNINGS. — The celebrity of Major Jack Downing has created an intense and very natural curiosity in
the public mind to know something of his origin and
ancestry. Hoping that some of the down-east antiqua-
ries and genealogists will favor the world with the information desired, I submit to your disposal the following imperfect notice of Sir George Downing, one of the
Major's ancestors, which I have drawn from an interest-
ing and learned work now in a course of publication, in
numbers, entitled ' Memorial of the Graduates of Har-